RUNNING WATER

RUNNING WATER

The essential guide to the water services – how they work and the leisure facilities they provide

Charles Hall

Robertson McCarta

First published in 1989 by

Robertson McCarta Limited
122 King's Cross Road
London WC1X 9DS

© Charles Hall, 1989

Managing Editor Folly Marland
Designed by Bob Vickers
Line maps by Rodney Paull
Production by Grahame Griffiths

© maps, Robertson McCarta Limited
Printed and bound in Great Britain by
Butler & Tanner Limited, Frome.

British Library Cataloguing in Publication Data
Hall, Charles
    Running water: a guide to the history, works and
    leisure facilities of the water services.
    1. Water supply industries
    I. Title
    338.4'76281

    ISBN 1–85365–157–5 paperback
    ISBN 1–85365–169–9 hardback

Contents

Acknowledgements

I would like to thank all those connected to the water industry who generously gave me their help in preparing this book. I retain happy memories of long friendly talks with many more people than I can thank individually.

Charles Hall
1989

FRONTISPIECE: '*I may say in brief that he is one of the contriving and organising minds of the age; a class of mind of which there are very few and still fewer who apply those qualities to the practical business of government. He is, however, one of the few men I have known who have a passion for the public good; and nearly the whole of his time is devoted to it in one way or another.*' *John Stuart Mill on Edwin Chadwick (1800–90), the social reformer who contributed more than anyone to the improvement in British nineteenth-century sanitary conditions* (Mary Evans Picture Library)

Introduction

Something is wrong with the water industry when a large section of the population uses filters of unproven efficiency, prefers to buy bottled water costing a thousand times more than tap water, has to consult a book to find out whether the bathing water at the beach is likely to be clean or not, and is nervous of swimming in the local river.

In the last few years the water authorities have come under attack from three fronts: the Government demands a new structure, the EEC lays down new laws and the public is no longer content to be unquestioning and passive. Fundamental changes have been thrust upon the water industry in the last 40 years and it is now expected to adjust once again to a new way of life.

The obvious change is privatisation and this will affect the customer as much as the industry – although the only thing everyone is certain of is that we shall all pay higher bills. Far-reaching changes are likely to come via the EEC, whose Directives are stringent, clear cut and affect all sections of the manmade water cycle, but the biggest change of all is likely to be the shift in public opinion. Once grateful that any water came out of the taps at all, and impressed that it looked clean and drinkable, people now want the highest standards for water in the environment and their homes. More alarming still, when they challenge the experts they often know what they are talking about.

No one I have spoken to has suggested that the water industry will gain any benefit from privatisation that could not have been obtained without privatisation. Although short of money and a bit low in morale because of the questions hanging over it, the industry is largely well run, and it must be assumed that the Government will be the major beneficiary of any changes. Privatisation is Government flavour of the month; slapping down a successful public utility gives a warm glow to ardent party supporters; the sale will put a great deal of money in Government pockets and save them a lot more at a time when the EEC is forcing greater investment to conform to its Directives.

The high proportion of people in the water industry wearing ties proclaiming their support for the Third World charity Water Aid shows a care for others that is typical of the many dedicated and unassuming men and women who work in it – an honourable tradition of public service, like teaching and nursing. It has much to be proud of in its often spectacular achievements of the past and its forward-looking ingenuity and research in the present. The water authorities worked away quietly in the background and few people realised the extent of their responsibilities for all aspects of the water cycle. At the same time, the public has never been so aware of, and concerned about, the environment; not just as an emotional reaction to dying seals but as a sound appreciation of the issue involved – the interrelationship between ourselves and the planet we live on.

By taking a broad look at water supply and examining some of the work of the authorities, this book hopes to show how they have come to play such an important part in our natural environment and how privatisation may affect this relationship in the future. We live in a country of startling and subtle beauty. It is shameful and degrading that any of its rivers, estuaries and seas should be polluted, or that any water is less wholesome than it could be. Let us hope that the changes about to take place in the industry are ones that we can be proud of.

From the Earliest Beginnings

With such an array of indispensable structures carrying so many waters, compare if you will, the idle pyramids or the useless, though famous, works of the Greeks.

Sextus Julius Frontinus (AD 79)

From an international point of view, the British were late developers in their water-supply systems. Living in a country that many people feel has too much rainfall, the needs of our earliest communities could easily be met by the nearest spring or river.

Roman water supply in England anticipated the majority of technical developments for the next 2,000 years. Water was channelled over great distances, reservoirs were constructed, there were hot and cold supplies, private supplies to houses, taps and metal pipes with joints, and even mechanical hand pumps. These were not necessarily commonplace, but they all existed in various towns, and pipework was certainly quite usual, made of wood, fired clay and lead. Taps, in the form of bronze or lead stopcocks, have been found on cisterns and pipes. No aqueducts survive but their remains have been discovered in several Roman towns, including Dorchester, Exeter, Leicester, Lincoln and Silchester.

Roman baths are well known for their grand scale and impressive facilities. They were large enough in many English towns to cater for several hundred people bathing and socialising each day. In addition to the cold, warm and hot rooms (*frigidarium*, *tepidarium* and *calderium*), there were water-flushed latrines and, in Wroxeter, an open air swimming pool.

Roman wells have been found all over England and these were a more usual source of supply for private houses. They are not often very deep, although one has been found which is 26 m deep by 132 cm wide. Vitruvius suggested that where wells would have to be deep, it would be better to build cisterns to collect rainwater, possibly arranged in groups, with water percolating from one to another to help to purify the supply.

When the Romans left, the population continued to take water as they had done before the legions came – from rivers, springs and wells. Wells became an increasingly important source of supply in the communities which grew up in the Saxon period and they remained an important source throughout the Middle Ages for both urban and rural populations. Typically they would be 8–15 m deep and usually 90–120 cm wide, enough space for one man to work in while another lifted the spoil to the surface, and they would be lined with stone or brick if the surrounding ground was soft.

It was the monastic institutions which pioneered the construction of water-supply 'engineering' in post-Roman Europe. By the end of the twelfth century, the Cistercians had abbeys with aqueducts in England, France, Germany and Italy, and this was also typical of all the other great orders.

The first recorded example in England was at Canterbury in 1153, where Prior Wibert of the Benedictine monastery brought in a supply

An aqueduct by Alex Graham. The nine major Roman aqueducts brought 175 litres per head per day to a population of about one million people, a rate of supply reached by London in the 1940s. (Photograph: Victoria and Albert Museum)

from springs 1.2 km away to a conduit house. Here it passed through a perforated plate to remove the largest impurities, then through five settling tanks, was then carried in lead pipes on a bridge across the moat, penetrated the city wall and was divided and conducted to various points in the institution: kitchen, infirmary, lavatory basins, etc.

It should be remembered that the systems of this first period of supply were almost always 'open ended'; a spring or stream was diverted along pipes or channels, filled tanks at one or more strategic points and then ran to waste.

Leats and Conduits

There are various names for the channels which brought water from springs or rivers into the towns. Leat building was originally associated with mining and milling. The leats were often several kilometres long

Water carrying was a thriving trade before piped supplies became commonplace. In the fifteenth century the Company of Water Tankard Bearers in London had 4,000 members. (Water Authorities Association)

and at first they were always open ducts, 1–2 m wide and about 25–50 cm deep. They are generally associated with the West Country, supplying towns like Plymouth, Honiton and Wells, places where high ground with plentiful rainfall was accessible to the town.

Conduits are generally urban and shorter, taking their water from local sources like streams and springs. They were usually covered over or enclosed in lead pipes and had stone or lead cisterns, troughs or fountains at their heads where the public could collect water.

One insoluble problem related to the exposure of the leats to bad weather. Any long period of freezing temperature brought the town's supply to a standstill and this was one of the first reasons for the replacement of leats with pipes. Later, the health risk to open channels from pollution was recognised and this made their enclosure a priority.

The conduits were constructed in an attempt to resolve the problems arising from supplies becoming polluted or inadequate as towns grew more rapidly in the Middle Ages. Waste pits and septic tanks were polluting the wells, and sewage, industrial waste and offal were beginning to destroy the quality of the rivers.

The 'New River'   The construction of the 'New River' was probably the most ambitious project of its day. It had been suggested for some years that water could be brought into London from springs in Hertfordshire, and a number of proposals were considered by the city authorities and Parliament. Powers were finally conveyed, in 1609, to Hugh Myddelton, by Act of Parliament, to make 'a new river for bringing water to London from Chadwell and Amwell in Hertfordshire'.

Myddelton was the Member of Parliament for Denbigh, a goldsmith and merchant with some experience of mining. With the help of finance from 28 other merchant adventurers, he proposed to complete the scheme within four years. This proved to be hopelessly overambitious; the distance to be covered was about 64 km. The project also met with such strong opposition from local landowners that work had to be suspended, and in spite of being granted a five-year extension, the project proved to be beyond the financial resources of Myddelton and his associates.

King James I already knew Myddelton and had become interested in the project because part of the river ran through the grounds of his palace at Theobalds Park. The king was approached for help and agreed to provide half the cost in return for half the profits. Work was resumed, such a powerful ally presumably silencing the objecting landowners. The completed channel was 3 m wide and averaged 120 cm in depth. The fall of only 5–7.5 cm per 1.6 km over such a distance was achieved

The opening of the New River – 'Myddleton's Glory' – was accompanied by much celebration. (Thames Water)

by following the land contour and carrying the water over particularly low ground in timber troughs lined with lead. Considering the simple measuring tools available at that time, it was an impressive piece of engineering .

The New River originally ended at the Round Pound in Clerkenwell, from where it was fed into a cistern for distribution. In 1709 the company began to raise part of the water to another small reservoir in the Pentonville Road, so that houses on higher ground could be supplied. This was first done with a windmill, the base of which still remains today. In 1720 that was superseded by horse-driven pumps and in 1768 by one of John Smeaton's steam engines.

Developments in Engineering

The foundations of nineteenth-century water supply rested on the technical developments of the industrial revolution. Water courses and water driven 'engines' were derived from experience with mills, while the later steam engines, adapted from those used in the mines, and reservoir construction owed much to the pioneer work of canal builders. A constant supply of water under pressure, the dream of many early engineers, was not possible until pipes could be cast reliably, reasonably cheaply and with effective joints. Supplies fed by gravity were adequate in many areas and remain so today, but it was seen that for large urban areas like London, pumping by some means would be necessary, both to lift water up to higher areas as the New River Company had done at Pentonville, and to supply enough water in the first place. Wind power was unreliable and horse power slow, so it was logical to apply the water power that was doing so much work in other industries for lifting the water itself.

A Dutchman (or possibly German) called Peter Morice was the first person in England to use a mechanical pump driven by water. Installed under one of the arches of London Bridge, it drove pumps capable of forcing a jet of water over the steeple of the nearby St Magnus's Church.

The Royal Society was founded in 1661 and frequently heard papers on hydrology and hydraulics. Even the fashionable interest in water and fountains in landscape gardening added significantly to the knowledge of water control.

In the last years of the seventeenth century there was a tremendous outburst of waterworks activity, much of it inspired by George Sorocold of Derby, England's first professional water engineer.

The water was generally pumped to small reservoirs from which it was distributed through the streets by wooden pipes. Private supplies through 'feathers' were normally taken off through thin lead pipes. Plugs for fire-fighting water were often fitted at regular intervals, but the wood could be hacked open at any point in an emergency. Lead mains were occasionally used but are much less common, both on account of cost and the difficulty of using lead sheets in large sizes.

Right: *George Sorocold of Derby greatly improved the tide-driven water pumps under the old London Bridge when he rebuilt them in 1701. They remained in use until the bridge was dismantled in 1822.* (Thames Water)

The wooden mains were vulnerable to damage, leaked badly and needed frequent replacement. Experiments were made with iron connections between wooden pipes and with earthenware and stoneware pipes. Even stone pipes were being cut at this time. Cast iron pipes had been used occasionally, on a small scale, in Germany to carry water since 1455. In the early years they were expensive, unwieldy and difficult to joint effectively, but they were increasingly used between 1745 and 1800 and then very quickly replaced the old wooden pipes in the early years of the nineteenth century.

The worst problems with joints were largely overcome by the end of

the century, although leakage is still responsible for very large losses of water. Steel, asbestos-cement and concrete pipes all came into use in the first few years of the twentieth century, followed by plastic and polythene in the 1950s.

James Watt built his first water-supply engine for Hull in 1795 and from the early years of the nineteenth century onwards such engines took over as almost the only source of power in the water industry, apart from gravity, until the twentieth century. They were first used for lifting water from rivers, for land drainage and for filling service reservoirs, and later for drawing water from wells and for sewage disposal. They were still being installed in the 1930s.

The water closet (WC) was designed in 1596 by Sir John Harrington and had been considerably improved by the end of the eighteenth century by men like Joseph Bramah, but it needed a regular supply of water to make full use of it, and good drains for it to be really healthy, and neither of these was to be available generally for some time.

A continuous supply became available in Nottingham in the 1840s and in Birmingham in 1853, but Exeter's first constant supply, in about 1880, is probably typical of most smaller towns. Private supplies were restricted to the wealthier households.

The growing general use of WCs from the 1820s onwards was not entirely beneficial to health; if there were sewers, they fed straight into the local river, often affecting supplies, and their discharge into pits frequently affected wells.

Edwin Chadwick and Sanitary Reform

In general, the population of the country increased by 47 per cent between 1800 and 1831 and at an even greater speed in the manufacturing towns of the north where the industrial revolution was accelerating. Overcrowding was made worse by land taken for railway construction, industrial development and the desire to house as many workers as possible in a small space near their work at a time before any form of public transport was available.

Under these conditions it is hardly surprising that local sources of water were becoming polluted with sewage and manufacturing wastes. An ideal breeding ground for disease was being created. It was the arrival of cholera into these conditions, in 1831–32, that finally aroused the authorities to the necessity of improving matters. The disease spread through all the larger manufacturing towns, causing 5,300 deaths in London and 16,427 over the country as a whole. In spite of this warning, improvements came slowly and the next serious epidemic, in 1848, was even more tragic, killing 72,180 people nationally.

Edwin Chadwick was an assistant to the Poor Law Commission and became Secretary to the Poor Law Board when it was set up in 1832.

Following an outbreak of typhoid in Whitechapel, he persuaded the commissioners to allow a committee of respected doctors to make an enquiry into the sanitary conditions there. Their report impressed the authorities enough for them to extend the enquiry to the whole country and publish, in 1842, the *Report on the Sanitary Conditions of the Labouring Population of Great Britain*.

The report had a powerful effect on public opinion and resulted in the Government setting up a Health of Towns Commission to investigate conditions further. The work was again very much under the control of Chadwick whose advocacy of a constant supply and new designs for sewers was impassioned and so much in line with what we believe now that it is difficult to understand why respected engineers like James Simpson and Thomas Wicksteed argued, often with equal passion, against him. The recommendations of the two reports led directly to Lord Morpeth's Public Health Act of 1848.

The Public Health Act 1848 and the Central Board of Health

Lord Morpeth had hoped that his Act would fulfil Chadwick's aim of making a constant supply available to every house, together with drains, sewers and street paving. The final Act must have been a disappointment since its powers were permissive rather than mandatory. It established a Central Board with the power to set up Local Health Boards if ratepayers wished or where the death rate exceeded certain limits.

Opposition to the board became very active. Coming from so many sides it proved too much and the members were forced to resign in 1854. Chadwick never held public office again, but had the satisfaction of seeing his ideas eventually accepted as a matter of course by all engineers.

The Waterworks Clauses Act 1847

Chadwick is also thought to have been influential in preparing the Waterworks Clauses Act. Water suppliers, whether municipal or a private company, had previously got statutory rights for their operations by obtaining a private Act of Parliament. These private water-supply Acts are, in effect, unique contracts setting out rights over such things as catchment areas, supply areas, property, powers to install pipes and conduits in public places, even charges and quantities of water.

The new Act was intended to standardise waterworks practice throughout the country. Its 94 clauses covered mundane details like the right to dig up pavements but, far more important, it also laid out what Parliament believed to be good practice and, as such, it became the foundation stone of modern supply.

Municipal Undertakings v. Private Companies

The technical means of supplying water existed and the legislative support was appearing, but the various reports on the health of towns showed that, in practice, water supplies were generally not very efficient and tended to favour the better off. The idea of public involvement in health and living conditions was only just emerging and public bodies did not have the means to raise finance by long-term borrowing. It was largely left to the joint stock companies of private enterprise to raise the capital for waterworks construction.

In 1801 about 6 per cent of the largest towns were supplied by statutory joint stock companies, a figure that rose to nearly 55 per cent by 1851. Supplies could not keep up with demand, particularly from growing industrial needs and the financial returns were low in relation to capital outlay.

The Gas and Waterworks Facilities Acts of 1870 and 1873 provided for the construction, maintenance and continuance of water undertakings. The 1875 and 1878 Public Health Acts enumerated, among other things, the general powers of local authorities over water supply, and contained provisions for rural water supply. The result of local pressures and enabling legislation was that, by 1901, 90 per cent of the largest towns had municipal waterworks and four-fifths of consumers were supplied by local authorities. Even the London companies, influential bastions of private enterprise, were finally amalgamated under the Metropolitan Water Board in 1902.

The section of the community that did least well from these improvements was the rural parishes whose supply would never be economical on financial grounds alone. Rural District Councils were empowered to contribute to the costs after 1929, and under the Rural Water Supplies Act of 1934 the Government gave £1 million towards parish supplies, the first time the Exchequer had given money specifically for water-supply purposes. A further £15 million was given in 1944 towards supply and sewerage. It became a duty to provide water for rural communities and by 1987 99.2 per cent of the population were connected to a public water supply.

1900–45

Three royal commissions sat in the first years of the twentieth century, to report on sewage disposal, salmon fisheries, and canals and waterways. They each recommended that control of rivers, for all water conservancy purposes, should be with a central authority, but no action was taken. In 1910 a Water Supplies Protection Bill was introduced, which aimed to create controls to ensure that the general public interest was protected when demands for resources conflicted. A joint select committee considered the bill, recommending the appointment of local boards, under a central authority. The only direct result, however, was the commissioning of a survey to detail every English and Welsh water undertaking.

The Parliamentary Return of Water Undertakings (England and Wales) 1914 was a 'Domesday Book' of water supply. It was one of those gifts to historians, which draws a comprehensive picture of a particular activity at a particular time.

The following list gives a good idea of the interesting variety and make up of the 2,160 undertakings existing at that time.

Local authorities	786
Joint water boards	35
Statutory companies	200
Other private companies	84
Private proprietors	1,055

The sheer number and variety of undertakers worked against their ability to exert influence on Government policy. Any influence that they did have was through individuals, but three professional groups emerged at this time, who were to change this situation: the Institution of Water Engineers, the British Waterworks Association and the Water Companies Association. When, in 1922, the Minister of Health (a post created in 1919) wanted to look at water supply, he set up an Advisory Committee selected from these three bodies.

In 1934 the three bodies felt that Parliament should move further towards a national policy and convened a Joint Conference on National Water Policy. Its report resulted eventually in the formation of a Central Water Advisory Committee appointed by the Government.

1945–74 Such developments finally produced the Water Act of 1945, the first significant restatement of waterworks law since 1847. Its importance in general terms was that it firmly gave the Minister of Health considerable powers over most aspects of water supply.

The post-war expansion of a population with higher living standards, the final connection of rural areas to mains supplies and greatly increased industrial use began to make serious demands on resources. It was felt that the time had come to rationalise the water-supply position and a Water Resources Act was passed in 1963. This set up 29 new river authorities based on the old river boards, while the suppliers and local authorities remained independent.

One of its most significant clauses created a Water Resources Board to oversee the authorities and to work out a Government policy for water resources. In spite of being a Government department, the board was outspoken, realistic and single-minded in revealing the problems that faced undertakers. Unfortunately, its advisory status gave it no powers to act and the water authorities seldom had the finances to follow its recommendations. A change of Government in 1970, and with it the creation of the Department of the Environment with its own Water Directorate, brought about the demise of the board when the Water Act of 1973 was introduced.

This Act created the ten regional authorities, who, under the Secretary of State and the DOE, took full responsibility for every detail of water supply except the 29 statutory water companies, which remained independent, and some local councils which undertook to work for the authorities as agents for sewage work.

The Work of the Water Services

The Structure of the Industry

Electricity, gas and railways supply straightforward quantifiable commodities; the water industry's responsibilities cover a whole range of services from clear-cut water supply and sewage removal to the looser interpretive work of river management, flood control and sea defences. These functions can usefully be divided into three areas of activity.

1. **Direct services to a customer**
   Water supply and the treatment and disposal of sewage.
   Controlling the quality of drinking water.

2. **Indirect environmental regulation**
   Planning and regulation of water resources and supplies.
   Testing the quality of rivers and coastal waters and ensuring this quality through the control of sewage and industrial and farm waste discharges.
   Overseeing fishing, fisheries and navigation.

3. **Community services**
   Land drainage, flood protection and sea defences, highway drainage, the furtherance of nature conservation, recreation and amenities.

A concept of one body being in charge of all these aspects of the water cycle grew up in the late years of the nineteenth century and gradually came to be seen as an ideal. Since the water cycle takes place locally within the catchment of individual river basins, this ideal came to be known as integrated river basin management. In the past 50 years the water supply story has seen the successful establishment of integrated river basin management as a working arrangement and its very recent deconstruction in order to turn parts of the industry into saleable commodities.

No other public service utility has had to undergo the changes which have taken place in water supply over the last few years. In the mid-

1940s, 1,200 companies and local authorities were supplying water and 1,400 local authorities were responsible for sewerage and sewage disposal. The 1945 Water Act encouraged the amalgamation of many suppliers and, as a move towards complete river basin management, set up river boards to assume general responsibilities for resources, including navigation and fishing, in 29 catchment areas. The 1973 Water Act took this management to a logical conclusion and the remaining 157 water and 1,393 sewage undertakings, together with the 29 river boards, were amalgamated to make the ten water authorities which have been in operation for the last fifteen years. Twenty-nine private water companies were an exception to this general movement and they remained independent suppliers working as statutory agents under the authorities.

The 1989 Water Act separates the direct service activities of the authorities from their regulatory and community functions and this new way of working has now to be tested in practice. The ten regional water authorities are now Water Service plcs (WSPLCs) which supply water and sewerage services directly to the customer, while a new body, the National Rivers Authority, will manage all the other river basin functions in a similar way to the old authorities. There will be some overlap between the WSPLCs and the NRA in such areas as resource planning and river regulation and final control of these matters is to be left in the hands of a newly created post, the Director General of Water Services.

Finance   At present, the work of the water authorities is financed in a number of different ways, a situation which may be simplified when privatisation is complete. Most domestic customers pay a water rate which covers unmeasured water supply and sewage disposal, while businesses, particularly the larger ones, pay for these services according to the amount they are used. There are special charges for the treatment of industrial effluent, which depend on what has to be removed from it. Land drainage and flood protection work is financed by a precept on the county council rates and sometimes grant-aided by MAFF. Some environmental work qualifies for DOE grants. Licensed water abstractions by farmers, industry and the private water companies are paid for by volume.

Most authorities offer their professional services and expertise to individuals, other companies and foreign governments, in the latter case in training students from overseas, and for projects abroad. An idea of the income from these 'enterprise activities' can be gained from the 1986/87 accounts of Thames Water:

The ten water authorities
of England and Wales.

NORTHUMBERLAND

NORTH WEST

YORKSHIRE

SEVERN TRENT

ANGLIAN

WELSH

THAMES

WESSEX

SOUTHERN

SOUTH WEST

	£000
Thames Water International	563
Water services	
Pipework, etc., on customers' property	10,743
Virology & materials testing	137
Horticulture	74
Water space (recreation facilities at piers and the Thames barrier taken over from the GLC)	44

Only pipework and testing made a profit in that year.

Small incomes are derived from fishing, and in some cases from navigation licences and payments by clubs for recreational facilities. In most instances, the income does not match the expenditure and the services are seen as a contribution to the community and good public relations.

Domestic water rates are usually assessed on the rateable value of a house. Once the new poll tax has been introduced, however, houses will no longer be rated. Pressure is therefore being put on water suppliers by the Government to install meters on domestic premises, and all regions are at present running test schemes to study the feasibility of this. This would appear to be ideological since no one in the industry actually thinks it will save money, although it might save some water. It has been found in the past that when the public have been asked to make water savings in drought years, there is only a 10–15 per cent improvement. This suggests that very little water is wasted and certainly not enough to justify the cost of installing and checking meters. As this cost could be very high and would have to be paid for by the public, it seems a retrograde step.

The largest part of the cost of water is paying for the capital projects and maintaining the infrastructure. It has been a tradition, considered fair in the UK, for that cost to be shared equally by all users. Ironically, one of the benefits to suppliers could be that they would get a better idea of where the 25 per cent or so of water goes which enters the system and then unaccountably disappears.

A considerable difference in the cost of water between regions results from the varying geography of the UK. Upland areas with high rainfall gain an unfair advantage over the low-rainfall, flatter counties. In the past this difference was adjusted by a system of balancing payments, but this has now been stopped in the interests of financial realism. This, again, breaks the tradition of fairly sharing distribution costs which has characterised other public services.

The Statutory Water Companies

From a very early date it was a common procedure to apply for an Act of Parliament to supply water. There are several examples of this from the sixteenth century: the 'Acte for Presvacion of the Haven of Plymouth' of 1585, for instance. Water could be, and often was, supplied without an Act, but such an Act could give the undertaker important rights over land use and virtually guaranteed such a supplier the monopoly of a given area. In return, a successful applicant would agree the conditions and terms of his supply. Parliament was, in effect, the contractual body for water supply.

The increases in population were accompanied by a parallel increase in the number of water suppliers taking out parliamentary Acts – these statutory suppliers could be either private companies or municipal undertakings. The very large number of water undertakers makes them difficult to trace, let alone determine which were statutory, but it is known that by 1944 there were 123 statutory companies in the British Waterworks Association and 85 in the Water Companies Association. The 1945 Water Act encouraged water suppliers to join together in larger units, and private companies and local authorities amalgamated in various combinations which left 29 private statutory companies in existence by the time of the 1973 Water Act.

A spirited defence of their private status in the years after the Second World War has left them as independent profit-making companies, although there have been quite tight restrictions on their profits and various restraints over their operations. In the shadow of the water authorities, they have been something of an anachronism, but they should now blossom financially in the sunlight of the lifted restrictions associated with privatisation. In the past, the companies' dividends and profits were severely limited; following privatisation, they will be allowed to convert to PLCs and run their companies in the same way as any other. As a result of this their share values have increased up to tenfold in anticipation, mostly through pressure from French buyers who have wider experience in the public utilities field than British investors. The companies are proud of the strong links with their Victorian past and often retain the manner of elderly gentlemen involved in good works. It would be a pity if the loss of their traditional restraints put them in the hands of businessmen more interested in money than water.

They are mostly substantial companies – four of them supplying water to over a million people each – and altogether they serve one quarter of the population of England and Wales. They have no operations other than the supply of water, which they undertake, in their statutory areas, on behalf of the water authorities. Their history has been emphasised in the chapter on the regions because it is available, in a way that that of suppliers taken over by the authorities has not been, and it gives a good idea of the nineteenth-century background of water supply. This will have been unfair if it gives the impression that they are old-fashioned in their work, as they play an equal role with the water authorities in the research and development of new ideas in the water industry.

The water authorities take a rather superior attitude to the companies, generally giving the impression that they have an inferior role in the industry because they have fewer responsibilities. They do not always make it clear that the companies supply 25 per cent of England and Wales's water. The companies, in their turn, seem to view the authorities with some suspicion, hinting that the authorities are too big and diverse to get on with the job of supplying water efficiently. It should be said, though, that both sides appear to enjoy good working relations with each other.

After privatisation, the authorities would presumably like to be in possession of many of the companies (Thames Water have openly stated this), but since they are not legally allowed to hold shares in the companies until after privatisation, they are probably going to be too late. Several companies are now owned outright by French companies and more than half have a large French stake – these companies do not share the typical British mistrust of foreigners and perhaps should be seen as better Europeans than most of us. Essex Water Company cited the possibility of being taken over by a water authority as a good reason for coming to an arrangement with the French.

Lyonnaise des Eaux is typical of the French firms which have large stakes in several English water companies. It works in all areas of drinking water supply, treatment, distribution and waste water treatment, and serves 18 million customers in Europe, America and Asia. Its other interests are in waste and rubbish management (collection, treatment and construction of equipment); energy technology (production of electricity and gas, distribution and management); communications (thirteen cable TV networks); mortuary services (40 per cent of French funerals), and leisure and health facilities.

It had been thought that because the companies were already private there would be little change with privatisation. It seems now that the changes for them will be as great as those for the authorities. Many will mourn the passing of these historic and slightly eccentric British institutions – others will see the change as an opportunity.

Public Involvement

The nomination of members to the water authority boards was altered by the 1983 Act. They had previously had committees of about 30 members, some appointed by the Secretary of State for the Environment and the Minister of Agriculture, and some nominated by local authorities, continuing the tradition of local government involvement in water and sewage services. The nominees were usually local councillors, who, it was thought, would look after consumers' interests. The Government felt that the system was unsatisfactory because, they said, few people either realised, or were concerned, that they were represented (and, one suspects, because members lacked commercial experience).

The new board membership was smaller, about eight to fifteen members, and entirely appointed by ministers. They were more orientated towards financial and managerial considerations, and consumer interests were to be looked after by consultative committees. One feels that this change had a far-reaching effect on the industry; the new 'business-like' orientation at the top made the commercial ideology of privatisation much more acceptable in the higher levels of the authorities' management.

Anglian Water, for instance, has a board of twelve members, of whom ten were appointed by the Secretary of State for the Environment and two by the Minister of Agriculture, Fisheries and Food. Four of these members work full time for Anglian: the managing director and the directors of operations, finance and technical services. In addition to the contribution which public members could make from their experience in finance, industry, and national and local government, each was given special responsibility for a particular area. These were land drainage, customer relations, performance and audit, finance, capital programmes and government relations, water quality and scientific matters, and fisheries, recreation and conservation. These special responsibilities are, unfortunately, not typical.

In the same region six Consumer Consultative Committees (CCCs) each represented a division and members were appointed by the board from nominations by interested groups. The local authorities held the majority of places, but others were chosen to make as diverse a collection of interests as possible. They hold two meetings a year, discussing subjects ranging from consumer charges and capital investment to privatisation and pollution incidents. The chairman and deputy chairman of each committee hold liaison meetings with the chairman of the board to convey the committees' feelings. The 1973 Act specified that board meetings should be held in public but the 1983 Act changed this. In the absence of that openness it is hard to tell what influence the consultative committees have.

The new Act also authorised the creation of regional Recreational and Conservation Committees. Generally these have more influence, partly because their interests are more specialised. Some regions take them more seriously than others, of course. North West's RCC had 25 members representing seven district or county councils, the CPRE, the NCC, the CC, the NFU, the RSNC, the Country Landowners Association, tourist boards and nine sports interests, including one for the disabled. They held three meetings in the year 1986–87 and discussed, among other matters, privatisation, catchment areas, fencing, access and bathing. The board and the committee seem to have both a genuine respect for each other and a positive working relationship.

Privatisation, the New Water Bill

We have absolutely no intention of privatising the water industry.

Government statement, Dec 1984

The Government has now decided to transfer the ten water authorities in England and Wales to private ownership . . .

Government statement, Feb 1986

Essential utilities affecting public health and safety have previously been regarded as a proper area to be under national and local control. The supply of services is now to be put into private hands and new public bodies set up to oversee their activities. The principle of integrated river management will largely be abandoned.

Water Services Public Limited Companies (WSPLCs)

Only the responsibility for the supply of water and sewage services will remain with the existing ten regional authorities. They will be free to develop whatever enterprise activities they choose and will be 'financially' as independent as any other PLC – capital investment has previously been strictly controlled by Government. Their regulatory functions will be taken over by the National Rivers Authority and their services to customers will be supervised by the Director General of Water Services.

The National Rivers Authority (NRA)

The NRA will have a strong regional presence, with an office in each of the ten water authority regions; it is expected to employ about 6,500 staff, which is about 10 per cent of the number presently employed in the industry. The Water Bill has not yet been passed but the Government thinks that the NRA will be responsible for:

- Maintaining and improving the quality of inland, coastal and underground waters, control of pollution, the operation of the system of effluent discharge consents and the maintenance of public registers of information.

- The management of rivers and other water resources, including issuing abstraction and impoundment licences.
- The provision of amenities and management of recreation, and the furtherance of conservation in carrying out their functions.
- Land drainage and flood defence, the improvement and development of fisheries, and the navigation functions of the water authorities with such functions.

The creation of the NRA will remove the anomaly, inherent in the 1973 Water Act, that the water authorities were both poacher and gamekeeper over the control of pollution and sewage discharges, and any NRA would have been welcomed by many, with or without privatisation. A big question mark still remains over the size of its teeth and the strength of its will. A national body with the powers *and the will* to really improve the quality of inland and coastal waters could be an important step for environmental protection. Are the new gamekeepers (formerly employed by the water authorities) who move over to the NRA going to be tough with their former colleagues – or will the 'friendly persuasion', that has failed so miserably over pollution control in many parts of the country, continue?

The Director General of Water Services

The WSPLCs will have a monopoly of water supply in each region and the Director General's organisation, expected to employ 80–100 staff, is expected to protect the consumer in the manner in which OFTEL operates for telecommunications and OFGAS for gas. The Director General's duties will be:

- To monitor the activities and performance of all the water companies against the conditions set out in their licences, and, where necessary, to enforce those conditions.
- To ensure that customers are protected from unjustified price increases, reductions in services or diminution of essential infrastructure, while enabling the water companies to finance their operations.
- To ensure that the water companies carry out their functions efficiently and effectively, and to facilitate competition within the industry.

The Director General will be independent of any Government ministry and accountable directly to Parliament.

New Customer Service Committees will replace the old Consumer Consultative Committees of the authorities. They will be appointed by the Director General and will advise and report to him. The new committees will have a new statutory duty to investigate customers' complaints.

The extent to which the public will be protected by the Director General is, of course, unknown and it is difficult to make comparisons with OFTEL as the water industry is so much larger and more complex. From the public's point of view, the 'success' of privatisation – is the service good, is the price fair, is the company doing a good job – will depend on how strictly and effectively the Director General carries out his obligations.

Water Resources

There is three times more water in the earth's crust than all other materials put together. It is visible in the sea, ice, rivers, lakes and rain; invisible in the ground and the air. Of this, 95 per cent is the saltwater of the oceans which cover three-quarters of the earth, and most of the rest will remain as ice or locked up in the ground. However, a small fraction remains which constantly circulates from the sea, to the atmosphere, into rain, onto the land and back into the sea, as part of the natural water cycle. Most of the water which evaporates from the sea falls back on the sea as rain, but about one-tenth of it falls on land. Unfortunately, a large proportion of this literally goes with the wind and is lost again by evaporation, but we are left with a vast amount of water each day from which to take our supplies.

We all know it rains a lot in Britain, but we also know that we don't get that much on our heads each day. Britain's rain doesn't fall evenly, either geographically or seasonally, and the basic work of water supply is to take it from where there is a surplus to where it is needed. Warm air holds more moisture (water) than cool air, so when air cools the moisture condenses and falls as rain. Air cools when it rises and three factors are responsible for the resulting distribution across the UK.

1. Warm wet air, blowing in from the Atlantic, is pushed upwards by the mountains that stretch along Britain's west coast, causing the air to cool and rain to fall in those areas (*orographic rainfall*).
2. The same warm wet air may be lifted by the cold air associated with depressions and the resulting warm 'front' will carry a belt of rain right across the country.
3. A hot day can cause large volumes of air to rise, creating 'thunderclouds' and extensive heavy rain (*convection rainfall*).

This pattern is responsible for the wide difference in rainfall in England and Wales. Welsh Water receives an average of 1,334 mm a

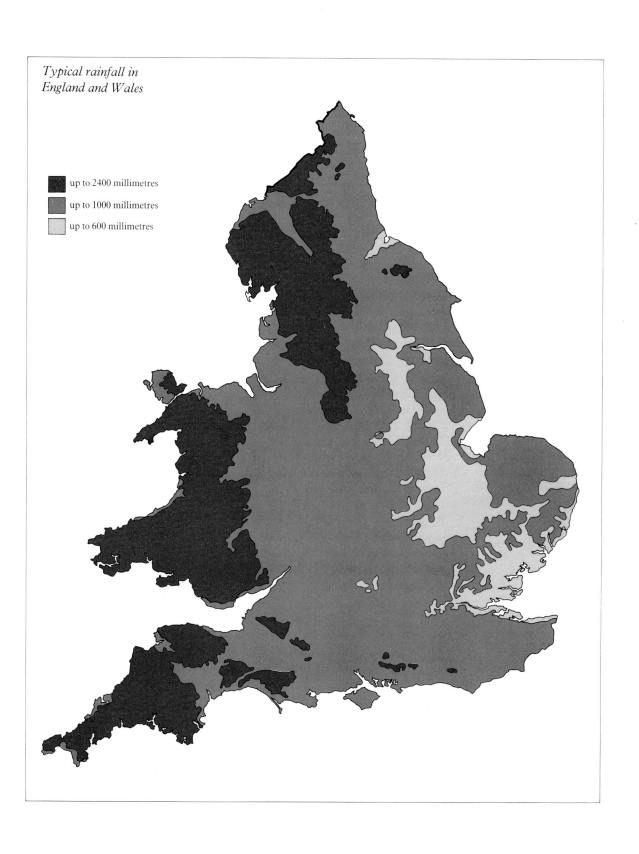

Typical rainfall in
England and Wales

up to 2400 millimetres

up to 1000 millimetres

up to 600 millimetres

year (1941–70) and Anglian Water 611 mm. Since approximately 500 mm are lost through evaporation across the whole country, the Welsh are left with 870 mm but Anglia with only 150 mm of *effective rainfall*. Worse still, orographic rainfall remains fairly constant, so in very dry years the east is more affected than the west and Anglia's rainfall can fall as low as 25 mm. On top of this, population numbers are high in the south east where the least rain falls, and low in the areas of maximum rainfall on the west coast. A further problem is that most rain falls in the winter, particularly the rain which falls on high ground and from depressions, while demand is greatest in the summer. Fortunately, our requirements, in relation to the amount of rain that falls, are quite modest, about 16 million cu m out of the 515 million cu m a day which fall.

In England and Wales we make use of water from three sources:

Groundwater

This is normally taken to mean water from under the ground, but should really include springs, in addition to supplies from wells and boreholes.

Springs

A number of springs were used in the ninteenth century but their yield, which was often not great anyway, tended to decline with the advent of pumps used to bring water from below ground. The presence of springs usually indicated a good groundwater supply, and wells and boreholes were frequently built on their sites. The source of the New River supply to London originally came from springs at Amwell and Chadwell. There are a few springs which, as a direct source, give a large enough quantity for public supply; the largest group are at Havant and give a reliable yield of 104 Ml per day. Naturally, there are many springs contributing indirectly to the catchments from which water is abstracted, particularly on the chalk of southern England.

Aquifers

Rain which falls onto the ground remains at first near the surface where it is known as *soilwater*. As more falls, it coats the particles of soil nearest the surface and runs deeper into the ground. The level below which the ground is saturated with water is known as the *water table*. Above this level the soilwater moves up, by capillary action, as water above it is removed by plants or evaporation, or down under the force of gravity. If the strata beneath the soil are porous, groundwater may be present in large quantities and go down to considerable depths. If, in addition, the strata are permeable, the groundwater will move under hydrostatic pressure, and can be extracted by pumping. The rocks or strata are

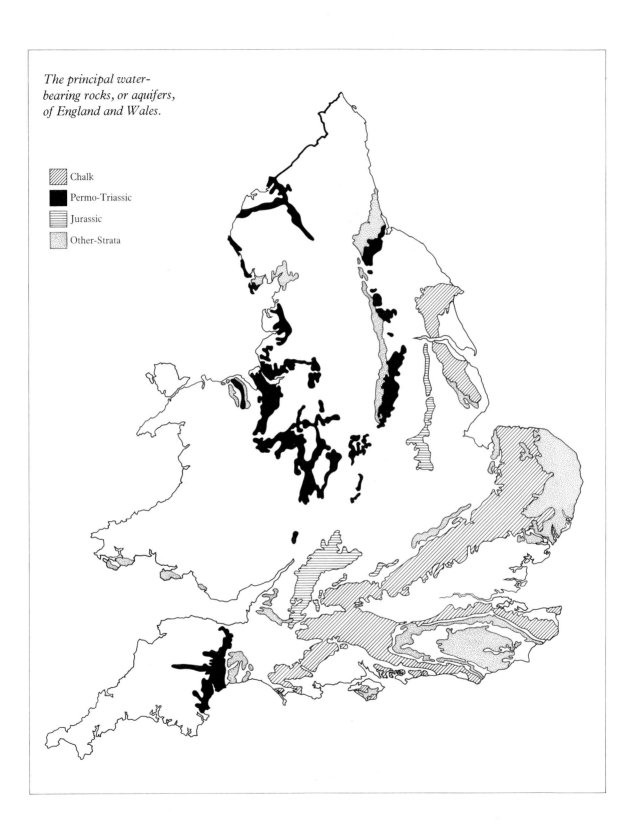

*The principal water-
bearing rocks, or aquifers,
of England and Wales.*

Chalk

Permo-Triassic

Jurassic

Other-Strata

then said to be *aquifers*. Rocks or strata that do not allow the passage of water are impermeable and said to be *aquicludes*. Clay is porous and holds water, but the small size of the clay particles does not allow the water to be abstracted and clay is therefore an aquiclude.

Chalk, in spite of being relatively impermeable itself, carries large quantities of water in cracks and fissures and is the most important of our aquifers. It covers much of the land between Weymouth and the Wash, with smaller deposits in east Yorkshire and Lincolnshire. There are nearly 13,000 sq km near the surface of England and an estimated extra 18,000 sq km more below ground; it is 90–500 m thick and yields roughly 40 per cent of our pumped groundwater.

The other major aquifers are the Bunter and Keuper sandstones which are found in the Midlands and the north west. There are about 4,500 sq km that outcrop and roughly another 3,000 sq km underground. The sandstones are generally thicker than the chalk and are an important source in Nottinghamshire. There are a number of smaller aquifers, like the magnesian limestone which supplies Hartlepool. An unusual aquifer is at Dungeness where about 15 sq km of shingle, between 3.5–6 m above sea level, have been deposited by the sea. This was the only source of supply for the Littlestone-on-Sea and District Water Company, now part of the Folkestone Water Company, which still has 28 wells there pumping good quality soft water.

The amount of water available in an aquifer is not as important as its dependable yield – public water supplies have to be reliable and it is not good management to pump more water out than will be naturally replenished from surface water. The quantity taken depends on the size of the aquifer, its permeability and its rate of replenishment or 'recharge'. The water level may vary by anything up to 46 m either through seasonal fluctuations, depending on rainfall, or as a result of pumping.

Water is pumped from aquifers through wells and boreholes. Wells are usually wide (anything from 1–3 m) and relatively shallow (say 15–125 m). They were traditionally dug by hand and usually lined with brick, cast iron or concrete. In self-supporting strata like chalk or sandstone, horizontal galleries, known as adits, were often constructed at the base of the wells. Usually about 1.8 m high and 1.2 m wide, they could be as long as 3–5 km. These not only improved yield but provided additional storage to even out fluctuations in demand. The larger wells are normally associated with nineteenth-century steam pumping stations where space was needed for the cumbersome mechanical pumping gear.

Boreholes are generally narrow (usually less than 1 m) and deep (mostly 30–300 m), although a few are considerably deeper. They are always made mechanically, by drilling or percussion boring. They often go down through one stratum into another and are frequently sealed in their upper lengths to prevent the intrusion of loose material and polluted or unwanted surface water.

Electro-submersible pumps are normally used in boreholes nowadays, as they are more flexible and easy to install and maintain. The first electric motors were positioned on the surface from where they drove long spindles to the pumps at the bottom of the shaft, and many of this type are still in use. One detail of their mechanics provides an interesting insight on modern technology: the bearings on the spindles were originally made of lignum vitae and lasted for many years; they are now made of a 'special' rubber – which breaks up in less than twelve months.

Diesel engines were sometimes used for a short period after steam, but steam was so reliable that it was not until labour and fuel costs rose in the twentieth century that they became uneconomical by which time electricity was the natural alternative, especially because it lent itself to automatic operation.

Aquifers are used extensively abroad to store water artificially. Instead of pumping water out, you can just as well pump it in, using the aquifer, like a sponge, as a natural reservoir. This is done with river water in Germany along the Main, the Rhine and the Ruhr, while in Holland they have found that rainwater can usefully be stored in sand dunes. Experiments have been carried out since the 1890s in England, but either caution or the easy availability of other sources may be the reason for this method not having been tried. Thames Water has recently done the most work on this and a scheme may soon be in operation.

Aquifers provide about a third of our water supply and the natural filtering which takes place in the rock makes it very clean. The only disadvantages are the cost of pumping, which can be high, and, recently, the presence of nitrates and pesticides in some areas where the aquifers are associated with agricultural land, as in East Anglia and the Midlands. The hydrogeology of aquifers is now fairly well understood and this allows them to be manipulated with considerable sophistication.

Impounding Reservoirs

We have seen that most rain falls on high ground and there were several good reasons why water undertakers in the early nineteenth century took advantage of this by building reservoirs to impound the available water.

1. Demand was continuous during the year, but water was more plentiful in winter. Build a large enough reservoir and you could have reliable supplies all the year round.

The shared Wimbleball reservoir was completed in 1978 and acts as a regulating reservoir for the River Exe in South West Water's region and an impounding reservoir for Wessex Water, who pump their supplies from it. (Photograph: South West Water)

2. Water from lowland rivers was becoming increasingly polluted as the population grew; the upland areas were relatively uninhabited and the water was clean and usually soft.

3. If the geology of a valley favoured the retention of water, very large reservoirs could be constructed by building one dam across the foot of a valley.

4. The reservoirs' height above the towns allowed the water to be taken down by gravity. The capital cost was very high even when labour was cheap but, once constructed, running costs were very low and they needed little maintenance.

The first dams were constructed of earth with a clay centre wall. When properly made they were very reliable and many still survive today from the first half of the nineteenth century. Overflow arrangements were a source of trouble when they ran in pipes through the embankment, but it later became normal practice to build them in tunnels in solid ground beneath the dam. Masonry dams were favoured for the very large reservoirs built towards the end of the nineteenth century. They remain as some of the most impressive examples of Victorian civil engineering still in use. Concrete buttresses have replaced masonry where this type of dam is appropriate but several recent dams have been constructed with earth embankments, although with the modern refinement of a waterproof membrane.

Many streams and rivers impounded for reservoirs were a source of power for mills further downstream, and in canal-building days it was normal to pay compensation to their owners for their losses. In some cases the millers preferred a guaranteed supply of water to be released, which came to be known as compensation water. The quantity is specified by the Act of Parliament that each scheme needed to allow it to proceed and in some cases this could be more than the amount withdrawn for public supply. When Bolton Waterworks wanted to impound water from the Daddy Meadows springs in 1824 (Springs reservoir), they were required to construct Belmont reservoir to supply compensation water to the millers and other riparian owners of Eagley Brook. They built another reservoir in 1843, taking water from the Shaley Dingle stream (Dingle reservoir), and were then required to raise Belmont by another 4.9 m. This made the total compensation flow 15.6 Ml a day, while the total supply available from Springs and Dingle is only a little over 4.5 Ml per day. Working watermills are scarce on our rivers today and the benefits of compensation water are now largely environmental.

Abstraction from Rivers

Rivers are both an obvious source of supply and an obvious place to throw rubbish, so they have not been a very popular source. However, the pressure of urban growth throughout the last 100–150 years has made many exceptions to this: London has had a continuous supply from the Thames since the sixteenth century. Unfortunately, those areas that did use river water had the worst outbreaks of disease and were often noted for the poor quality of their water. London has made use of sand filters since 1828, long before any other area in England.

The increase in water consumption since the last war, and projections for further increases that were made in the 1950s, brought about a return to the use of lowland rivers because other sources were running out, and because better treatment now made it a practical possibility.

Abstracting lowland river water has two big advantages over an impounding reservoir.

1. The further downstream that water is abstracted, the larger the catchment area feeding that intake. This can amount to many times the quantity that could be obtained from an impounding reservoir and piped supply.
2. Water can be taken in, used and returned again several times on its way downstream. I suppose this rather disagreeable thought can be looked at positively – the fact that the water in the Thames is used six times between Oxford and Teddington is a wonderful example of shared resources.

Regulating Systems

The problem of reduced summer flows has largely been overcome by regulating schemes. Water is taken from the catchment area when there is a surplus (normally in winter) and is released when flows downstream fall below predetermined levels (normally in summer). The usual method is to construct a 'regulating' reservoir in the catchment area. In practice this also acts as an impounding reservoir without the cost of a pipeline, since this is provided by the river, with the advantage that water need only be released when river levels are low. Several very large regulating schemes have now been built, the largest of which is on the Dee.

An important side effect of these schemes is the possibility of flood control – a large-storage-capacity upstream reservoir can be filled by very heavy rain and prevent flooding downstream. The level of the Clywedog reservoir on the upper Severn is lowered by 1 November each year to make space for 8,400 Ml of possible floodwater and is only allowed to refill by 1 May for possible demands over the summer. It has been found in practice, however, that the flood relief value does not altogether match the theory. There is a clear benefit immediately downstream of the dam at Llanidloes, but the dam only takes 2.5 per cent of the catchment of the Severn reaching Shrewsbury for instance, which is not enough to give significant relief. Of the average River Dee run-off from the catchment areas 33 per cent is controlled by regulating reservoirs and this clearly gives greater opportunities for control.

Well and borehole water is used to regulate rivers in the same way as reservoirs but usually on a much smaller scale since groundwater is being pumped all the year round and there is not likely to be a surplus in summer. It does form part of schemes where river flows without regulation allow abstraction to take place most years but cannot always be relied on. The groundwater may then be used as a back up in very dry summers.

Pumped Water Storage

Areas like East Anglia, whose geography and rainfall patterns make them unsuitable for impounding reservoirs, were often forced to be more dependent on rivers. The usual problem of low summer flows was overcome by constructing storage reservoirs into which water could be pumped when flows were high. This had the very useful additional advantage of improving the water quality. Some of the fine organic and other matter settles out naturally, the action of light kills undesirable bacteria and the oxygen level is improved. Some of these reservoirs are used all year round. Acting as a buffer between the river and the treatment works, they may contain only a few days' supply. Others only take winter floodwater and remain on standby in case of very dry summers. Rutland Water is one of the largest and takes water from two rivers, the Welland and the Nene. Distinctions between reservoir types can become blurred when additional water is pumped into an impounding reservoir from a river.

Development of Resources

Development of resources in the past could be taken to mean finding more water, but the decline in industry and the levelling out of population figures give all the authorities reason to believe they have adequate supplies until the end of this century. Severn Trent is the only one about to build a major new project, the reservoir at Carsington. This does not mean that developments are not taking place, but these could better be described as managerial, aiming to make more efficient use of the supplies we have, largely as a result of computerised techniques.

Many ideas put forward for the future have more to do with using what is already available. It would be possible to connect the Thames to the Severn system or Yorkshire to Kielder Water in Northumberland, bringing water from an area of surplus to an area of need. Estuary barrages could save very large quantities from going out to sea, but they would be very expensive and environmentally undesirable. Public feeling is fairly strongly against further impounding reservoirs on loss of amenity grounds.

River Management and Flood Control

The management of our larger rivers is a balancing act between the different and often conflicting requirements of many users and there is no solution that will satisfy every interested party. Water resource engineers, navigators and fishermen all want plenty of water, but high levels will create problems for land drainage and flood control. Environmentalists may want a different rate of river flow to the sewage works managers who have to discharge effluent into it. In this century several Acts of Parliament have gradually introduced the concept of overall river basin management in England and Wales. In 1915, 2,160 or so water undertakings existed, in addition to local authorities responsible for land drainage, flooding and sewage. The 1973 Water Act finally reduced the remaining 1,600 assorted river and drainage boards, various companies and local authorities' water and sewage interests down to the ten existing regional water authorities, with complete control over all aspects of river management.

Rainfall is one of the most important aspects of planning in river management and some records exist from the eighteenth century. After 1825 records were made regularly, with Victorian enthusiasm, by both amateurs and professionals. The British Meteorological Society was founded in 1850 and followed by the English Meteorological Office in 1854, which was a branch of the Board of Trade.

Measurements have been made in a standardised rain gauge since 1866 and by the end of the nineteenth century there were about 3,000 separate stations recording data; there are about 7,000 today. Our climate is changing and for this reason a convention has grown up of comparing annual rainfall against an 'average' of the last 35 years only. The climate between the years 1881–1915 and 1915–50 was from 4–14 per cent wetter over different parts of the country. The highest ever 24-hour fall recorded in Great Britain was 28 cm in Dorset in 1955.

River flow records have more rarely been kept in the UK and hydrologists have often had to use marks on bridges and buildings to estimate maximum and minimum flows, but systematic gauging has now been in force since the Water Resources Act of 1963. Forecasting, as a management aid, has become very high tech in recent years. Satellites can measure the proportion of absorbent ground surface and help predict the amount of water that will run straight into a river system; radar is used in conjunction with the Meteorological Office to track weather systems across the Atlantic; telemetry is permanently recording data on rainfall and river levels and flows, and a mass of information is available on computer records to help analyse the outcome of any weather pattern.

All this information can now be used in computer models which take in all aspects of the control and use of a river, and these are now used for all the larger river systems, to make maximum use of the water available, economise on costs of abstraction and for flood warning and control.

River Management

No river in England or Wales exists in anything like its natural state. Over the last 2,000 years they have been a resource which has attracted industry and trading and people have channelled them to suit their needs. For the first settlers they were convenient for raiding and marking boundaries, but as kingdoms expanded all our large towns grew up on their banks and they became the most important routes for commerce until very recent times. They were the most important source of mechanical power for many years and the experience gained by millers in controlling their flow was subsequently put to use in controlling the levels of smaller rivers for navigation. Farmers made use of the fertile land and soon learnt the value of constructing open drainage channels to improve soil condition and make the land more workable.

Land Drainage

The history of land drainage in Britain is difficult to trace and opinions differ on early practitioners. It is not clear whether channels dug by the Romans at a number of sites in England were for navigation or drainage or both. Romney Marsh, consisting of 20,000 hectares of land below the level of high tide, is the oldest known area to use artificial means for draining agricultural land and the first area to have a properly constituted drainage authority. The 'lords bailiff and jurors of Romney Marsh', dating from 1232, had the power to make a levy on landowners for the maintenance of sea walls and drainage channels. This body continued to function until it merged with the Romney Marsh Main Drains Catchment Board in 1930.

In 1508, in the reign of Henry VII, an Act was passed 'concerning The Commissioners of Sewers to be directed in all parts within the realm'. This was succeeded by a number of further Acts which culminated with an Act in 1601, setting up Commissioners and Courts of Sewers. Several nineteenth-century Acts concerned themselves with land drainage but without any system of management or control, and it was only the urgency of food production during the First World War of 1914–18 that gave impetus to the establishment of area drainage boards with powers under the Minister of Agriculture. At this time there were 51 commissioners of sewers, 49 elective drainage boards and 219 other local authorities with drainage responsibilities, and the situation remained messy.

A Royal Commission reported, in 1927, that 517,500 hectares were flooded because of defective drains, and a further 192,600 hectares required draining. It was estimated two years later that £18 million worth of food production had been lost for these reasons. The Land Drainage Act 1930 constituted 46 catchment boards with vested powers to correlate drainage throughout their areas. It was still found necessary for special powers to be taken during the Second World War and a number of these provisions were made permanent in the River Boards Act of 1948, which brought all drainage in 32 river catchment areas under their own authority.

Internal Drainage Boards (IDBs)

The principle of river basin management being under the control of the water authorities breaks down with these curious institutions. Land drainage in many areas is, in practice, in the hands of internal drainage boards. There are 214 of them and they have been described as 'private clubs for farmers, with the power to levy rates'. Members must own at least 4 hectares of land, or occupy 8 hectares or be nominated by someone who does; there is little competition for places so elections rarely take place – existing board members simply nominate others. Inevitably, the boards consist of farmers and are dominated by farming interests, in spite of the fact that most of their money comes from urban ratepayers and Government grants.

The Dun IDB in Yorkshire receives 93 per cent of its rates from its 2 per cent of urban ratepayers, although 98 per cent of its land is agricultural. In 1980 for instance, they received £17 million in grants and appear to be accountable only to an assistant secretary in MAFF. They do not have to make ecological studies; they can enter land and carry out work without notifying anyone; their cost/benefit analyses are secret; and they do not have to show that they have chosen the least environmentally damaging scheme, although they did go too far in claiming to be exempt from the clause in the 1968 Countryside Act requiring public bodies to have regard for conservation – and were reprimanded by the minister.

The 500,000 hectares of land in England and Wales covered by the IDBs include some of our most sensitive wetland habitats, occupied by many of our rarest birds and plants, but the boards, not surprisingly in view of their make-up, have shown little consideration for any interests other than farming. The 1988 Water Bill, claimed as a major advance for the environment, leaves the organisation of the IDBs unchanged.

Flood Prevention

There are two sorts of flooding. Flash floods are caused by very heavy rain falling on areas where it cannot run away if more rain falls than the drains or gutters can hold – urban concrete or low lying ground already saturated are typical causes. These floods usually subside as quickly as they appear and are not very damaging.

The other type of flood is caused by rivers having too much water in them, which then rises out of control beyond the banks. These circumstances have been responsible for the worst floods in England, often associated with serious damage and fatalities. Flooding of this type can mostly be allayed nowadays with structural flood prevention schemes and careful control of river levels, but however much money is spent, it is not possible to guarantee protection from something that is a one in every 100–200 years eventuality. When the River Lud in Lincolnshire flooded in 1920, it was carrying 33 times its average annual maximum water and the flood caused 24 deaths. According to subsequent calculations, it was found to be theoretically impossible for the 12.5 cm of rain which fell to have created such a flood; the river rose 5 m in fifteen minutes and created rivers up to 30 m wide in normally dry valleys. It would clearly not be feasible to structure rivers to cope with 'extraordinary' events like this.

Structural prevention in 1986–87, like improving banks, dredging, realigning lengths of river, building weirs and sluices and making flood relief channels, cost the water authorities nearly £35 million that year. Their other line of protection is early warning. If flooding is seen to be likely from the analysis of incoming data, the police and the local authority are alerted. They pass on the warning to householders and businesses likely to be affected, and arrange for possible road closures. Although this cannot prevent the disruption of people's lives which a flood may cause, it can appreciably reduce damage and hardship.

Sea Defences

As the high watery walls came rolling in, and, at their highest, tumbled into the surf, they looked as if the least would engulf the town. As the receding wave swept back with a hoarse roar, it seemed to scoop out deep caves in the beach, as if its purpose were to undermine the earth.

Charles Dickens, the storm at Yarmouth from *David Copperfield* (1850)

Water authorities took on the responsibility for sea defences, along with that of land drainage, because, ultimately, all river, flood and drainage water which is not abstracted for public use has to be discharged into the sea. In addition to defence in relation to rivers at their conjunction with the sea in estuaries, it was thought logical to extend responsibility to the protection of all land against tidal flooding. The distinction should be made between sea defences which protect from flooding and those which prevent the erosion of the coast; they may often be the same thing but not always.

It has been known for some time that risks of tidal flooding have increased, and expensive precautionary steps have had to be taken in recent years to protect a number of areas. The main reasons for this increased risk are that the east side of Britain is tilting into the sea, at a rate of about 30 cm per century, along an axis from Bristol to Newcastle, and, at the same time, the oceans appear to be increasing in volume. If a tidal surge from the North Sea coincides with a high spring tide, high water may be 2–3 m above the average. The populations

The floods at Sea Palling, Norfolk in 1953 when seven people were drowned. Life-destroying floods have been recorded in this low-lying area since 1287. Although reasonably well protected now, a question mark must remain over the future if, or when, the greenhouse effect raises sea levels. (Photograph: Anglian Water)

likely to be affected are very large, but the projects do not excite public imagination in a way that others do which can be seen to be immediately useful. It is a sad but characteristic failing that we tend not to notice these defences unless they do not work. It would appear that they are at present suitably matched to likely high seas but a question mark stands over the future as the 'greenhouse effect', or global warming, could appreciably raise sea levels.

Britain's tilt is reflected in the cost of sea defences for 1986/87: Northumbrian spent nothing, Southern spent over £5 million and Anglian spent nearly £11 million. A large part of these expenses is grant-aided by the Government.

Much of our coastline is on the move as sand and shingle are picked up by the action of the waves and deposited somewhere else. This drift can be slowed down, and in some cases prevented, by building groins at right angles to the shore, but if too much erosion takes place there may be a danger of flooding. In cases like this, the beach materials can be picked up and replaced where they first came from, or a similar material can be used to construct an artificial beach. These 'natural' defences have several advantages. They can look much nicer or may even be indistinguishable from the originals; they are often cheaper, and they are more efficient at breaking the power of the waves. Hard, solid barriers take the full force of the waves in one place, but beaches gradually remove the waves' power over a large area (Southern Water's Seaford beach is a good example and is described on page 175).

In areas where it would be impossible to build such natural defences, or where there is exposure to severe wave action, hard sea walls have to be constructed, usually of concrete. In many cases a combination of both methods can be used, with a shingle or sand slope backed or topped by a concrete crest. Marshes and tidal river estuaries, which are usually sheltered from the full force of the waves, are often protected by earth embankments surfaced with stones or concrete blocks.

Water Treatment and Supply

Our sister Water, very servicable and humble and precious and clean.

St Francis of Assisi (1181?-1226)

There is no such thing as pure natural water. Water is a dilute solution of a large number of chemicals and often holds a number of substances in suspension. Some of its contents may be beneficial or even essential

Water abstraction from the Thames has always carried the risk of disease. The dangerous and sometimes illegal practices of some nineteenth-century companies were a public disgrace. (Thames Water)

for human health, while others may be undesirable or even toxic. Furthermore, all natural waters vary enormously according to the different chemical and biological 'load' that they pick up. Groundwaters collect their constituents from the rocks that hold them; rainwater picks up ingredients from dust and chemicals in the air; river waters may carry large quantities of living and dead organic matter and minerals and acids from the soil, as well as manmade pollutants.

The extent of variation may be imagined from looking at groundwaters – they are usually considered the purest supply. A current textbook lists 121 sources, all with an entirely different chemical make up. It is not the purpose of treatment to get rid of all these 'impurities' – they give the water character and life. The EEC even specifies minimum concentrations of certain substances which make water hard, as they are considered beneficial to our health. Spa waters gain whatever medicinal effects they have from their chemical content and are drunk for this very reason, despite their sometimes dubious taste and appearance.

In spite of the Victorian interest in health and civic affairs, there was no national legislation specifically covering water quality in the nineteenth century and, even more extraordinary, practically none until the EEC Directive of 1980. The Waterworks Clauses Act 1847 did specify that all statutory water undertakings were required to supply 'pure and wholesome' water but made no attempt to define this, nor did any subsequent Act until the EEC Directive. This does not, in any way, mean that it had not been a subject of concern (the writings of Victorian water engineers and health officials show a frequent and serious involvement with the subject), merely that it was not considered to be a proper subject for legislation. Routine chemical analyses of water supplied to London were begun in 1858, followed by regular bacteriological examination in 1885, and it may well have been felt that these matters could safely be left in the hands of scientists. Chlorination has practically eliminated water-borne disease since the Croydon outbreak, and suppliers have turned more of their attention to appearance and taste in the last few years. Pressure groups are also now demanding a reassessment of health aspects and some of these are considered below.

The World Health Organisation published International Standards for Drinking Water in 1958 and European Standards for Drinking Water in 1961. These formed a basis for many authorities to work from, but the EEC Directive (80/778/EEC) now defines a mandatory standard to which all European suppliers must work. This has certainly been welcomed by the public as its parameters are clearly defined and leave no room for argument. The welcome has been less than wholehearted from the water authorities, who challenge the stringency of the limits –

Group	Parameter	MAC	GL	Units etc.	Derogations applied for	
					Supplies no.	Volume Ml/d
A	colour	20	0	mg/l Pt/Co scale	16	156
	turbidity	10	0	mg/l SiO$_2$	3	55
	odour	{ 2 at 12° C	1	dilution no.	9	274
	taste	{ 3 at 25° C	1	dilution no.	9	274
B	pH	5.5† to 9.5★	6.5 to 8.5	pH	3	331
	conductivity	1500★	400	us/cm	2	4
	chlorides	400★	25	mg/l	2	4
	sulphates	250	25	mg/l	3	9
	magnesium	50	30	mg/l	3	60
	sodium	175	20	mg/l	2	4
	potassium	12	10	mg/l	10	45
	aluminium	0.2	0.05	mg/l	50	959
C	nitrates	50	25	mg/l	49	311
	nitrites	0.1		mg/l	4	10
	ammonium	0.5	0.05	mg/l	4	6
	trihalomethanes	100★	1	µg/l	13	164
	iron	200	50	µg/l	53	861
	manganese	50	20	µg/l	71	1183
	zinc	2000★	100 to 5000	µg/l	0	0
D	lead	50		µg/l	★★	★★
	pesticides	0.1 to 0.5		µg/l	††	††
E	total coliforms	0		{ membrane	23	40
	fecal coliforms	0		{ filter	37	100
F	total hardness	60†		mg/l Ca	4	364
	total				266	3000

† minimum required concentration ★ values set by Government
†† EC being asked to review limits ★★ areas still being drawn up

Drinking water parameters set by EEC Directive 80/778 and supplies affected by derogations in England (September 1987). (Table: Water Authorities Association)

and have the problem of keeping to them. There are 66 parameters covering taste and appearance as well as safety (to health) and they are classified in groups as follows:

A Organoleptic
B Physico-chemical
C Substances undesirable in excessive amounts
D Toxic substances
E Microbiological
F Minimum concentrations for soft water

The limits are demanding and this is, to some extent, recognised by the fact that under Article 9 of the Directive Government derogations can be applied for in groups A, B, C and F to take account of 'situations arising from the nature and structure of the ground in the area from which the supply in question emanates', or 'situations arising from exceptional meteorological conditions' and where it does not 'constitute a health hazard'. Compliance with groups D and E, which relate to 'toxic and microbiological factors', may be delayed under Article 20 for geographically defined population groups. In addition to the maximum admissible concentrations (MAC), guide levels (GL) are given which are often substantially lower. The table on page 47 lists those parameters for which derogations have been sought under Articles 9 and 20, with the quantity of supplies involved.

The major point which the British Government and many suppliers in Britain feel to be unfair is that compliance depends on never exceeding the MACs. They think that a three-monthly or annual average should be acceptable (as in World Health Organisation [WHO] guidelines). While there are good grounds for accepting this argument from a supplier working within the spirit of the law, it is felt in many quarters that our Government's bad record of rule-bending in the EEC lays all of its actions open to suspicion. As the guide levels are often so much lower than the MACs, there seems a good case for trying to conform to the law rather than altering it. The substances causing most concern at present are:

Aluminium

Evidence published in January 1989 suggests a correlation between the incidence of Alzheimer's disease, a form of senile dementia, and aluminium in drinking water. Soluble aluminium occurs naturally and widely in water, particularly where acidic upland water leaches it from rocks or the soil – for this reason it has the second largest Article 9 derogation by quantity. As only a very small part of our dietary intake of aluminium comes from water, the link with Alzheimer's disease is puzzling. It is, however, a particularly worrying suggestion since, in addition to its widespread natural occurrence, aluminium sulphate is used widely in the industry as a coagulant in water-filtering techniques. Although research is in its early stages, it will undoubtedly lead to pressure to remove the derogations on aluminium as soon as possible. Other coagulants are available – but often with their own disadvantages.

In July 1988 20 tonnes of aluminium sulphate were put by mistake into the drinking water supply at the Lowermoor treatment works near Camelford in Cornwall. This incident must be one of the worst in recent British water-supply history, not only for its serious possible repercussions, but also because of the disastrous way in which the situation was handled by South West Water – mistaken assumptions, wrong decisions and bad communications with the public. Around 20,000 people are reported to have suffered illness, with many still affected, and with an unknown prognosis for after affects. Approximately 61,000 salmon and trout were killed in attempts to clear the mains and the Rivers Allen and Camel may take three years to recover.

Lead

Lead is a proven toxic agent in water and has been held responsible for a high incidence of insanity in areas associated with disused lead mines. Several recent studies have shown that almost any intake of lead can have an adverse effect on children's intelligence, and a number of countries would like the accepted EEC levels for lead to be lower.

Although lead was the traditional material used for domestic water pipes, it is not normally soluble, although certain waters, said to be 'plumbosolvent', can carry lead from these pipes into the supply. All suppliers now treat water to reduce plumbosolvency and the old pipes are less common. However, it would be sensible for anyone who does have extensive lead piping to consult his or her local water supplier.

The situation is serious in Scotland where far more lead is in use in supply pipes and cisterns. Towns like Glasgow and Edinburgh are said to have the highest levels in Europe, some at the point of being clinically dangerous. It is quite common for EEC standards not to be met but the Government's attempt to gain a further delay in implementing them for the whole of Scotland is now likely to be challenged by the European Parliament.

Nitrates

In excessive quantities, and usually in association with bacteriological contamination, these are the cause of methaemoglobinaemia (blue baby syndrome) in bottle-fed babies. The condition is very rare and has not been reported since 1972 in the UK. A connection between nitrates and stomach cancer has been suggested but does not appear sustainable on current evidence. In some areas, particularly Anglian and Severn Trent, contemporary agricultural practices are creating a serious problem, with nitrate levels exceeding EEC limits in supplies. They are not easily removed. Experimental treatment plants are in operation and have proved effective but the processes are expensive to run and some have byproducts which are difficult to dispose of.

Some authorities are able to mix high-level with low-level supplies, to comply with the Directive, but this is not practical in badly affected areas. The Water Research Centre, Severn Trent, the DOE and MAFF have all contributed to a study of farming practice and groundwater movement which included computer modelling and cost-benefit analyses. This showed that land-use control would be feasible, either by whole catchment restrictions (say a 20 per cent reduction in production) or local protection zones (involving forestry, for example). The question of who will pay for the implementation of such schemes is a hot potato currently being tossed round among the DOE, MAFF, the NFU and the water authorities. Until someone grasps it, there is no scope for progress to be made. Friends of the Earth's suggestion that all nitrate fertilisers should bear a tax to pay for either treatment or compensation for the protection zones seems a workable and fair application of the 'polluter pays' principle. The difficulty of keeping to the EEC Directive is very real and although the dangers to health may be exaggerated, that should not be a reason for complacency.

Pesticides and Organic Compounds

Many organic compounds may be dangerous to health in very small quantities and are, at present, the subject of worldwide research. Several pesticides, industrial solvents like trichloroethylene, and some chlorination byproducts like trihalomethanes (THMs) are considered a potential source of human cancer by scientists, including those at the World Health Organisation (WHO), and nobody yet knows how safe they are in very small quantities. Some of WHO's recommended levels for pesticides are lower than those of the EEC.

A survey undertaken by Friends of the Earth shows that the EEC limits for individual pesticides (1 part per billion) were exceeded in 298 sources and supplies between July 1985 and June 1987; those for total pesticide content were exceeded on 76 occasions in the same period. A DOE report has estimated that a tenth of all groundwater sources may be contaminated with trichloroethylene above the level of WHO limits.

The WRc is researching the use of granular activated carbon in removing these 'potentially hazardous substances', and was due to publish a review in 1988 on the toxicological significance of some of them. The Government, in the meantime, would like flexible standards to be established, which relate more directly to the proven health risk of each chemical. This may well be reasonable in the long run but at the present time there is very little information to go on and a more cautious approach seems sensible. The priority recommended by Friends of the Earth would be to prevent further pollution now, with the use of the 'best available treatment technology' on suspect sources as soon as possible.

Water Treatment

Water treatment is the term used to describe the processes which improve the quality of water and ensure that it should be as safe as possible before delivery to the customer. These range from the passive – leaving water in a reservoir to improve – through various filtration methods and, finally, to some form of disinfection.

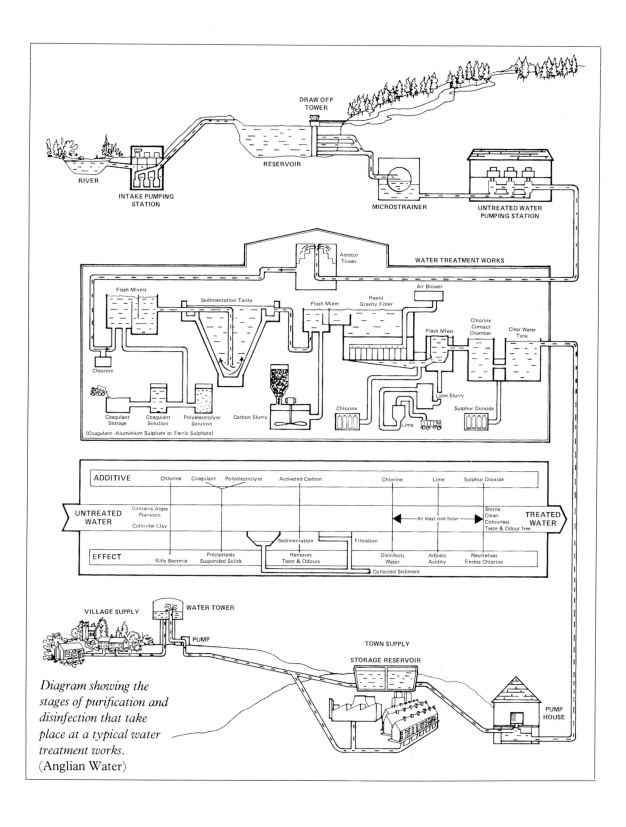

Diagram showing the stages of purification and disinfection that take place at a typical water treatment works.
(Anglian Water)

Treatment should make water safe and healthy by:
- destroying harmful bacteria;
- removing harmful minerals and pollutants such as pesticides;
- controlling hardness and acidity.

It also aims to make water aesthetically pleasing by:
- removing unpleasant tastes and smells;
- removing colour and suspended matter.

There is no set treatment for water because of the enormous variations in its quality. All suppliers use one or more of the following methods in different combinations and with minor variations.

Storage

In addition to the practical advantages for supply of keeping water stored in reservoirs, very real improvements to its quality do take place. It has been said that 'an adequately stored water is a safe water'. Roughly speaking, the longer the better, but after ten days' storage between 75 and 99 per cent of the harmful bacteria die out, the actual amount depending on weather, temperature and sunlight. At the same time, suspended matter settles to the bottom, sunlight improves colour, and hardness and organic impurities can be improved by exposure to air and algae. The average time for storing Thames water varies from fourteen to 120 days and is probably typical of most pumped storage reservoirs. If the water is rich in nutrients, filtration problems may arise from the growth of algae. Steps can be taken at the storage stage to reduce this, but the disadvantages are thought to outweigh the advantages.

Screening and Aeration

Water is passed through coarse screens to remove any objects roughly over the size of a grain of sand, the main object being to prevent the entry of fish, weeds, sticks, etc., to the works. It is sometimes aerated in cascades, or mechanically with air pumps, to remove certain odours and dissolved gases. Aeration can also oxidise some mineral salts, taking them out of solution into filterable form.

Coagulation, Flocculation and Sedimentation

A coagulant, usually aluminium or iron sulphate, is added to the water and thoroughly mixed. This produces a floc (from the Latin *floccus*, a fleece) of coagulated suspended matter which attracts and filters out the smaller particles. These are collected in the sedimentation tanks, either settling out on the bottom (horizontal flow) or, more usually nowadays, forming a blanket near the top of the tank, through which the water has to pass (upward flow). The mechanism of coagulation, or agglomeration, is physically and chemically complex, but sophisticated controls now allow the whole process to operate automatically. Dissolved air flotation is a closely related technique, using air to carry particles to the surface from where they can be removed by scrapers.

Rapid Gravity Filters

These are normally used in conjunction with coagulation techniques to remove any particles or floc that might remain in the water supply. They are open tanks through which water is passed either downwards or upwards through 90-cm layers of sand and/or anthracite, which act as the filters. These filters are fast and simple to clean, but are not effective enough to be used on their own except with good quality groundwaters and very clean upland sources. Pressure filters are the same in practice but the filtering medium is enclosed and water is pumped through under pressure.

Slow Sand Filters

This is one of those simple methods which are so successful that, with only small modifications, they can remain useful for years. The credit for the idea normally goes to James Simpson who introduced them at the Chelsea Waterworks Company in 1829. He was probably responsible for their widespread use in Britain thereafter, but was really only developing the work of a number of earlier engineers in Scotland in the early nineteenth century – the full implications of the benefits of the process were not realised until many years later.

In this method water is strained through several layers of sand in large basins in a similar manner to the rapid gravity filter, although the sand is more carefully graded, with some layers containing much finer sand. The water passes through very slowly and, in addition to the straightforward physical straining, a number of complex micro-biological actions are simultaneously taking place. Organic and chemical deposits on the surface of the grains make a base on which algae, bacteria and protozoa establish themselves and form a fine living mesh that breaks down further organic matter, decomposes plankton and uses up nitrates, phosphates and CO_2 while releasing oxygen in their place. Huge numbers of bacteria develop below this and break down any remaining organic matter; a clear clean drinking water comes out at the bottom. The importance of the biological role in removing harmful bacteria and viruses was not realised until quite late in the nineteenth century, but the method was so effective that it became almost universal for cleaning river water and is still often used today as the only other treatment apart from chlorination.

The system is a delightful example of people setting up an apparently simple operation and finding millions of primitive lifeforms both helping them and benefiting themselves from the situation. However, this benign mutual co-operation has the disadvantage of being rather too slow for contemporary needs and inadequate for coping with the very heavy loads of pollutants in lowland rivers. Also, although the process for cleaning the beds has been automated, it remains a difficult and skilled operation.

Polishing

These processes, sometimes called 'tertiary treatment', are additional treatments which may not be essential but greatly improve the aesthetic quality of drinking water. It is a measure of the water undertakers' concern for public opinion that considerable reseach has gone into this area over many years. The process most often associated with it is filtration through granular activated carbon.

Disinfection

However effective any treatment can be, it cannot guarantee the absence of pathogenic material, and all water in public supplies has been disinfected since the 1937 outbreak of typhoid in Croydon. Faecal contamination is the source of human pathogens in water and the indicator used by all analysts looking for it is the presence of *Escherichia coli* (known as *E. coli*), the measure of which will be found on all analyses of water. The EEC Directive stipulates a zero count for microbiological content in supplies, but the occurrence of bacteria is so universal that they normally need to exist in large numbers to be harmful.

The most common substance used for disinfection is chlorine, which is added in sufficient quantities to kill all bacteria and leave a little over for the journey to the customer, to make sure that old or leaking pipes cannot contaminate supplies. If there is a high risk of infectious material in a supply, or large fluctuations of such material, as there might be from some lowland rivers, for instance, a much greater dose of chlorine is given and any excess removed before the water finally enters the mains, a process known as superchlorination. Other methods used for disinfection are treatment with the gas ozone and exposure to ultra violet light, but they only account for a tiny proportion of supplies in comparison to the chlorine method.

To read water authority literature one would assume that water-borne illness was a thing of the past. This is unfortunately not so. Cases of gastro-enteritis, dysentery and paratyphoid B have all occurred, one incident in 1966, for example, infecting 4,000 people. The cause is usually a combination of contamination and faulty chlorination. At

Bramham, Yorkshire in 1980, after 3,000 people contracted gastroenteritis, it was found that a brief sewer blockage had allowed sewage to enter an aquifer and get from there into the public supply. The equipment dosing that supply with chlorine appeared to be working normally and the chlorine was being used up at the correct rate, but it was subsequently realised that it was running to waste through a leaking pump gland. The infection was not particularly serious, but does show the importance of effective methods of disinfection.

Adjustments

Two 'adjustments' to water are regularly made. The first concerns pH which is a measure of acidity or alkalinity. Many of the treatment processes work best at a specific pH and the water is adjusted to suit this. Before going into the supply it is neutralised so that it is not so acid that it would corrode pipes (plumbosolvency is one particular risk already mentioned) and not so alkaline that it leaves deposits of scale.

The second adjustment is control of the hardness in water. Very hard water is neither pleasant nor popular and is softened to bring it within certain limits. Very soft waters have been associated with cardio-vascular disease and some waters are artificially hardened. Fluoride can only be added at the request and expense of a Medical Officer of Health. Since supplies nowadays are rarely specific to health areas and may, anyway, be routed to different areas at different times, a question mark hangs over the future of fluoridation.

Sewerage

And thou shalt have a paddle upon thy weapon; and it shall be, when thou wilt ease thyself abroad, thou shalt dig therewith, and thou shalt turn back and cover that which cometh from thee.

Deuteronomy 23

Privies in rural China were set up near the household gate and enticements offered to passing travellers in the hope that they might leave a valuable contribution of manure for the next season's crops. No such common-sense attitudes prevail in Britain where even to mention the subject is 'not quite nice'. We have no socially acceptable word for shit or crap in everyday use and have to rely on circumlocution or quasi-medical terms like stools and motions when talking to the vicar.

Unfortunately, urban living and the industrial revolution, in particular, brought so many people together in one place that it became

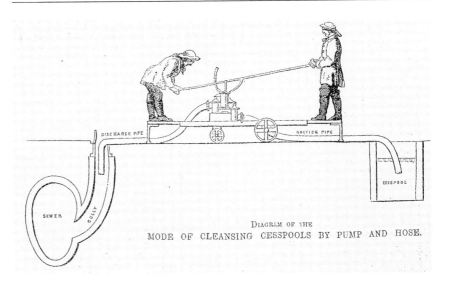

An illustration from Henry Mayhew's London Labour and the London Poor. *Mayhew's fascination with London's hidden life extended to sewage and sewage workers. He devotes many pages to their working conditions and rates of pay, as well as to statistics relating to sewerage.*

DIAGRAM OF THE
MODE OF CLEANSING CESSPOOLS BY PUMP AND HOSE.

impossible to ignore the stuff and by the nineteenth century it had become essential to find a disposal system. Things that are desirable in a rural society may be a nuisance, or even dangerous, in an urban one. Night soil men had traditionally removed it from the wealthier urban homes, but could not cope with rapidly growing demands on them. Victorian reformers put their minds to this as much as any other challenge and the dedication of men like Edwin Chadwick helped to bring in the Public Health Act of 1848. This Act was a disappointment to those hoping for powers to improve the insanitary conditions in the larger towns, but, in establishing a Central Board of Health, it was the start of the role of the Government in public health, and ancestor to the Ministry of Health.

In 1857, Parliament appointed the first of several royal commissions to look at sewage disposal, the last of which sat from 1898 to 1915 and recommended a number of standards which are still widely used. At the same time, other commissions examined the discharge into rivers and produced the Rivers Pollution Prevention Act in 1876, which remained substantially in use until recently. It was revised in 1951 as the Rivers (Prevention of Pollution) Act, and is now largely replaced by the Control of Pollution Act. They were all intended to protect rivers from pollution by sewage discharges, a subject which remains contentious.

The Public Health and Local Government Acts put the responsibility for sewerage in the hands of local authorities. This remained an effective system for many years, but the large number of these bodies, somewhere over 1,000, did not fit in with the concept of overall river basin management and sewerage was brought under the control of the water authorities in the 1973 Water Act. This has proved an extremely expensive legacy since numerous works (the majority in at least one authority area) were found to be out of date, neglected and discharging polluted effluent. In a few works, the discharges flowing out were found to be even more unhealthy than the sewage flowing into them! The sewers were also decaying; in many cases they were over a hundred years old and frequently not large enough for the population they served.

Victorian sewers, which still form the basis of today's urban networks, were usually constructed to take rainwater from gutters and streets as well as sewage. This presents a serious problem today because the larger loads the sewers carry do not allow sufficient space for storm water. The raw sewage that overflows from the network is a regular contributor to pollution incidents. Since the 1920s, water from roads and gutters has often been channelled separately and discharged directly

An aerial view of the Beckton Sewage Works, which treats the waste of nearly two and a half million Londoners. Britain's largest sewage works, it was first brought into operation in 1864. (Photograph: Thames Water)

to the rivers. This has made sewer flows more predictable but is, in itself, another frequent cause of river pollution from accidents and one which cannot be prevented without the buffer of a sewage works. Many sewers are quite adequate for most of the time, but not large enough for the daily morning and evening peaks combined with larger rain flows. The Water Research Centre (WRc) is investigating 'sewer flow attenuation', a technique using retention tanks to hold back high flows for slow release over longer periods. These would allow existing sewers to work beyond their apparent capacity and save the enormous capital costs of constructing new ones.

There are 6,435 sewage treatment works in England and Wales and some 250,000 km of sewers. The state of the works and the sewage network remains one of the big financial problems of the water authorities, and sewage disposal is certainly going to be one of the great challenges of the future. The two together account for about a third of the operating costs of the industry and close to half of the capital expenditure, with one of the largest chunks going to the rehabilitation and improvement of old sewers.

The WRc has worked extensively on techniques for sewer improvement in recent years and has been at the forefront of work to indentify the most cost-effective approach to renewal and to develop and assess new methods of updating the infrastructure. Crisis maintenance – repairing sewers as they collapse – is more expensive and socially disruptive to street users than preventive maintenance, so critical areas of the system are identified and their condition assessed by inspection or, if necessary, remote-controlled photography. Flows are monitored with probes and sensors fitted inside the sewer and a computer model constructed which helps to analyse the significant factors affecting improvement. In this way, not only can the most important areas be pinpointed for structural repair but the hydraulic performance of the whole system can be improved. This is enormously important in those places where the sewers are only just adequate to cope with the demands of bigger populations. It is fortunate that the Victorians built on a large scale and the size of their sewers often made up for any deficiencies in flow. By improving this flow, many can be made suitable for the heavier loads they now carry.

Sewage Treatment   The quantity of organic matter in sewage, and hence the loading of sewage works, is measured by its BOD (biochemical oxygen demand), the amount of oxygen required to oxidise the organic matter. The total BOD removed by sewage works in 1986/87 was over 1.3 million tonnes, which means that our rivers had 1.3 million more tonnes of oxygen than they would have had if the sewage had not been treated. The

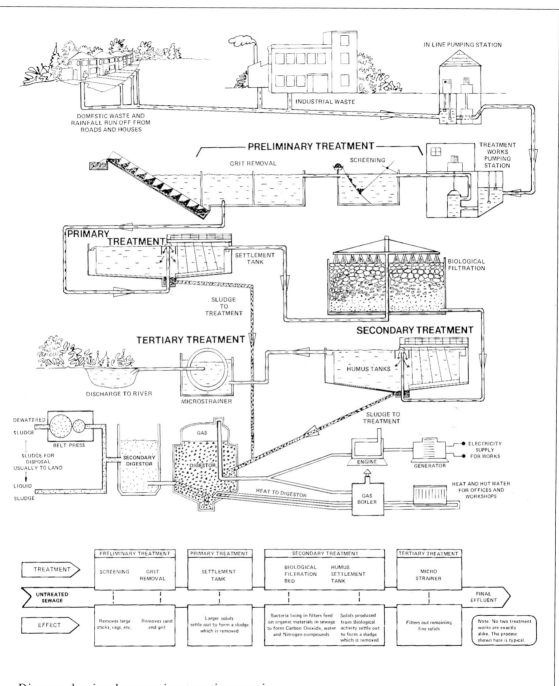

Diagram showing the stages in separating organic matter from liquid sewage at a typical sewage works.
(Anglian Water)

amount of oxygen in water reflects its ability to support life, so BOD is also an important measure of river water quality. The primary aim of sewage treatment is to remove the organic matter and thereby preserve the oxygen in our rivers for sustaining a rich flora and fauna. Although much of the bacterial content is removed at the same time, large quantities remain in the effluent and are destroyed by natural processes in the river water.

Preliminary Treatment

Sewage arriving at the works includes paper, cloth, sticks and other objects which are removed by screens. Grit is allowed to settle in special channels.

Primary Treatment

The sewage is then passed through settlement tanks where any particles and solid matter settle to the bottom as sludge. This takes from two to six hours and the sludge is taken continuously from the bottom for different treatment. This should remove about 70 per cent of the suspended solids and about 50 per cent of the BOD.

Secondary Treatment

The effluent now undergoes a biological treatment to remove most of the remaining pollutants. Bacteria are encouraged to oxidise the organic matter and most works use one of the two following methods to bring this about:

Biological filtration takes place when the effluent is dripped over beds of clinker or similar material. As in water treatment, the filtration is not specifically physical but encourages the formation of colonies of micro-organisms, worms and insects on the surfaces, which degrade the organic matter to a fine humus.

Activated sludge is the name given to a culture of bacteria mixed with the effluent and allowed to act in open tanks, usually with some form of extra aeration, which again reduces the organic matter to humus.

The liquid resulting from either process goes through another settlement tank which removes the humus and activated sludge. It should now have had at least 95 per cent of its organic load removed and can be discharged straight into a river or go for further treatment. In the UK, all effluents released must conform to a 'consent' which determines their quality. The consent will vary according to the capacity of the river to absorb the remaining organic content of the effluent. An effluent released to a large, fast moving river can have a lower consent than one released to a slower, smaller river or one from which drinking water may be abstracted further downstream. If the quality of effluent from primary and secondary treatment does not meet the standard of the consent, it can be given tertiary treatment to improve it further.

Tertiary Treatment

The final effluent is a clear liquid containing very little organic matter, but still with an enormous quantity of faecal and other bacteria which die off rapidly and naturally in our rivers.

> *Pebble bed clarifiers* are shallow beds of gravel supported on a perforated floor, usually in the humus tanks. The effluent passes upwards through the bed which traps any remaining particles.

> *Irrigation over grassland.* The land is divided into grass plots and the effluent runs on through a system of channels. It flows over the surface and is collected by a second series of channels. Where there is suitable land available, this is cheap and effective. The plots are rested in turn, the grass being cut and the accumulated solids removed periodically.

> *Sand filtration* removes fine particles of organic material. It takes many different forms; both slow- and high-rate processes may be used in both upward and downward flow units.

> *Microstraining* has a similar effect to sand filtration. The effluent is passed through a very fine steel fabric stretched on a partially immersed rotating drum. Continuous spraying with the strained liquid keeps the fabric clean.

Sludge Treatment

Sludge settled out from the primary tanks is often pumped straight into the sea where this is practical, or is pumped for stabilisation, a biological or chemical treatment which destroys the harmful bacteria and changes the sludge from an unacceptable, smelly and foul brew to a more wholesome form before disposal. The usual treatment in Britain is a biological one – anaerobic digestion – but several other methods are in everyday use.

The sludge is heated to 30°C in primary digesters, from which air is excluded, for a period of three to four weeks. A controlled decomposition takes place in which anaerobic bacteria convert most of the organic matter present in the sludge to gas, principally methane and carbon dioxide. During this time the nature of the sludge changes from its original state to a black sludge with a tarry odour and the consistency of thick cream. It is then taken to secondary digestion tanks where it

Sewage pipes by George Scharf (1788–1860). Scharf was a Bavarian who worked in London for most of his life, recording in intimate detail the street life and activities of the time. (British Museum Print Room)

cools and consolidates. If the sludge is to be transported any distance by land or sea, it is usual to take as much water from it as possible to save costs. There are a number of mechanical methods for doing this, like pressing and centrifuging, or it may be air dried. 'Cakes' of sludge typically contain about 20–50 per cent solids.

Methane is a valuable byproduct of this process and its efficient use makes considerable savings in energy costs. It is typically used to drive turbines for generating electricity for the works pumps, etc. In turn, the waste heat from this process is often used to assist in heating the primary digesters. This bonus of getting something for nothing has aroused the suspicions of businessmen in the industry and various pilot plants, exploring digestion methods with lower energy requirements, have been set up.

Storm Sewage

Sewage works often receive rainwater as well as sewage. They are designed to accommodate average dry weather flows (DWF) plus an allowance for heavy rain. Under storm conditions, the flow may be greater than the capacity of the works. When this happens the extra flow can be run into stormwater tanks which can hold it for treatment later. If the storm continues and the tanks are full, the overflow usually runs into the nearest river; this undesirable state of affairs is not considered serious as the tanks should act as primary settlement tanks and any pollution is very much diluted by the rainwater. Unfortunately, sewage networks may also be overloaded and discharging raw sewage themselves. It seems that pollution problems do arise in many rivers after storms, particularly where older sewage works are involved.

Sludge Disposal

This is an area in which interests are bound to conflict. The authorities have the equivalent of nearly a million tonnes of dry sludge solids to dispose of annually and, wherever they go, someone or something is going to be affected. The ideal end product is a saleable landfiller or fertiliser and sales of composted sludge, for instance, make a small contribution to offset expenses.

Agricultural Land

The most desirable environmental answer is to put sludge onto agricultural land where it can be recycled usefully, and it is commendable that about half the total disposed of goes this way. It is rich in nitrogen and phosphates, the exact amounts and how quickly they are released depending on how it is applied. Liquid undigested sludge is usually injected into the soil to avoid smells; liquid digested sludge is particularly suitable for grazing and silage; sludge cakes can improve soil structure on very heavy or very light soils. The pressure to dispose of sludge is so great that it is usually available free of charge to farmers. There are, however, a number of difficulties:

1. The bulk is enormous; four ships leave London each day for instance, carrying a total of 11–12,000 tonnes of sludge. It is inconceivable that this quantity could be taken through the streets, and even if it was it would have to go huge distances to find enough land to put it on.
2. Grassland could take fairly regular applications, but arable land is nowadays only out of production for a few weeks in the autumn and the sludge would have to be stored somewhere until it could be used.
3. In addition to pathogenic organisms which might remain from inefficient treatment, sludge from trade and industrial discharges can contain either toxic, or potentially toxic, elements (PTEs). British codes of practice will be reinforced by an EEC Directive on the protection of the environment from the use of sewage sludge in agriculture. These will set limits on the organic and chemical make-up of the sludge and the chemical content of the soil to which it is applied. Much of our sludge does not at present conform to these parameters and this may be a good reason for caution in disposing of it anywhere in the environment – on land or in the sea.
4. The authorities work to tight budgets, set at present by the Government. Many operations are carried out on a cost-effective basis that has traditionally given a low priority to the environment. It is true that the authorities are about to have new masters, but business interests are already very much reflected in official attitudes. Alternative methods of disposal could be very expensive to implement and change will not come about until the majority of people choose different priorities.

Landfill

Sludge has been a useful landfill but the number of sites available is limited and likely to decrease as competition for such sites grows. The chemical and toxic parameters which apply above may be relevant to landfill which could leach these elements into groundwater.

Incineration

This has never been very popular in Britain because there are cheaper alternatives like dumping in the sea. It is expensive because the sludge needs to be fairly dry before it will burn. It also leaves large quantities of ash, and in the past has led to atmospheric pollution, although this problem can now be prevented with improved technology.

The Sea

In districts near the coast, sludge and effluent, usually raw (untreated) are discharged straight into the sea. The numerous outfalls for this were built too near land, even above low tide levels sometimes, and have been the cause, amongst other things, of our polluted bathing water. All the authorities with coastal towns are now building long sea outfalls which will carry the sludge to a point where it will be dispersed rapidly by the currents. (The organic matter is oxidised by the oxygen in the saltwater and the bacteria destroyed, mostly by the action of sunlight.) The long outfalls are still being built and their satisfactory performance will be assessed over the next few years. The Royal Commission on Environmental Pollution and the Coastal Anti-Pollution League have endorsed their use and most scientists are favourably disposed. The investment has been enormous: £150 million in the four years to 1985 and about £70 million a year since then.

There have been suggestions that sludge could be sterilised before discharge into the sea but the chemical reactions involved are likely to create more problems than they solve. Since the action of saltwater on bacteria is known to be effective, and the risks of virus infection are exceedingly low, there seems little point in pursuing that path. The greatest dangers arise from chemical and toxic pollution and the long-term effects of releasing large quantities of nutrients into the water. The release of nutrients into closed systems has triggered several ecological 'disasters' in recent years, but it is not clear at present to what extent our seas are such closed systems. At one level, all systems on the planet are interdependent and it is dangerous to interfere.

Sludge can only be dumped at sea under licence from the Ministry of Agriculture and Fisheries, which monitors the dumping grounds and sets conditions for quantity, solids content and quality. The bulk of treated sludge from the London and Manchester areas is disposed of in this way, with smaller amounts from other sources. It is expensive to reduce the bulk of sludge; for sea dumping it consists of about 5 per cent solids – like a thick soup.

Pollution Control

... where men are wasteful and dirty, and let sewers run into the sea, instead of putting the stuff upon the fields like thrifty reasonable souls; ... there the water babies will not come, sometimes not for hundreds of years ...

Charles Kingsley, *The Water Babies* (1863)

This is probably the area of greatest public concern about the water authorities. One of the few serious criticisms of the 1973 Water Act was that water authorities would be both fox and hound in the area of pollution, and it is certainly true that they remain major polluters themselves. The situation should have been helped by the Control of Pollution Act (COPA) Part II, but its extraordinarily delayed implementation and the ambivalent role of the Secretary of State only confused matters. The tightening of pollution controls has now had to be left somewhat in abeyance until it can be seen who takes responsibility under the new structure of a privatised industry.

The water industry's responsibility for the control of pollution is authorised by statute but often carried out in a tradition of gentlemanly negotiation which has not been notably successful, especially when very large sums of money need to be spent. Perhaps the water authorities have been rather cowardly and irresponsible in hiding behind Government lassitude but it is difficult to blame them when their spending limits have been kept low for many years. It is fortunate that the EEC has been in the background with a strong arm to push the British Government towards accepting its Directives.

Among other priorities, COPA Part II concerns the protection of water from pollution. Five out of its 36 sections were implemented by 1976 but it was announced two years later that the rest would be delayed for another year because

... their implementation would place water authorities in a position where they would have to incur substantial capital expenditure on new and improved sewage treatment works, at a time of increasingly severe restrictions on public expenditure and of great public pressure to minimise their charges. Industry, also under severe economic pressure, would be similarly affected.

In the event, it was not until 1985 that all of COPA Part II was implemented.

Sewerage was the responsibility of local authorities before 1974 and was paid for out of the rates. Although eligible for a Government rates support grant, the 'no votes in sewage' attitude of most local councils was responsible for many sewers and sewage works being in very poor condition. This meant that in 1974, at the very time when the Government introduced the Control of Pollution Act, the water authorities took over many rivers heavily polluted by inefficient sewage works, which could not possibly be improved overnight or even for several years in some cases.

On the assumption that COPA would be implemented, the DOE, which was at that time responsible for fixing the acceptable levels of discharge from sewage works (the consent), permitted the water authorities to 'rationalise' their consent conditions to the *current* quality of the river rather than to a true river quality *objective*. A further twist given to the implementation of COPA Part II was the introduction of an exemption order in 1983, which allowed various discharges exemption from the Act and, in effect, made COPA meaningless in those areas until the Government chose to lift those exemptions.

This rather bizarre setting of quality standards to meet the consent rather than the consent to meet the standards has been typical of the Government's approach to the environment. It may well be responsible for the feeling among the water authorities that provided they do the best they can in the circumstances, the consents are not too important. Thirteen years after the introduction of COPA and three years after its full implementation, something like 20 per cent of all sewage works still fail to reach their consent standards.

The Royal Commission on Environmental Pollution pointed out in its tenth report (1984) that almost the only exceptions to the exemptions were those necessary to meet Britain's legal obligations to the EEC and it emphasised its 'belief in the benefits of a continuous and progressive approach to environmental improvements rather than piecemeal reaction to pressures of the moment' and stressed 'the importance of tackling pollution problems in an order of priority which has been determined on its merit, not on grounds of expediency or merely in response to the pressure of international obligations'. The situation is very much the same now.

For the authorities, doing the best they can in the circumstances is not an unreasonable defence following the heavy squeeze put on them by the Government over the last few years, partly to save money and partly to prepare them for privatisation. The Secretary of State for the Environment said in 1986, 'In the last six years we have made the water authorities fit and ready to join the private sector'. This, unfortunately, refers to the appearance of their accounts rather than the state of their assets. It seems a very cynical attitude which gives the profit that can be made from selling the authorities priority over concern to improve services and the environment. In this context it is worth noting that the national performance aims, agreed with the Government, concern themselves entirely with financial comparisons and have no categories covering performance *in practice* whatsoever.

The money that the authorities can borrow for capital projects is set by Government 'external financing limits'. These have been cut as follows:

	1983–84	1984–85	1985–86	1986–87
£M	358	287	237	109

In addition to this they were also required to repay their existing debts before their due repayment dates, which has brought down investment financed by borrowing from 80 per cent in 1975 to about 10 per cent today. To make matters even worse, their profit targets were raised in the same period, from 1.0 per cent to 1.6 per cent. These measures have not only been a constraint on investment but have, of course, raised customers' charges. It has not been unusual for assets in the water industry to last 100 years or more and a policy of such heavy payments now from current income is very unfair on the industry and the customer at a time when more investment is urgently needed to bring standards up to the higher levels demanded by the public and the EEC.

In addition to the water authorities being responsible for fixing the consents for other people's waste discharges, they are the body which monitors river quality and initiates prosecutions when a pollution incident takes place. This is an area where traditional attitudes of persuasion still play a major, but apparently ineffectual, part since pollution incidents have risen from 12,500 in 1980–81 to 21,095 in 1986–87. A breakdown for the year 1985–86 shows the number of incidents and the extent to which prosecutions were made as a result:

	Industrial			*Farm*	*Sewage*			*Total*
	oil	*chemical*	*n.c.*★		*works*	*sewers*	*n.c.*★†	
	4,588	660	2,481	3,513	333	406	3,398	19,665
prosecutions	9	4	93	142	0	0	0	253

★not classified and includes some from the two previous categories
†includes private discharges

One has to feel some sympathy for the authorities faced with so many incidents; litigation is expensive and extremely time consuming and, of course, in many cases the polluter may be extremely difficult to identify. For example, finding conclusive proof in the large number of farm pollution incidents can be impossible in an area where all farmers are using the same techniques. More importantly, many authorities feel they have no moral right to prosecute until they have put their own houses in order.

Nevertheless, the situation is extremely unsatisfactory. Few areas publish useful figures but one that does so reveals that 12 per cent of trade effluent samples did not reach their consent standards. (This was a mainly rural area and the number is worse in the industrialised regions, see page 232) All the authorities have invested in improvements to their own works and most predict compliance with the consents by the 1990s although the new EEC Directives may be in force by then, which could alter the consent standards, particularly for industrial wastes.

River Water Quality Proof of the effective control of effluent and industrial waste should be found in the regular surveys of river water quality undertaken by the authorities, but the results are disappointing. The parameters and testing procedures have altered over the last few years and make direct comparisons difficult. The present classification may be summarised as follows:

> *Class 1a* waters of high quality suitable for potable supply abstractions and for all other abstractions; game or other high-class fisheries; high amenity value.
> *Class 1b* waters of less high quality than Class 1a but usable for substantially the same purposes.
> *Class 2* waters suitable for potable supply after advanced treatment; supporting reasonably good coarse fisheries; moderate amenity value.
> *Class 3* waters that are polluted to an extent that fish are absent or only sporadically present; may be used for low-grade industrial abstraction purposes; considerable potential for further use if cleaned up.
> *Class 4* waters which are grossly polluted and likely to cause nuisance.
> *Class X* insignificant water courses, not usable, where the objective is to prevent nuisance developing.

There was a slight decline in the length of Class 1a and 1b rivers between 1980 and 1985 and recent results show no obvious change for the better. Some good rivers deteriorated; some poor rivers were upgraded. The fact that no overall improvement can be shown is disquieting since over 4,000 km remain in Classes 3 and 4. There can be little doubt that greater progress could have been made, given sufficient political will, and one can only wait to see how the situation develops in the hands of the National Rivers Authority.

It should be mentioned that many environmentalists find the laboratory testing procedures for river water quality to be crude and would prefer to see more biological monitoring. The DOE itself said, in the 1975 River Pollution Survey, that,

> ... animal and plant communities form valuable indicators of pollution because they respond to intermittent pollution and to new and unsuspected pollutants which may be overlooked in a chemical sampling programme.

Furthermore, the response to pollution shown by a living community can be detected for some time after the polluting event ... There is no doubt that *in situ* assessments of water quality in biological terms are extremely valuable.

Most authorities use some biological techniques but there is no concerted work on this, apparently due to lack of money.

Bathing Water Quality

The water authorities' problems with pollution of seawater result both from the direct disposal of sludge and the fact that river pollutants tend to end up in the sea. The state of Britain's beaches has been the subject of widespread concern and shows that action can be taken to improve the environment when the issues are clear and when an institution with muscle, like the EEC, is demanding action. The Government's role in this episode is particularly shameful and made an important contribution to our poor reputation as environmentalists in Europe. In 1975, the EEC asked member states to list those waters in which bathing was 'traditionally practised by a large number of bathers' and then monitor them for sewage pollution. It set mandatory and guideline values for various physical, chemical and microbiological limits which should be met by 1985. The DOE listed 27 beaches, a ludicrously low figure in relation both to other countries and to the facts – Brighton and Blackpool were not even listed! Under threat from the European Court to produce a figure with some relation to reality, 397 beaches were listed and in 1986, ten years after the Directive, the results of monitoring were produced.

	pass	fail	total
Anglian	18	10	28
Northumbrian	9	10	19
North West	10	20	30
Severn Trent	0	0	0
Southern	38	27	65
South West	96	13	109
Thames	0	2	2
Welsh	28	19	47
Wessex	32	6	38
Yorkshire	20	2	22
Total	251	109	360

Note: Compliance has been assessed on the directive's rules where at least 20 samples have been analysed. In other cases, provided that at least 12 samples have been analysed, the water was assumed to comply where not more than one sample failed the numerical standards.

Bathing Water Quality Table (Water Authorities Association)
Nearly 400 British beaches should conform to the EEC bathing water quality Directive 76/160, although the Royal Commission on Environmental Pollution recognised 600 that are popularly used by swimmers.

These showed that some 40 per cent failed to meet the standards and the outcry was so great that every authority has taken action to improve the situation, mostly with the construction of long sea outfalls. The improvements are already beginning to show, as an estimated 70 per cent of beaches now comply and it seems quite feasible that nearly all beaches will do so by the mid 1990s. Admittedly, this is ten years later than the Directive intended, but it would be unfair to blame the authorities for Government tardiness. The several hundred million pounds the authorities have spent on research and improvements demonstrate their desire to conform to the EEC ruling.

Sewage Disposal at Sea

Sludge dumping at sea is normally considered as a separate issue from the general disposal of sewage in seawater. This rather unrealistic difference stems from legal considerations; the dumping of wastes at sea is controlled by licence from MAFF, and discharge into coastal waters requires a consent from the Secretary of State. In practice, this arbitrary distinction is confused further by the fact that most contaminants enter the sea through rivers anyway.

The fact that Thames Water, for instance, is the largest identifiable dumper of sludge in the North Sea makes it an obvious target for criticism, but looked at as part of the total load it is a very small proportion. Our long coastline and strong tides have, for years, made it easier for Britain than for other Europeans to use the sea as if it were a bottomless pit for wastes, but we should not take all the blame. We contribute roughly a quarter of the nutrient load to the North Sea and about a third of the metals and organic matter. What is really worrying is the traditional attitude, still surviving in some circles, that it does not matter because there is no proof that we are doing any harm.

You do not wait for a patient to die before you have final proof of his illness and, further, perhaps more aptly, much illness nowadays is not readily identifiable. More and more, diseases related to immune deficiency and our way of life take precedence over a clearcut pathology. The North Sea has for some years been recognised by those fishermen and others who work on it as unhealthy and damaging to their interests. We may not at present know quite what the illness is, but that should be all the more reason for caution. The Germans have a concept which does not readily fit British ways of thought. This is called *Vorsorgeprinzip* (literally, anticipation principle) which stresses the need for a cautious and preventive approach which would seem particularly appropriate in the circumstances.

In the light of present information, it is surely important that the pollution load carried by the North Sea, of persistent toxic and bio-accumulating substances, must not be increased and more positive steps must be taken by our Government to ensure their limitation. It must also be a matter of urgent research to know more about the effects of discharging such a large amount of nutrient into the sea. Through the DOE, MAFF and others, the Government is funding work on large-scale projects, but it may be precisely the small-scale work which they have cut from the budget of the Institute of Terrestrial Ecology that would be most useful in this area.

Industrial, Farm and Other Effluents

The water authorities' sewage effluent discharges require the consent of the Secretary of State under the Rivers (Prevention of Pollution) Act 1961. They are, however, largely monitored by the authorities themselves. This should change under the new Water Act. The water authorities both authorise and monitor the discharge of other people's wastes and these make a substantial contribution to the sewage system. In the year 1986–87 it amounted to 1,117 Ml per day which, in terms of oxygen demand, was about 30 per cent of the total waste going for treatment. Some idea of the different effluents can be gathered from

Brewing	19	5	5	20	5	54
Brickmaking	—	—	—	—	—	—
Cement making	6	1	2	1	2	12
Chemical and allied	69	44	7	4	10	134
Coalmining	—	—	—	—	—	—
Ethanol distillation	—	—	—	—	—	—
Electricity generation	1	—	3	—	—	4
Engineering	30	136	59	14	33	272
Food processing	137	90	225	85	109	646
Gas and coke	5	—	5	3	—	13
Glass making	6	4	—	—	1	11
Glue and gelatine	1	1	—	—	—	2
General manufacturing	32	60	14	20	16	142
Iron and Steel	—	—	1	—	—	1
Laundering & Dry Cleaning	120	91	70	75	46	402
Leather tanning	8	1	3	2	39	53
Metal smelting	1	—	—	—	—	1
Paint making	3	1	—	2	—	6
Paper and Board making	2	2	2	2	1	9
Petroleum refining	1	1	—	—	—	2
Plastics manufacturing	2	1	—	—	3	6
Plating and Metal finishing	117	69	12	14	32	244
Pottery making	—	—	1	—	—	1
Printing ink, etc.	75	6	25	7	16	129
Quarrying and Mining	2	7	—	—	—	9
Rubber processing	5	—	1	1	—	7
Soap and Detergents	2	2	—	1	2	7
Textile – Cotton & Man-made	1	3	2	—	—	6
Textile – Wood	—	—	—	—	—	—
General Farming	42	43	27	15	66	193
Unclassified	225	64	45	105	221	660
Total	912	632	509	371	602	3,026

The categories and numbers of trade effluent discharges to sewers in the Anglian region 1986/87. (Table: Anglian Water)

the list of consents given by Anglian Water for 1986–87. The total number of these consents for England and Wales in that year was 29,312.

The sections concerning consents under COPA Part II are an unusual example of openness in a country that does not greatly value this quality. Requests for a consent must be advertised publicly and make clear the nature and quantity of the discharge. Both the public and the Secretary of State can raise objections. Apart from the right to protect certain trade secrets, registers must be kept, which are open to the public and record the following information:

- Applications for consents.
- Consents given and any conditions attached thereto.
- Samples of water and effluent taken by water authorities, information produced by analyses of these samples, and steps taken in consequence of this information.
- Certificates granted by the Secretary of State exempting applications, consents and conditions, etc., from publicity.

The water authorities also have a duty to make regular reviews, and consents may be varied or revoked.

As larger proportions of water are now taken from rivers for consumption, it has become more urgent to look at the movement of all toxic substances in the water cycle. Many industrial solvents and organic pesticides are thought to be highly toxic in small quantities and the Water Research Centre is investigating ways of removing them from water supplies. They are even appearing in groundwater supplies that were traditionally thought to have been cleaned by the filtering action of the aquifer.

A particularly difficult area for the authorities to deal with is pollution from roads. Sometimes runoff goes straight into streams and rivers and in other places it enters the sewers. In both cases, a polluting incident can be damaging and difficult to control. It is not unknown for chemicals to be deliberately dumped down road drains for example. Chemicals entering sewage works can upset a biological process like activated sludge and then endanger rivers from pollution by the resulting improperly treated sewage. Constant monitoring is essential.

'The Polluter Pays' There is a widely accepted principle that the polluter should pay for the pollution he or she causes. It is far too widely accepted in practice that pollution control is expensive and demanding and that polluters should be indulged if they have problems. The difficulties are certainly formidable; industries which have been polluting for years can be faced with crippling bills to pay to clean themselves up, even to the extent that they might be forced out of business. Do you put people out of work for the sake of a clean environment?

It should not have to come to decisions like this, if the Government had, or in some cases would, make its intentions absolutely clear and give advance warning that it was going to act in a positive manner. The messy business of exemptions from the Secretary of State would then not be necessary.

Conservation

Come brethen of the water and let us all assemble
To treat upon this matter which makes us quake and tremble
For we shall rue it, if't be true, the Fen be undertaken
And where we feed in fen and reed, they'll feed both beef and bacon.

The Powtes Complaynte (c. 1700)

The 1981 Wildlife and Countryside Act imposes on water authorities the obligation to 'so exercise their functions ... as to *further* the conservation and enhancement of natural beauty and the conservation of flora, fauna and geological and physiographical features of special interest' and they should also 'have regard to the desirability of protecting buildings or other objects of archaeological, architectural or historic interest'. These duties took the authorities into areas outside their traditional activities but many have now built up a strong team of experts as well as establishing consultation procedures with interested parties when new projects are planned.

For several historic reasons the water authorities find themselves the guardians of some of our most important natural features. The nineteenth-century habit of constructing reservoirs on high ground, often in isolated places with protected catchment areas, is the most impressive legacy and these comprise the greater part of the 182,000 hectares owned by the industry. They form quite a high percentage of several national parks – 15 per cent of the Peaks for instance – but, perhaps more importantly, they have also preserved large areas of land which have not been so designated. The Elan Valley group of reservoirs, an astonishingly beautiful and dramatic sight, do not have protective national park status, although this was once proposed. This guardianship has been traditional and passive, part of the industry's policy of protecting its supplies; with the Countryside Act a more active participation was demanded and this has, to a great extent, been given.

The huge output of glossy brochures on how much the authorities have done for the environment can produce a 'methinks thou dost protest too much' reaction and could imply a superficial concern with appearances rather than an understanding of some of the complex issues involved. It's hardly worth patting yourself on the back for building a frogs' ladder at a disused sewage works if you control a river that can hardly support any life at all! However, public relations officers invariably underestimate public intelligence and behind the 'simple stories make good copy' attitudes there exists, at nearly all levels of the industry, a serious concern for the natural world. Some regions do more than others, and the concern is often apparent in very different ways, but each authority not only plays some part in furthering conservation in its area, but has built consultation procedures and conservation techniques into its working practices. All projects, from river maintenance to the construction of a new reservoir, are now carried out with advice from the relevant environmental groups at the earliest planning stages.

The River as a Corridor for Wildlife

The damage done to plant and wildlife habitats in the past has been considerable and any relief that one feels is tinged with sadness that change has come about so late. For example, in Bedfordshire records have been kept for the last 200 years which show that 30 per cent of the wetland species of flora have been lost. Land drainage was the principal cause. It was usually associated with increased agricultural production and much of it has been recent; one species has been lost every three years since the Second World War (30 per cent of the 38 species gone). Some 27 species of wetland flora are currently under threat of extinction nationally and a reduced incidence of birds and other wildlife associated with aquatic environments has been apparent for some time, in particular the low numbers of once-common wet-meadow-breeding waders.

With losses like these in mind, the House of Lords Select Committee, reporting on the water industry in 1982, said,

The Committee are concerned that the duty imposed on the Water Authorities by Section 48 of the Wildlife and Countryside Act 1981 will not be properly operable until survey work on their river corridors has been completed. Without surveys some features of scientific interest will be discovered only when they have been effectively destroyed.

The concept has grown in recent years of the river and its banks as a corridor for many types of plant and wildlife, not just a specialised habitat, but something more like a lifeline around and along which a diverse and rich number of species have a dependent association. Some surveys had already been undertaken but the Lords committee's promp-

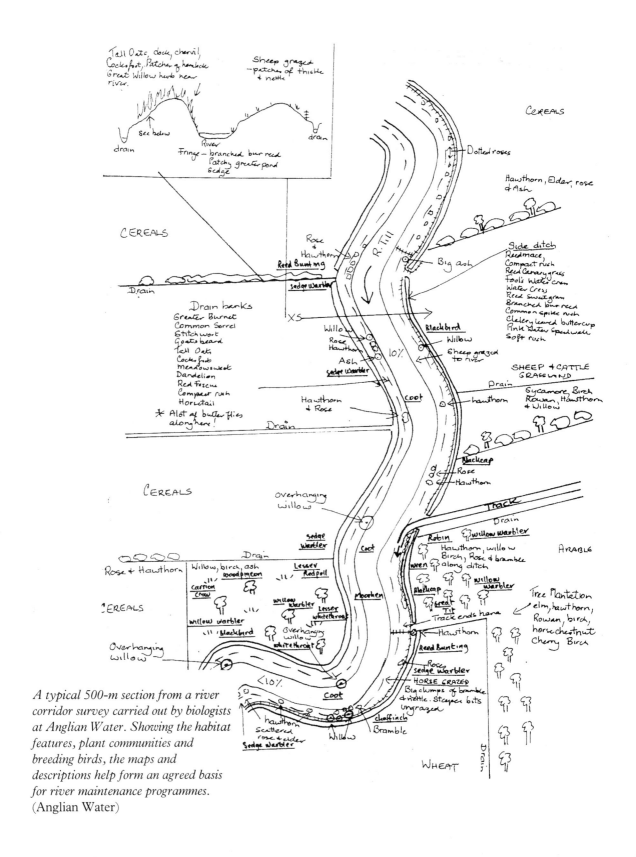

A typical 500-m section from a river corridor survey carried out by biologists at Anglian Water. Showing the habitat features, plant communities and breeding birds, the maps and descriptions help form an agreed basis for river maintenance programmes.
(Anglian Water)

ting established the River Corridor Survey as an essential tool for managing rivers in sympathy with the needs of wildlife. The DOE, in conjunction with the Nature Conservancy Council, brought together all the groups with an interest in the rivers and agreed to a methodology which could be used nationally.

These surveys try to record the distribution and abundance of all species using or living in or near the river, and detail the nature of the river bed, the water, the banks and the land on either side. In doing this they attempt to determine the relative value of the wildlife features and their sensitivity to the environmental impact of engineering and maintenance work. The Water Research Centre, among others, is working on techniques in this area. The local databases built up from the surveys in different areas are all compatible with each other and are therefore of value to the water industry as a whole, as well as to other bodies like the British Trust for Ornithology and the Botanical Society.

The surveys may have a conservational and a practical value. It was found in Lincolnshire that mowing reduced floral diversity by 57 per cent. A new policy of mowing only one bank saved £70,000 in maintenance costs and is likely to initiate a threefold increase in bird species breeding and a fourfold increase in the overall numbers of birds. The data can contribute directly to efficiency in operations, for example in helping to predict the build up of weeds and thereby making management decisions on clearing them more cost-effective.

Land Drainage and River Management

The establishment of river corridor surveys as a basis for assessing the effect of engineering works on the environment should not imply that land drainage and other work before this had been carried out without regard to wildlife. The Water Space Amenity Commission published its *Conservation and Land Drainage Guidelines* in 1980, after widespread concern was expressed not just about the loss of traditional wildlife habitats, but the bleak visual impact of many drainage schemes. It is luckily now some years since it was thought that drainage channels had to be clean, straight and preferably concrete. The Nature Conservancy Council, the Countryside Commission and the RSPB, as well as the DOE and MAFF, have made authoritative advice available and have all worked with the authorities on methods of flood alleviation and land drainage which can be efficient, sensitive and enhance the potential for wildlife in a given situation.

Reservoirs

Reservoirs make an important contribution to the habitat of many water birds, in particular for wildfowl whose traditional sites are lost. The large estates they often depended on are now broken up; many wetland areas are now intensively cultivated and there has been greater disturbance to them following the postwar increase in public mobility. There are over 550 drinking water reservoirs in England and Wales, with an area in excess of 14,100 hectares. Many of these are too high, too bleak or too small to support wildfowl populations, but about 50 carry in excess of 250 birds and at least fifteen of these support over 1,000 birds.

With the opening up of reservoirs to the public, the conflict between the interests of birds and recreational activities became apparent and a number of studies showed that birds were not only disturbed but in some cases were leaving altogether. All the large reservoirs are now zoned for different activities, with separate nature reserves, usually with restricted public access, to ensure that birds remain as undisturbed as possible. Every new reservoir built now includes a purpose-built nature reserve, planned in consultation with environmental groups and many of these are run by county or local conservation trusts.

The planning was so successful at Rutland Water that in 1984 the whole 1,255-hectare reservoir was designated a Site of Special Scientific Interest (SSSI) by the Nature Conservancy Council. The nature reserve itself has 142 hectares of land attached to three lagoons containing 60 hectares of water. The level in these can be controlled to maintain a margin of rich feeding grounds throughout the year. This has attracted up to 7,000 wildfowl at a time in the autumn and over 200 species of birds have been recorded; there is also a diverse animal and plant population. The Leicestershire and Rutland Trust for Nature Conservation manage the reserve in conjunction with Anglian Water.

Other Nature Reserves

A number of nature reserves have been created in disused parts of sewage works where the lagoons make shallow lakes whose banks and borders can be planted for cover. Exeter, Bristol, Sheffield and London have all converted abandoned sections of their works in this way. South West Water, at Exeter, have used 5 hectares of filtration lagoons at their Countess Wear Sewage Works to construct a mixed habitat of water, reed bed, marsh vegetation, willow scrub and open ground. Buntings and several different warblers breed there, including the unusual Cetti's warbler and over 140 visiting species have been identified. There are a large number of dragonflies and damselflies and these include seven nationally restricted species. This site is now also a registered SSSI.

Disused reservoirs and gravel, clay and peat workings have all been made available to conservation groups to run on licence from the authorities, usually for birds, plants and animals, but at least one exists for butterflies. Several coastal sites, including Pagham harbour, are managed as reserves by various authorities.

Buildings and Industrial Archaeology

The water utilities have handed down to us some extraordinarily handsome Victorian buildings and probably the finest stationary steam engines in existence. In early pumping stations the two are frequently interconnected since the form and structure of the buildings housing steam plant were dictated by the machinery they enclosed. The mechanical, moving parts of the engines were supported by the walls and pillars which made up the fabric of the building; even the roof structure was frequently designed for the needs of lifting gear.

The second beam of the Ryhope Pumping Station, Sunderland being lifted into place c. 1868. The engines are preserved as a working museum by a private trust.
(Photograph: Sunderland and South Shields Water Company)

These are the poor relations of conservation. There is a fine legacy of Victorian water towers, water and sewage pumping stations and early mechanical equipment by which the authorities and companies are really a bit embarrassed. Wildlife conservation can, and should, be incorporated into working systems that are alive and healthy. Redundant buildings and equipment are 'dead' and can only be preserved as museums by spending money and getting little back in return. Independent trusts have taken over several of the steam and other engines and have converted the premises to successful working museums, often with the help of tourist authorities. South Staffordshire Water Company and Yorkshire Water both have museums, but the other companies and authorities generally appear to feel that this sort of activity is not part of their brief and that others should do it for them while they get on with more important things.

Several water towers and pumping stations are listed buildings, but it appears that many others which should be so designated are not; their authoritative and functional presence seems to imply that they are above such classification. The large number of fine pumping stations that have been pulled down in the last few years makes it important to try to preserve those that remain as well as possible. North West Water and Severn Trent are to be congratulated for attempting to make comprehensive inventories of their buildings. Severn Trent's lists include a record of the history, a description of style and condition, and the present use of each building. This should surely be standard procedure for all authorities.

The water tower in Colchester, a particularly fine structure dating from about 1880, which dominates much of the town skyline, became redundant recently and has been sold to a religious group as a Christian 'power' centre. Outline planning permission was given for a change of use as offices or flats, but there would have been considerable difficulties in conversion. The actual tank, when removed, will leave a huge space, in addition to large spaces on other floors.

Archaeological Sites   Such sites are affected in many ways by water authority activities, the most obvious being the construction of reservoirs. The appropriate local or county archaeologists are usually aware of such large capital works and most authorities have contributed to the cost of any excavations or other work thought necessary. Only Thames Water employs an archaeology officer to make systematic assessments of how all capital and maintenance programmes will affect archaeological sites and to recommend appropriate action. The Countryside Commission has recommended that the water industry generally should adopt this responsible approach.

Documents and Early Photographs

Detail from a 25 × 20-cm glass negative of the Hampton Pumping Station at Hanworth, Middlesex, c. 1920. (Photograph: Thames Water)

The fate of documents in the industry is confusing and depressing. When the 1,200-odd undertakings came together in the 1960s and 1970s, it was with thoughts of the future rather than the past. The private water companies have the best kept records, presumably because they were not losing their identity or their sense of a long and proud service to the public – coupled with a tinge of civic self-congratulation. Many have fine engineering drawings, early letters, minute books and other company records, often looked after by capable amateur historians. Other companies have some of these things lodged in local town or county archives and a few have them 'somewhere'!

The situation in the authorities is generally worse; at best the local authority records have been passed to local archives, but frequently nobody appears to have thought much about records at all, or seems to care very much where they are. This hardly appears to have 'regard to the desirability of protecting ... objects of ... historic interest'. It is extremely worrying to find a superb set of Edwardian photographs, for instance, in a divisional office that 'someone thought they might do something with one day'. This should not be taken as a criticism of any individuals, for such things are appreciated and valued, but in a very organised industry, if there is no one delegated to do a job, it doesn't get done. Some system ought to be adopted, either nationally, regionally or divisionally, to co-ordinate the care of these early documents and photographs – if possible, cataloguing them or, if financial restraints prevail, handing them over to county archives *and keeping a record of where they went.*

Privatisation and the Environment

The most worrying objections to privatisation come from conservation groups and have been eloquently stated in the booklet *Liquid Assets,* published jointly by the CPRE and RSPB. Their concern for water quality and pollution control *ought* to be met by an NRA that does its job properly – there is little one can do but wait and see. Their fears that the development of assets by the new WSPLCs may be at the expense of the environment seem justified, as no protective legislation exists in the new Water Bill to cover such eventualities.

In the past, authorities have often allowed surplus land to be used for nature reserves but it is almost inconceivable that a private company, perhaps even owned by a large construction group, would willingly hand over any land with a potential development value of, perhaps, several million pounds. Thames Water's ring main will release five reservoir sites, which, they hope, will raise over £50 million towards paying for it. This land, if it 'belongs' to anybody, surely belongs to the public and should be used for the public good. To quote from *Liquid Assets:*

The environmental value of these sites ranges from green field sites, such as the Kempton reservoirs, which meet the NCC criteria as SSSIs, urban SSSIs such as Barn Elms, to urban green sites of significant conservation and public amenity value in deprived inner city areas, such as Stoke Newington.

It is true that the normal planning procedures would apply to any developments but the Secretary of State, with whom any appeals would end up, has not shown himself to be particularly concerned for environmental issues. It is pointed out, furthermore, that WSPLCs may have a strong influence on planning decisions by virtue of the advantageous position they hold on supplying water and sewage services.

In a less dramatic way, but also difficult to control, the profitable recreational facilities are already threatening wildlife. Anglian Water recently extended its fishing period on Rutland Water (see above) into the winter months, which are the most crucial to wildlife, selling the rights on a long lease to a private management company without consulting the NCC – a legal obligation under the Wildlife and Countryside Act. There has been speculative buying and selling of land on the site and plans have been passed for a country club/hotel with time-share chalets, a golf course and possibly another hotel.

The CPRE suggests that to protect the water authorities' many unique land holdings 'requires either vesting ownership or restricting covenants of these assets with conservation bodies'; this would lower the sale value of the industry and is unlikely to be acceptable to the Government, but one must fear for the worst without some stronger form of control.

Recreation and Amenity

More people have lived in towns than the country for over 100 years now, but the attraction of the countryside is stronger than ever. Few farm labourers long for a walk across the mountains in the way that an office worker does and the relative affluence of our society, our extra leisure time and vastly increased mobility, have greatly increased the pressures on rural recreation since the Second World War. In particular, the conjunction of water and land has always been fascinating to people. It provides contrasts that are especially rich aesthetically, it increases the variety of habitat and range of flora and fauna, and it has, in recent years, been our favourite place to play. In spite of our climate the British are not richly endowed with large expanses of water and some of our best known lakes, like Windermere, result from human interference to increase their size. The water industry owns more of our inland waters than anyone else, and the nineteenth-century practice of purchasing catchment areas alongside the reservoirs has made it one of Britain's largest landowners.

Bristol Waterworks Company allowed fishing on Blagdon reservoir in 1904, but this was a notable exception and the water undertakers generally showed great resistance to the idea of public access to their amenities. Water is an industry in which traditions are strong, and the 'keep out' policy, reasonable before filtration and disinfection became

Sailing on Scammonden Reservoir. (Photograph: Charles Hall)

routine, remained sacred to many managers. The Government finally went some way towards meeting the demands of the public with the passing of the National Parks and Access to the Countryside Act in 1949 and this marked a turning point in official attitudes. More specifically, the 1948 Report of the Gathering Grounds Sub-Committee stated:

It is a commonplace of history and of natural history that over-developed defences may stifle the life they are designed to protect and it would not be in the national interest if, dissatisfied with effective practical security against typhoid, the water industry were to pursue theoretical perfection in this one field of public health [protection of catchment areas] at the cost of seriously limiting facilities for healthy exercise ...

The committee suggested that other lines of defence against infection existed and that, provided precautions were taken, public health should not by itself be a reason for denial of access.

The Water Resources Act 1963 and the Countryside Act 1968 gave express powers for river authorities and water undertakers to provide facilities for water recreation. This was anticipated at Grafham Water, completed in 1966, where the enabling Act of Parliament authorised sailing, picnic areas, a nature reserve and, for the first time, unrestricted public access to most of the water's edge.

The emphasis on recreation was shifted further by the Water Act 1973 which stipulated that:

Every water authority and all statutory undertakers may take steps to secure the use of water and land associated with water *for the purposes of recreation* and it shall be the *duty* of all such undertakers to take such steps as are reasonably practicable for putting their rights to the use of water, and of any land associated with water, *to the best use for those purposes.*

(my italics)

In spite of the rather woolly 'reasonably practicable' steps, the new water authorities took the provision of recreation as a responsibility, some of them even grasping it with enthusiasm. It has now become an accepted part of operations; all new reservoirs in the last twenty years have planned recreation and amenity areas and all authorities have introduced at least some facilities on their older reservoirs.

Recreation can be broadly interpreted and includes the physically active sports as well as the quieter occupations like birdwatching. This passive or 'conservationist' aspect was encouraged by the Countryside Act 1968 which provided that,

In the exercise of their functions relating to land under any enactment every Minister, Government Department and Public Body shall have regard to the desirability of conserving the natural beauty and amenity of the countryside.

For the water authorities this was spelt out in the Water Act 1973; Section 22 requires them to regard:

... the desirability of preserving natural beauty, of conserving flora, fauna and geological or physiological features of special interest, and of protecting buildings and other objects of architectural, archaeological or historic interest ...

The conflict that arises between active sports and conservation has been resolved on smaller reservoirs by designating them to different activities. The extremes of this policy are the 'honey pot' centres set up to attract the crowds drawn to anticipatory sports, which leave other areas as sanctuaries, sometimes with no public access except to conservation groups or trusts. Most modern reservoirs are large and zones for different activities are planned from the outset. They all include nature reserves with restricted access at a considerable distance from the active sports. The antisocial sports like water skiing are generally confined to a few centres and further restricted by time, day of the week, numbers and season.

Grants are available from various public bodies, like the Countryside Commission, the Sports Council and local authorities, to share some of the expense of providing amenities, and users, either individually like anglers, or corporately, like sailing clubs, are expected to contribute to costs. Generally speaking, revenue does not cover outgoings and, for the present (prior to privatisation), the authorities see the provision of amenities as a public service that will be good for public relations. They are very popular and in many cases suffer from overuse; on public holidays for instance. South West Water has estimated that at least 2.5 million people visited its sites in 1988.

Fishing

Our plenteous streams a various race supply,
The bright-ey'd perch with fires of Tyrian dye,
The silver eel, in shining volumes, roll'd,
The yellow carp, in scales be drop'd with gold,
Swift trouts, diversify'd with crimson stains,
And pikes, the tyrants of the wat'ry plains.

Alexander Pope, *Windsor Forest* (1713)

The involvement of the water authorities in recreational pursuits usually ends with their provision of a facility for that pursuit – with fishing it goes much further. Habitat, fish stocks, breeding, enforcement and research are actively promoted by all the authorities and nearly £9 million were spent on these in the year 1987–88. Since revenue from licences and other 'fish' sources amounted to a little over £5 million, it can be seen that the responsibility to develop fishing and a good quality fish environment are seen as a public good that goes beyond the maintenance of professional and amateur fishing. It is for this reason that the fishery activities of the authorities will be taken over by the National Rivers Authority after privatisation.

Estimates of the number of people who fish regularly vary enormously, but it appears that 2–3 million people are involved. They are catered for on over 400 reservoirs in addition to all the rivers. There does seem to be a decline in the number of rod licences issued recently, however, but no reasons for this have been put forward. Small reservoirs are generally let to angling clubs which manage them and the stocks themselves, while the larger sites are managed by the authorities or leased to commercial operators to develop for profit. It seems likely that these commercial operations will increase in the next few years.

Checking licences and enforcing by-laws are duties often carried out by honorary or part-time bailiffs, but the serious business of detecting and apprehending poachers has to be done by professionals. In areas like Wales and Northumberland this has become quite dangerous and bailiffs are given special training with police dogs, sophisticated communications and image-intensifying night surveillance equipment. Fast patrol boats are now used on the larger estuaries. Legally caught salmon are now being tagged in an effort to prevent sales of poached fish and a number of prosecutions of people buying untagged fish may help to make marketing more difficult – controls of this sort have not, however, proved easy to implement. The determination of poachers and the difficulty of patrolling enormous lengths of river make this a problem that is likely to remain for some time.

All regions carry out extensive surveys of fish stocks and have fish hatching and rearing facilities. The laboratories make regular checks on fish stock health and investigate incidents of disease and mortality as well as researching environmental factors affecting fish health. Some of this research covers areas that benefit water quality generally like the distribution of heavy metals.

THE TEN REGIONS

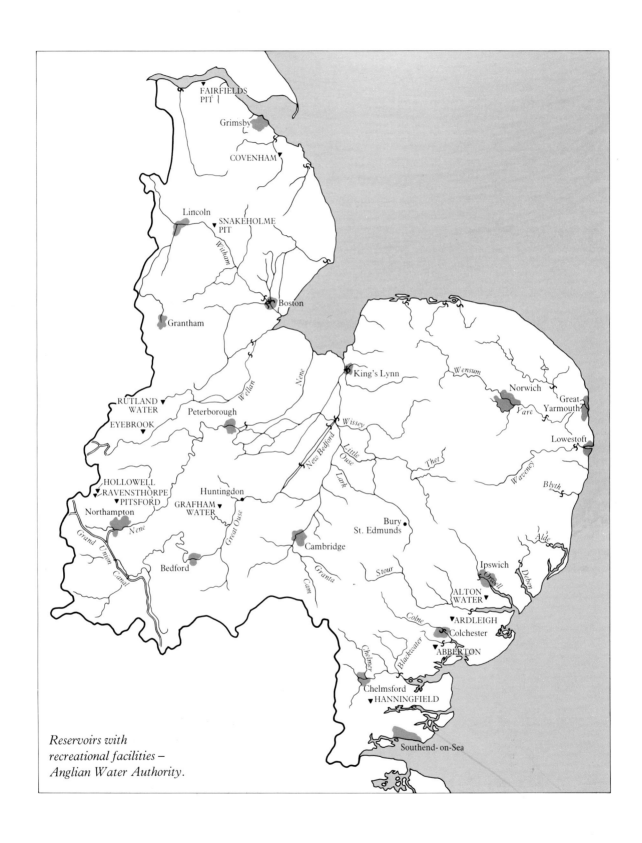

Reservoirs with recreational facilities – Anglian Water Authority.

Anglian Water Authority

Anglian Water is geographically the largest regional water authority. It covers the 30,000 sq km between the Humber and the Thames, and has the distinction of having the lowest rainfall in Britain and the fastest growing population. The land is mostly low, and rarely rises above 90 m, which may strike a stranger from the north as dull, but it has a subtlety and softness which grows on one and it is mostly regarded with affection by the inhabitants. Many writers and artists have been inspired by its varied qualities; Constable, Cotman, Crabbe and Benjamin Britten, for example, had strong associations with the East Anglian landscape. The region is one of small rivers, better known for their quiet gentility than their grandeur, meandering with no sense of urgency through water meadows lined with willow and alder. Much of the traditional flora and fauna of these meadows has been lost in the conflict between farming practice, flood prevention and conservation, but this charming picture can still be found. The population is growing fast but the area is large and growth is mainly confined to the towns, the population per square kilometre remaining lower than in the other regions of the south east.

Virtually all of the smaller rivers in the region are artificially impounded by mills, sluices and weirs, which retain a minimum head of water all year round. These mills and their associated sluices are of considerable historic interest, although their original purpose, for grinding corn and providing power, has long ceased to exist. In most instances they still retain the head of water even where the mill has been demolished or converted to other purposes. The retention of these structures is most important from a conservation viewpoint, both on historical and environmental grounds, as the river regimes that have developed over several centuries are based on the impounded reaches. If the heads of water were lost, the rivers would become mere trickles during dry-weather periods, with disastrous effects on fish and other aquatic life. A further historic reason for the impounding of many rivers is that they were developed as commercial navigations. The Stour is distinguished by being the earliest known statutory navigation, the Act to make the river navigable having been passed by Parliament in 1705.

Rainfall is the source of all our fresh water, but about three-quarters of the region's rainfall is lost in the form of evaporation, or used – mostly by plants. The remaining quarter is known as the residual

Opposite: *Wind and horse power were for many years the only forces available to pump water from the low-lying Fens and Broads. Olby Mill on the River Bure is one of many windmills being restored by local enthusiasts.*
(Photograph: Charles Hall)

rainfall and has to provide for human needs. The residual or effective rainfall (rainfall minus evaporation) averages only 147 mm per year, compared with 487 mm for the rest of England and Wales. Rainfall occurs fairly regularly, month by month, but most evaporation takes place in the summer, making it quite normal for the region to experience a 'drought' every summer in the sense that evaporation exceeds rainfall, soils dry up and river flows become very small. The close balance between rainfall and evaporation also makes the region vulnerable to periods of low rainfall; for one year in ten the residual figure is only 70 mm, 48 per cent of the average – the equivalent for the rest of the country being 390 mm or 80 per cent of the average. For a drought occurring one year in 50 (the kind of extreme drought for which public water-supply schemes are commonly designed) the rest of England and Wales might still enjoy 66 per cent of normal resources, but this region will have only 27 per cent. It can be seen that storage of water is necessary to maintain supplies throughout the year.

It is fortunate, therefore, that the solid geology of this area favours the natural storage of water. Boreholes and rivers give about 50 per cent each of the total supply. More recently, many farm storage reservoirs have been built privately. As a result of these large volumes of storage, public water supplies are, in general, not vulnerable to the short 'one-summer' droughts which often affect other parts of the country. Droughts of this kind are commonplace, but whereas a very dry summer is harmful to agriculture (because soil water is limited), it would take at least a 'summer-winter-summer' drought to create public water-supply difficulties.

East Anglia is an important agricultural region; cereals are widely grown and are the dominant crop on the heavier clay soils. Vegetables and fruit are concentrated in parts of the Fens, the Ivel valley and in parts of Essex. Over 65 per cent of English and Welsh fruit and vegetable production is in the Anglian region; potatoes and sugar beet are important on the Fens and lighter soils, which grow some 55 per cent of the national total.

The Fens

... a most terrible fen of immense size, which begins at the banks of the River Gronta [the Cam] not far from the little fort which is called Gronte [Cambridge]; now in fens, now in flashes, sometimes in black oozes swirling in mists, but also with many islands and groves, and interrupted by the braiding of meandering streams ...

Felix's *Life of St Guthlac* (c. AD 700)

The low, flat land has given us two extremely interesting landscapes, the Fens and the Broads. The Fens, the epitome of flatness, stretch

featureless, but dramatic in their very starkness, to an infinite distance. They have some of the richest agricultural soil in Britain, and, until recently, almost all of it fell into the official classification of first-class land. They are, today, England's most prosperous agricultural area. This prosperity has only been achieved after centuries of effort by people to control the environment; some parts are as low as 1.5 m below mean sea level (3.5–4 m below high flood level), making the fenland subject to regular and often disastrous flooding. Only in the last two decades have modern engineering and the expenditure of millions of pounds finally made the area secure.

Until the end of the sixteenth century the outflow of the many rivers, coming out against tides which were often backed by fierce winds, left much of the area virtually under water – some parts were dry enough for summer pasture, others remained wet the whole year round. Tradition describes a scanty local population with its special way of life – living in flimsy wattle and daub huts, the floors often awash, with roofs of thatched sedge, sleeping on beds of reeds with pillows stuffed with bullrush down. Known as the 'Breedlings', they were thought of as a people apart, among whom other Englishmen rarely ventured. Romantics may be disappointed to learn that this 'web-footed fenman' theory is roundly condemned by Oliver Rackham in his *History of the Countryside*. Here he points to the large number of magnificent medieval buildings in the area as proof enough of a flourishing culture.

Ague was certainly common, a mosquito-borne endemic maleria, in which fever and thirst alternated with severe pains in the arms and legs. The remedy was said to be brandy and opium.

The Breedlings were protective of their way of life and reacted with effective violence when the first overall plans for draining the entire Fen area were announced in the seventeenth century. For many decades sluice gates and other mechanisms installed had to be protected, not always successfully, by armed guards.

Local drains and canals had been cut in the past, notably by the Romans; who made extensive use of the fenland rivers for transport, but this was the first large-scale plan for the whole area. The work was commenced in 1630 by Francis, fourth Earl of Bedford, together with thirteen associates or 'gentlemen adventurers' whose efforts would be rewarded with some of the retrieved land – 'Adventurers' Fen' is still a common name in the district. They engaged the famous Dutch engineer Sir Cornelius Vermuyden, who had already demonstrated his skill with drainage works at Hatfield Chase in Yorkshire. Vermuyden was to design and supervise the work, which consisted principally of making two new straight cuts – the Old and New Bedford Rivers – from Earith to Salters Lode on the tidal River Ouse. This cut off the loop of the river through Ely, shortening the distance to the sea by 16 km. A flood storage reservoir of 2,066 hectares was created between the two new rivers, and embankments built to contain flood water and tides. In 1631 the first of the great cuts, known as the Old Bedford River, was dug, 21 m wide and 34 km long. A sluice at its upper end regulated the amount of water diverted from the river's ordinary course, and a tail sluice resisted inflow from the tidal water and the sea. The Civil War broke out in the 1640s and this diversion allowed the Breedlings to put a temporary end to the work.

After the war, work was started again and a greatly extended network of cuts, drains and sluices was completed in the 1650s, including the New Bedford River, or Hundredfoot, running parallel to the Old Bedford River. In 1651, the first Denver sluice was constructed across the Ely-Ouse at the lower end of the Hundredfoot. It excluded the tidal water from the south level rivers and turned them up the Hundredfoot, a beginning of all-the-year-round control. In 1713 disaster struck when a combination of high tides and exceptional floods burst the Denver sluice, and once again sea and flood water could flow unchecked into the south level rivers. Land was inundated, much of it became derelict and incursions of the tide were frequent. In 1715 a sturgeon measuring 234 cm long was caught in Thetford mill pool. The sluice was finally rebuilt in 1750 by a Swiss engineer called Labelye, and this remained in use until 1834 when it was reconstructed by Sir John Rennie. In 1848 the middle level main drain was completed, much of it with a 15 m bed width, and also an outfall sluice at St Germains, flowing into the tidal river.

Wind power was first used to pump the water, small mills delivering the water into drains, larger mills lifting this into canals and, finally, the largest mills lifting it into the rivers. Since the moisture content of wet peat may be as much as 800 per cent, the immediate effect of drainage was rapid shrinkage of the land, perhaps 30 cm in the first year, followed by 2–5 cm a year, hence the strange world of the Fens where rivers run higher than the surrounding land, and the separation of the drainage network into two systems, a high-level one carrying the upland rivers and a low-level one carrying the drainage water to the mills and pumps. Over the following years the efficiency of pumping followed the progress of technology, wind power being replaced successively by steam, diesel and electric pumps.

Pumping the water out of the lower-level system was never a particularly serious technical problem; the real difficulty was keeping it out, giving protection from flooding caused by the overtopping or breaching of the flood banks. Major floods from this source continued, culminating in the greatest flood on record, in 1947, when 16,000 hectares were flooded and many lives lost. In consequence, a scheme was prepared which allowed for floods about 5 per cent greater than that of 1947, coinciding with a spring tide. This was accepted and passed by Parliament in 1949 as the Great Ouse River Flood Protection Bill.

The problem of keeping the embankments secure arises from the nature of the fenland soil which is peat or silt overlying 'buttery clay' for a depth of 5 or 6 m above the underlying beds of harder Kimmeridge clay, gault or chalk. The embankments are really floating on the peat and buttery clay, and this affects them in three respects: liability to

This cast-iron post from the Great Exhibition was hammered into Holme Fen in 1851 so that its top was level with the ground. It now stands some 4 m high, a graphic demonstration of how fenland drainage has affected the peat. (Photograph: Charles Hall)

sinking, instability and seepage underneath them. The floodbanks sink as the underlying ground consolidates slowly under their weight. As they sink, the safe margin above flood level diminishes and they have to be heightened, and the weight of clay added to them in the heightening starts off a new sinking process. It can be seen that continually heightening the banks can never solve the problem and the solution has to lie in getting rid of the water within the banks, a solution proposed by Vermuyden 300 years before.

The obstacle to the discharge of the south-level waters through the Denver sluice is that in times of flood the water level from the old and new Bedford-Ouse outside the sluice was higher than the waters coming from the Ely-Ouse and its south level tributaries. However, the low water level at King's Lynn, under high flood conditions, is about 3.5 m lower than at Denver, so if you bypass the Denver sluice and bring the point of discharge to King's Lynn, advantage can be taken of this lower water level to enable the flood waters from the south-level rivers to get away. A relief channel was therefore cut from Denver, with sluice gates at each end, and, to ease the flood level in the Ely-Ouse itself, a cut-off channel from the River Lark near Mildenhall, crossing the Little Ouse and the Wissey, takes flood waters from all three and conveys them to the relief channel at King's Lynn. When the incoming tide rises, the tail gate sluice at King's Lynn closes, and the outflow of flood water ceases. The water is then contained in the relief channel until the tide once again falls, then the gates open and the discharge of flood water is resumed. It is a wonderful tribute to Vermuyden that the basic principles of this scheme, put forward in 1638 and carried out so recently, have largely overcome the problems of removing excess water from the Fens.

The Ely-Ouse Water Scheme

Another ingenious scheme, this time to make use of the water drained from the Fens, has recently been completed. In 1964, a Ministry of Housing and Local Government study highlighted the fact that expansion and development, and the general population increase anticipated in the south Essex area, could result in problems of water supply in the 1970s. The existing Great Ouse and Essex River Authorities investigated a scheme to transfer surplus water from the Ely-Ouse to the head waters of the Essex rivers to increase their flow and give extra water to the existing reservoirs. The Ely-Ouse-Essex Water Act 1968 was promoted jointly by the two authorities to implement this scheme. One great merit was that it utilised existing reservoir capacity, avoiding the loss of agricultural land to create new ones.

The Ely-Ouse River drains a catchment of approximately 3,662 sq km upstream of Denver and is fed by four main tributaries, the Cam,

Lark, Little Ouse and Wissey. It discharges into the tidal channel through the sluice at Denver. Surplus water from the eastern part of the catchment, which would otherwise be lost to the sea, is now transferred to the flood protection scheme cut off channel at Denver (provided it is not in use). If the level in this channel is raised by 60 cm at the sluice, the water can be sent in a reverse direction up the channel to Blackdyke, some 25 km to the south east. At this point water is drawn off into a tunnel 20 km long, which terminates at Kennett. Pumps lift the water from the tunnel and through a 14-km long pipeline over the watershed to the River Stour at Kirtling Green. Part of this discharge is drawn off at Wixoe, about 13 km downstream and pumped 10 km over further watersheds to the River Pant. The water is then pumped to the Hanningfield and Abberton reservoirs, a distance of 148 km and 141 km, respectively, from Denver. For about two-thirds of this length use is made of existing watercourses.

Nitrates A common worry of the general public about water supplies in this region is pollution from nitrates. It is not altogether clear at what level nitrates are a danger to health but they present a problem to water authorities who are required by the EEC to keep their level below 50 mg/l. Since the main source is the leached residue from arable farming, the problem is most widespread in the Anglian and Severn Trent areas. Low rainfall in the east makes the problem more serious as it dilutes the nitrates in other areas.

Arable farming has increased dramatically since the Second World War and the amount of nitrates applied has grown also. According to a study in the Midlands, nitrate application to cut and grazed grassland increased from 33 kg per hectare in 1963 to 230 kg in 1987; and for winter cereals from 67 kg per hectare to 168 kg. The rate of leaching amounted to 10–15 per cent from the grassland and 40 per cent from winter cereals. The leaching tends to be seasonal, particularly in rivers, most of which in the south east and east of England now exceed 50 mg/l in winter. A number of aquifers now exceed this figure and the most severely affected, like the Lincolnshire limestone, are above 100 mg/l; several boreholes have had to be taken out of service in these areas. It is generally agreed that if the present farming practices continue at the same rate, the nitrate levels will reach 150–200 mg/l in the east of England in the future.

Water typically takes many years to reach the water table – figures of five to 40 years have been suggested depending on the geology of the soil and rock – therefore even if no more nitrate was applied, there would still be a rise in the levels for several years to come. The setting up of protection zones, in which the use of fertiliser is restricted, is the most popular method among the water authorities of controlling nitrates, although even if they could be established tomorrow, some form of treatment would be necessary to remove the nitrate that is already in the soil. In spite of moves to cut down farm production, such zones are not likely to be set up in the near future since nobody can agree on who should compensate the farmer for any loss in profits.

Nitrate levels can be lowered by moving boreholes or abstracting water from different depths in the aquifer, although both of these techniques may result in lower yields of water which can also require more treatment. Blending different waters is the most widespread control in use at present, but this is technically more complex than the layman might imagine if the levels are to be controlled accurately – water is easily mixed on a small scale but not in large volumes. Surface waters are unlikely to present a problem if they are stored in reservoirs for any length of time as bacteria bring about a natural reduction in nitrates, often as much as 50 per cent in nine months for instance.

Anglian has experimented with two types of plant to remove nitrates using either chemical or biological treatment. The chemical method is similar to commercial water softening processes. Water is passed through beds of synthetic resin and exchanges nitrate for chloride ions. The process is straightforward but produces large quantities of brine, which are difficult to dispose of, and can also produce water with unacceptably high levels of chloride. Further work is being carried on in conjunction with the WRc in an attempt to overcome these problems.

The biological process artificially develops high levels of naturally occurring bacteria which break down nitrates into nitrogen gas – the pilot plant for this process is also operated in conjunction with the WRc.

The financial scale of the problem is very large. Anglian Water has estimated that it could cost up to £70 million over the next ten years to bring all the water within the EEC 50 mg/l standard, with possible running costs of £5 million per year after that. If nitrate removal treatment proved necessary, this might add some 30 per cent to the total water costs. The general public are very aware of the nitrate problems and are unlikely to accept lower standards. With the water industry undergoing large-scale changes, it is difficult to foresee how the situation will develop.

Cambridge Water Company

Population served: 266,000
Water supplied: 70 Ml/d
Length of mains: 735 km
Area: 1,173 sq km
All water pumped from boreholes in the chalk.

In medieval Cambridge water was taken from the river, shallow wells and an artificial defence channel, 'the King's Ditch'; all these sources were heavily polluted and caused a high incidence of disease. In 1352, the Franciscans brought water into the town from higher ground 2.5 km to the west, in a lead pipe. After the dissolution of the monasteries this supply was granted to Trinity College in 1546, and still supplies a fountain there today. In 1574, after a serious outbreak of plague, the Chancellor of the University wrote, 'our synnes is the principle cause; the other, as I conjecture, is the corruption of the King's Ditch'. He suggested that a conduit should bring water in from the Nine Wells, a group of strong springs, to flush the town's ditches and drains and create a public supply in the market place. This was carried out in 1610, partly by Thomas Hobson (of Hobson's choice fame), and is now known as Hobson's Brook; water from it can still be seen flowing along Trumpington Street.

In 1852 heads of colleges and leading citizens combined to form the Cambridge University and Town Waterworks Company and obtained an Act of Parliament to pump water from Cherry Hinton to supply the whole town, a joint management which continued until 1962.

East Anglian Water Company

Population served: 233,000 plus a large seasonal fluctuation
Water supplied: 69 Ml/d
Length of mains: 2,125 km
Area: 1,311 sq km
Water from 30 boreholes, Ormesby Broad and Fritton Lake, and intakes from the Rivers Bure and Waveney.

This company resulted from the 1963 amalgamation of the Lowestoft Water Company (1853) and the Great Yarmouth Waterworks Company (1854) with various local authorities and the Southwold Water Company. The engineer Thomas Hawksley was employed by both companies (and also by Norwich and Cambridge in the same region) and some of his buildings survive at Ormesby and Lound; the original beam engines still remain at the latter and are scheduled as an ancient monument.

The Norfolk Broads border the company's area and have been a source of water for the company since 1855, which makes the company one of the few to have an active interest in conservation. It has a 36-hectare nature reserve at Marsh Farm Fen near their intake from the River Bure, which is run in conjunction with the Broads Authority. Part of this is managed in the traditional manner, with reeds cut for thatching every winter, and the growth of milk parsley has been encouraged as it acts as host to the swallowtail butterfly – there are now large numbers of these in the summer. Another site is being developed at Fleggburgh Doles by the Norfolk Naturalists Trust and is a recognised Site of Special Scientific Interest. The Ormesby group of broads shelter one-fifth of the national population of breeding pochard duck, a species which is very sensitive to disturbance.

Essex Water Company

Population served: 1,400,000
Water supplied: 400 Ml/d
Length of mains: 6,000 km
Area: 1,540 sq km
Water mostly taken from surface sources, the Rivers Stour, Chelmer, Roman and Blackwater. Also imports water (see below).

Essex Water is one of the largest private water companies. It was formed by the Essex Water Orders of 1970, which amalgamated all the companies and undertakings in the area between Chelmsford and the north bank of the Thames, including Southend, Basildon, Tilbury, Romford and Ilford, a heavily populated area of 1,538 sq km. It is not possible to extract enough water locally to supply so many people and so much industry, and Essex Water therefore imports water via the Ely-Ouse scheme described on page 97 and from the Lee valley reservoirs and direct from the River Thames.

The company in many ways typifies the successful twentieth-century water-business. The Victorians had no romantic use for steam engines; they used them because they were the most efficient pieces of technology available to them. In the same way, Essex uses computer information

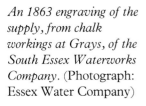

An 1863 engraving of the supply, from chalk workings at Grays, of the South Essex Waterworks Company. (Photograph: Essex Water Company)

systems and communications networks to make its company as efficient as it can possibly be. Essex can be refreshingly shameless in its belief that modern business methods can serve everybody well – shareholders, staff and customers.

This is the first water company in England to be bought by the French. Lyonnaise des Eaux has had a controlling interest since 1988. Two French representatives sit on the board but otherwise the same people run the company. There have been no problems with the takeover, the companies respect each other and see the merge as advantageous.

Tendring Hundred Waterworks Company

Population supplied: 128,000 (215,000 summer season)
Length of mains: 894 km
Area: 352 sq km
Water from boreholes and winter floodwater of the River Colne.

This company was founded by an indefatigable Victorian entrepreneur, Peter Schuyler Bruff, railway engineer and later the developer, in whole or in part, of the resorts of Frinton, Clacton and Walton. He obtained a parliamentary Act to supply Harwich in 1884 and the company eventually supplied all the other towns and villages in the north-east corner of Essex, including the University of Essex. Tendring, in conjunction with Colchester and District Water Board (now part of Anglian Water), planned and constructed the Ardleigh reservoir scheme. This draws flood water from the River Colne in winter and provides storage for its use during the summer when flows are reduced. Considering its small size, it has made impressive use of its space. In addition to sailing, birdwatching and ringing, it is recognised as one of the country's best roach fisheries and holds the British record for pike at 20.35 kg.

Reservoirs Open to the Public

ABBERTON, Layer-de-la-Haye, nr Colchester, Essex
490 hectares, 25,725 Ml, max depth 15 m
Birdwatching (an important site)
Coarse Fishing
Nature Reserve, SSSI
   WII Ramsar Convention.
   Picnic area & car park.

ALTON WATER, Tattingstone, nr Ipswich, Suffolk

158 hectares, 9,000 Ml, max depth 18 m
Nature reserve,
   Suffolk Wildlife Trust.
Sailing, rowing, windsurfing, sub-aqua and **fishing**,
   Alton Water Users Association
Picnic area and marked walk (13 km)

ARDLEIGH, Clover Way, Ardleigh, Colchester, Essex
57 hectares, 2,204 Ml

Sailing
Sub-aqua
Trout and coarse fishing (record 20-kg pike caught here)

COVEHAM, Grimsby, Lincs
88 hectares, 11,000 Ml
Waterskiing and **windsurfing** (club only)

FAIRFIELDS PIT
Nature reserve, SSSI
 Lincolnshire & Sth Humberside Trust for Nature Consv., The Manor House, Alford, Lincs., tel: (05212) 3468

GRAFHAM WATER, Perry, Huntingdon, Cambs
635 hectares, 59,000 Ml
Nature Reserve, SSSI
 The Beds and Hunts Wildlife Trust, Priory Country Park, Barkers Lane, Bedford MK41 9SH, tel: Bedford 64213
Sailing and Windsurfing
 Grafham Water Sailing Club, West Perry, Huntingdon, Cambs PE18 0BU, tel: (0480) 810478
Trout Fishing
 Piscators Ltd, The Lodge, Mander Park, West Perry, Cambs PE18 0BE, tel: (0480) 810531
Picnic areas, nature trails, licensed bar, restaurant and refreshments

HANNINGFIELD, South Hanningfield, nr Chelmsford, Essex
354 hectares, 123,000 Ml, max depth 17 m
Nature Reserve (access restricted to Essex Birdwatching & Preservation Society)
Trout Fishing
Windsurfing
Picnic area and nature trail, marked walk through ancient woods. enq., tel: Basildon (0268) 710101

HOLLOWELL
Fishing and Sailing

PITSFORD WATER, Pitsford, Northampton
283 hectares

Nature reserve (200 hectares), **SSSI, wildlife information centre**
 Northampton Trust for Nature Conservation, Holcot Visitors' Centre, tel: (0604) 781350

RUTLAND WATER, nr Oakham, Leicestershire
1,250 hectares, 124,000 Ml, max depth 34 m
Cycling, 40-km waterside track.
 Cycle hire, all types, all ages.
 Whitwell: Easter–31 Oct then weekends to Christmas, 9.30–7
 Normanton: weekends and school hols only, Easter–30 Sept, 9.30–7
Information Centre and Gift Shop, Sykes Lane car park
 1 April–end Sept, 1–4 (12–5 weekends and bank holidays). Winter Sun only.
Nature reserve and wildlife visitors' centre
 The Warden, Fishponds Cottage, Stamford Road, Oakham, Leics, tel: (0572) 4101 or (057 285) 378
Nature trails, adventure playgrounds, refreshments in season, barbecue facilities
Normanton Church Water Museum (opening times as information centre)
Pleasure Cruiser, *Rutland Belle*
 operates from Whitwell car park, 1st April – end Sept (not Mon except bank holidays), Charnwood Marine, tel: (0533) 693069
Sailing and **windsurfing**
 Whitwell Sailing Centre, Whitwell Peninsular, tel: (0780 86) 464
 also Rutland Sailing Club – residential centre, Gibbet Lane, Edith Weston, nr Stamford LE15 8HL, tel: (0780) 720 292
Sub-aqua and **Swimming**

RAVENSTHORPE
Fishing and **Nature reserve**
 Snakeholm Pit, nr Lincoln. (open to BBCS members only)
 Nature reserve for butterflies, enq. Hon. Memb. Sec., 'Holly Mead', Lowthorpe, Southrey, Lincs LN3 5TD

North West Water Authority

January 25th, Monday. We did not rise as soon as we intended – I made bread and apple pies – we walked at dusk to Rydale – no letters! it rained all the way.

Dorothy Wordsworth, The Grasmere Journal (1802)

Water supply in the north west is at its most romantic and really looks like water supply should. Heavy mountain rain is caught in lakes and reservoirs, carried through many kilometres of tunnels and enables the grateful citizens of Manchester and Liverpool to have cups of tea round the hearth. It was all planned and carried out so long ago that it is taken for granted as a natural part of life. North West Water's 8,000 employees would no doubt have their own thoughts about this, but it is a water undertaking whose history arouses a strong reaction in the public imagination and it is, indeed, a dramatic story. No one before had built such large dams, impounded so much water or carried it such a great distance – 154 km in the case of Thirlmere.

The population of Manchester and Salford grew rapidly in the first half of the eighteenth century, increasing by 47 per cent between 1821 and 1831, for instance. They had a small source of supply, but by 1846 less than a quarter of the population had its own piped water and those that had only received it for a few hours a day. Expectations of cleanliness were beginning to rise, however, and the connection was being made between an unpolluted water supply and good public health. Industry was expanding fast in the region and beginning to need water in quantities of millions of litres a day.

An Act of Parliament was passed in 1847 to build reservoirs in the Longendale valley, near Glossop in the Pennines. This is a very long valley, gently rising up to the moors, and the technical construction was made easier by building a chain of seven small (by today's standards) reservoirs, each one ascending a further step up the valley. This had the additional advantage that water could be brought into supply as soon as the first reservoir was constructed – it took 30 years to complete all seven. They look very much the same today as they did when they were built – a remarkable sight, climbing on and on up the long valley, the overflows of each one cascading down high weirs into the next,

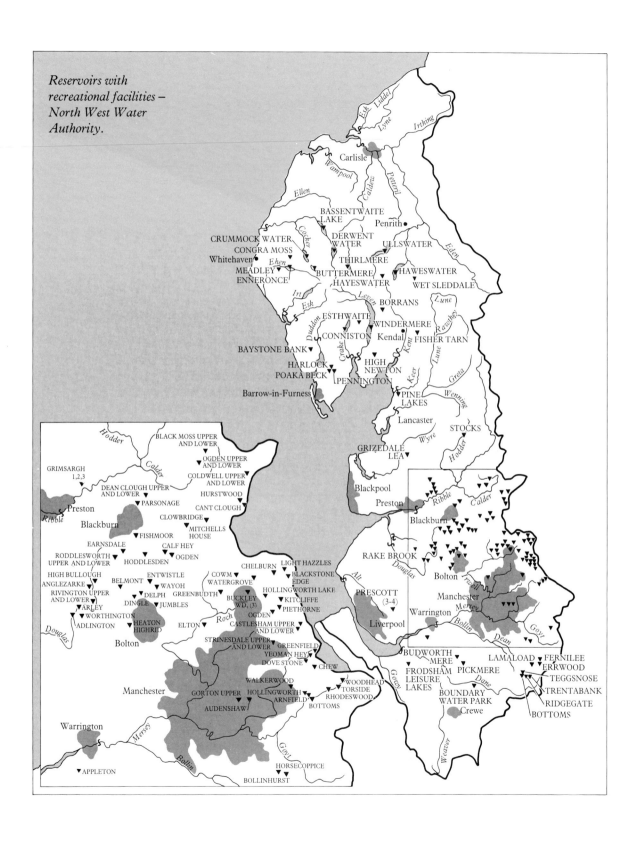

Reservoirs with
recreational facilities –
North West Water
Authority.

although these days the rather aggressive presence of national grid power lines somewhat detracts from the solomn and sparse beauty of the moors.

At this time Liverpool, known as the second city of the British Empire, had the same problems, and built a similar series of reservoirs at Rivington, on high ground to the north west of Bolton. In both cities development was taking place so fast that further supplies were seen to be needed before the reservoirs had even been completed; both had chosen very ambitious schemes which would, presumably, have appeared at the time to be adequate for all future possibilities.

By the 1850s the relationship between clean water and disease was generally accepted, but it was not the general practice to treat water; clean supplies were sought in large catchment areas which could largely be kept unpolluted by excluding the public. To find such a source, which would also give very large quantities of water, meant looking a considerable distance away. Manchester employed the eminent water engineer John Frederick La Trobe Bateman to advise it, and he suggested the Lake District as the most suitable source. He also felt that if Liverpool joined in a shared scheme, there would be obvious economic advantages for both cities. Liverpool, however, chose to develop its own scheme in North Wales, and with hindsight that may well have been sensible considering the size of demand in both towns. So Manchester began a long and uneasy affair with the lakes.

Manchester and the Lake District

Ullswater, Haweswater and Thirlmere were all suggested, but Thirlmere was initially chosen because of its greater height and rainfall, although the other lakes, and several more, were eventually added to the scheme. The plan was to carry the water to Manchester by gravity, so Thirlmere's 17 m of extra height was an important factor and its very high average rainfall of 2,360 mm compared well with other lakes; it subsequently broke records for high rainfall on 30 October 1977, with 178 mm of rain in one day.

Opposition to the Manchester scheme was very strong and local people, led by Thomas Leathes Stanger Leathes, Lord of the Manor of Legburthwaite and owner of Thirlmere, felt very bitter about the loss of this amenity. The lake had been in the Leathes family since 1577 and was known locally as 'Leathes Water'. Thomas Leathes forbade entry to his land to anyone from Manchester but surveys were still carried out in secret. Leathes died in 1876, leaving the estate to his son who, having spent many years in Australia, did not have such passionate feelings on the subject and sold the lake to Manchester. The town immediately applied to Parliament for an Act to take water from Thirlmere, but it took two years and nineteen sittings of a select

The protectionist policies towards land in the Lake District have helped to keep it undeveloped. It is ironic that we may now have to fight to keep it that way. (Photograph: Charles Hall)

committee before the Act was passed in 1879, with the important proviso that those on the route of the aqueduct should be entitled to supplies. This was the first time that a regional concept of water supply was proposed, an idea which would eventually culminate in the regional organisation of the water authorities under the 1974 Water Act.

Thirlmere was originally two lakes, but a dam was constructed along the northern end, which raised the water level by 16 m and created one 5-km long reservoir holding 40,900 Ml and capable of supplying up to 227 Ml a day. One does have some sympathy for the opposers who did indeed lose their local amenity; 5,000 hectares came under the water board's management and 'keep out' signs remained the most prominent feature of Thirlmere until the 1970s, at which time water treatment and new attitudes to public access resulted in the opening of many areas to the public, which had previously been forcibly denied.

The work on the pipeline began in 1890, much of it tunnelled underground. It is 2 m wide, with a flat floor, and 2 m high with an arched roof. The occasional sections crossing river valleys above ground were in cast-iron pipes. The masonry dam and the 154-km pipeline are notable achievements in civil engineering; the pipeline in particular is remarkable as there was a fall of only 50 cm per 1.5 km to give the gravity feed. The quality of surveying and construction must have been exceptional – the fact that the water takes 26 hours to reach Manchester gives some idea of the scale of the operation. The work took four years to complete and was officially opened in October 1894.

The supply proved adequate until after the First World War when Haweswater was again proposed as a source. Parliament was approached in 1919, but it was not until 1930 that work began on a dam to double the length of the lake and raise its level by 29 m, causing the submersion of the very attractive village of Mardale. The dam is a hollow buttress type, made from concrete poured into place on site. It looks solid, but two doors at the bottom allow entry to a long gallery on the rock beneath the buttresses, and here are the outlet pipes, control valves and a pump for local supplies. It is an eerie feeling to be inside the dam; the sound of rushing water in the pipes is disconcerting and when a pump motor starts up automatically with an explosive roar, people like myself, who might take such things in their stride in the open air, understand what it means to panic! A pipe was built to connect the supply to the Thirlmere aqueduct and the first water reached Manchester in 1941, the long delay being due more to the suspension of work during the depression than the war.

Later development allowed water to be piped to Haweswater from Swindale, Naddle, Heltondale and Wet Sleddale, the latter containing a further reservoir to hold flood water from the River Lowther before transfer to Haweswater. In the 1960s it was seen that further supplies would be needed for the predicted expansion in the 1970s and it was decided to take water from Ullswater and Windermere (Britain's biggest lake). Between them these two lakes can give up to 200 Ml a day. The quantity of water abstracted from these lakes is carefully controlled and should not affect their natural level.

These additional water supplies were complemented by developments in the distribution system; a second aqueduct, completed in 1955, carried bulk supplies from Haweswater direct to Manchester, and interconnections between the lakes gave greater flexibility. The Lake District Planning Board refused permission to enlarge or add to this pipe from Haweswater where it crossed the national park, so in 1978 an aqueduct had to be built across Shap to carry any extra water when demand was high. This necessitates pumping the water up a 19-km pipe across the fells to a point were it can fall by gravity to join the other pipes in the network.

Lancashire Conjunctive Use Scheme

There are 'fashions' in water supply just as there are fashions in more ephemeral interests like clothes and pop music, although the reasoning behind trends in the water industry must be less obscure than that governing the length of skirts. Sometimes needs have forced the pace of technology, as in the development of large impounding reservoirs in the last half of the nineteenth century. At other times the reverse may be true, as when the means to pump water from boreholes followed the development of steam power in the mining and manufacturing industries. In the 1950s, the return to favour of river-water abstraction followed a better understanding of water treatment and its technology.

A trend for the 1980s can be identified in the management of supplies to give a flexible, and therefore optimum, use of resources. In the past, source A would supply town A, and source B would supply town B. It is now more common to join sources together so that towns A and B could be fed by source A if it is the cheapest supply, using source B only when absolutely necessary. Once a source has been set up and the distribution system laid down, the greatest expenses are the cost of treatment and the cost of pumping. If there are high levels of organic matter in river supplies, they will need extensive treatment; borehole supplies are usually very clean and require little treatment, but can be expensive to pump. Lakeland supplies are relatively clean but a further balancing act is needed. Water from Thirlmere, for instance, can flow south by gravity at very little cost, and some additional supplies from Haweswater can do the same through the older pipeline, but if more water is needed it has to be pumped up over the Shap aqueduct at a cost of £3,900 a day. Any further supplies, from Windermere or Ullswater, add another £4,600 and £5,000 a day respectively. These are the maximum costs – in practice it may be possible to pump at night when electricity is half-price, although the highest demand, in the morning and evening, usually coincides with expensive electricity tariffs.

Other factors include the balance of reserves against seasonal variations in rainfall and demand, trying to keep pumping to periods when electricity costs are lowest, and maintaining quality and pollution control. The maintenance of satisfactory standards has become a more important issue since the EEC gave its Directives on water quality, and mixing supplies is one way of controlling this. If water from one source contains more of a particular chemical than it should, it can be mixed with a source which contains very little of that chemical. This does not mean that the authorities are 'getting away' with anything – all natural waters contain chemicals in varying amounts and nobody believes that a chemically pure supply would be desirable for taste or health. With regard to pollution, if a source becomes temporarily polluted by, say, spillage of toxic matter affecting a river supply, other sources can replace it until it is safe to use again.

The Lancashire Conjunctive Use Scheme (LCUS) was opened by the Queen in 1980 and allows the sort of controls described above. It enables water abstracted from the Rivers Lune and Wyre and from boreholes in the Fylde to be used, in conjunction with Lake District sources, to supply central Lancashire and Manchester. A main pipeline now circles round the chief Manchester conurbations, which will carry either the LCUS supplies or those from other sources like Longendale, giving the system flexibility at the consumer's end. It is probable that schemes such as this would be effective without electronics but their sophistication and popularity are certainly the results of recent advances in information technology. Telemetry (the automatic transmission of data like reservoir levels, river flows and treatment information to a distant control room) allows central monitoring of resources, computers make calculations about the best use of them and remote controls enable either computers or staff, many kilometres away, to switch between sources and turn pumps on and off, etc. It is now quite normal for large areas to be managed by very few staff in centralised control rooms.

The table of supplies which follows shows the quantities of water available from the different sources. They are not all interchangeable and it can be seen that about one-third of the water still comes from a local source rather than a network.

Lake Vyrnwy	220	million litres per day
River Dee	650	
Lake District	690	
Rivington	49	
LCUS	260	
Local sources	1,111	

(1982 figures)

Liverpool and Lake Vyrnwy

Manchester and Liverpool now come under the same water authority, but of course they had no such connection in the nineteenth century, so it is not really surprising that Liverpool preferred to find its own supply. The Liverpool Corporation Waterworks finally chose a site in the Vyrnwy valley on which to build an impounding reservoir. The dam was made large enough to create an 8-km long lake that would hold 60,000 Ml and was big enough to release the 45 Ml a day of compensation water that the Act of Parliament required in addition to Liverpool's supply. This was the largest artificial reservoir built in Europe at the time, requiring a masonry dam much larger than any previously constructed. Work started on this huge project in 1881 and was finally completed in 1892, when the first water flowed into Liverpool. Additions to the aqueduct have been made and a reliable yield of 205 Ml a day is available.

This was the first encroachment of English water undertakers into Wales and the start of continuing bitterness over the issues involved. At that time, the worst feelings must have been aroused in those inhabitants of the village of Llanwddyn who were to lose their homes when the valley was flooded. A church, two chapels, three public houses, 37 houses and ten farms were demolished before flooding. A new church and houses were built by the corporation for the inhabitants, who had no choice but to accept the situation. It is interesting to note that the population of 443 in 1871 showed a decline of 33 per cent since 1831 and the vicar at that time recorded 57 ruined houses that had been inhabited in 1800, although some were rebuilt, and some new houses were added, as not all of these were affected by the flooding. The number of families had dropped by 1 per cent in the 1971 Census and the population by 10 per cent, compared with 34 per cent and 50 per cent, respectively, for similar parishes in the same area.

I would not wish it to be a defence of the scheme or to suggest it was a satisfactory substitute for the loss of one's home but the construction clearly brought some continuing prosperity to the area. In 1950 the Liverpool Corporation contributed to a combined community centre and school for the village, which was then taken as a model for similar projects in the county. In view of the usual objections to access in the late nineteenth century, it is interesting that a sporting hotel was built on the lakeside in 1890, to take advantage of the fishing and shooting in the catchment area.

The disruption to the community during construction must have been extraordinary. One thousand men were employed, a few local but mostly English and Irish, all of whom would have to be housed in temporary accommodation. Stables had to be built for the horses drawing the stone from the quarries; roads had to be laid and facilities provided for eating and washing. At many sites where dams were built at this time, schools, hospitals and recreation facilities were provided for the men and their families. The work could be dangerous; it included blasting and handling huge weights with fairly rudimentary equipment. Ten men were killed at work and another 34 died during the construction period. Several large masonry dams were being built at this time so there must have been a very large number of good masons available; the work was universally accepted to be of the highest standard.

Some of the anomalies of the 1973 Water Act are most apparent around the Welsh borders. The boundaries of the water authorities follow the watersheds of the catchment areas, which results in large parts of Wales not coming under the Welsh Water Authority. At the same time historic arrangements take precedence over the boundaries; thus Lake Vyrnwy is in Wales, in a catchment area administered by Severn Trent, containing water that goes to the North West Water Authority. Technically, the straining tower (for drawing off water) is a North West Water island in a Severn Trent lake. Compensation water released to the River Vyrnwy is the responsibility of Severn Trent!

The Mersey Basin Campaign

Control of environmental pollution is not an optional extra; it is a fundamental component of national economic and social policy, and has many international implications.

Royal Commission on Environmental Pollution (10th report)

The Mersey Basin is the worst polluted river and estuary system in Europe according to the House of Commons environment committee. Its improvement must be the largest single problem facing any of the water authorities. The catchment area is about 4,500 sq km and serves as a drain for some five million people, the most concentrated urban complex after London. The pollution problem has been so big since the early nineteenth century that no institution has had the courage to face it. The population increased from 630,000 in 1801 to 2,400,000 in 1861 – a royal commission reporting in 1868 found that parts of several rivers had already been rendered lifeless by industrial waste; they counted 10,500 factories in the catchment of the Irwell alone.

Even today, the estuary receives over 600 Ml daily of untreated sewage and trade effluent, a load that the geography of the basin has difficulty in discharging, being shallow with a narrow outlet. It can take up to 30 days for pollution entering the tidal limit at Warrington to leave the mouth 48 km away. Faeces (known as Mersey trout locally), often mixed into balls with fats and oils, are a common sight on the water or washed up on the shoreline and beaches. Industrial effluents, including toxic metals and organic chemicals from the pesticide and pharmaceutical industries, have in the past caused devastating kills of birds and other wildlife. Until recently there were no fish in the estuary left alive.

The spirit and the letter of the Control of Pollution Act seem to be given little regard in the estuary, half (approx. 570) of the industrial discharges are known as 'deemed' consents; they were authorised before the Act, and are not formally controlled. Other consents are so loosely worded as to be meaningless, and discharges into the sewers are private (and secret) arrangements between industry and the water authority. Consents often appear to have been set to accommodate the discharge rather than to protect the environment. Furthermore, companies that do have consents have consistently breached them, often by very wide margins, without prosecution.

The environmental group Greenpeace have launched their own campaign to draw attention to pollution in the Irish Sea and, in particular, the quantity of dangerous heavy metals and organic compounds entering it from the Mersey estuary.

Some considerable efforts have been made since the 1960s towards environmental improvement but the cost of cleaning up is understandably daunting after so many years of neglect. For the sewage problem alone the authority needs to repair or renew half the 21,000 km of sewers, some 1,200 storm sewage overflows are unsatisfactory, 220 sewage works need upgrading and 375 new sewerage and sewage treatment projects are planned. The figure of £2 billion has been suggested for overall improvements which would bring all the rivers into 'fair', Class 2 condition.

The present initiative stems from proposals in North West's report *A Cleaner Mersey – The Way Forward*, which was published in 1980 and set out a fifteen-year programme to at least remove the more gross and offensive pollution from sewage works. Coming at a time when considerable interest was aroused in the inner city areas by the Toxteth riots and the *Faith in the City* report by the Church Commissioners, North West's proposals were taken into the wider context of work, leisure and environment in the huge areas of water and land affected by pollution. The original North West initiative was taken up by a broad group of interests headed by the DOE. They include the borough, district and county councils, development corporations and planning boards, as well as the Countryside Commission, Nature Conservancy Council, Sports Council, etc.

Some resentment is perhaps felt that the 'Mersey Basin Campaign', as it is now called, has climbed on the back of a water authority initiative and political cudos will go to those at the top rather than the bottom, but the developments envisaged for recreational, residential, commercial and industrial use go far beyond a water undertaking's brief and the money generated, from the Government and Europe amongst other sources, will be essential for improvements.

Improvements on land are visible at a number of riverside sites, in Liverpool, Wigan and Salford for instance. Improvements to the water are measurable rather than visable so far. The implementation of COPA in 1985 has not been as effective as it should have been – North West are reluctant to take a hard line with polluters until they have put their own discharges in order, but a number of the larger industries have installed treatment plants for their effluents. Birds overwintering in the estuary are reported to have increased and 30 fish species have been caught, mostly in small numbers but enough to prove that the system is showing signs of life. One good indication is the dissolved oxygen in the non-tidal river; from averages of below 20 per cent, too little to support fish, they have risen to 72 per cent – the lowest recorded at 45 per cent and the highest at 84 per cent. Metal and other pollution can, of course, still be present with improved oxygen levels and overall improvement may still be decades away, but these figures must be a cause for some optimism.

A more general environmental problem is raised by the disposal of sewage from the area, the sludge will be dumped by ship or long sea outfall and industry's discharges contain polluting chemicals and metals that will continue to reach the Irish Sea whether they are discharged directly into the river or into sewers. The poor record of industry keeping to its discharge consents suggests, at best, some disregard for the consequences to the environment. The practice of mixing domestic and industrial effluent is out of step with contemporary environmental thinking and, indeed, the EEC. Britain's policy of dumping sludge at sea is at variance with most of the other European nations and is likely to be banned in the next few years. Considering that the alternative, of putting it on land, will also not be available to sludge containing industrial waste, it is surprising that more imaginative planning and research have not been undertaken for a problem for which the solution will be very expensive – whatever course of action is taken.

Recreation and Access to Moorland

He said, 'All this land is my master's.'
At that I stood shaking my head,
No man has the right to own mountains
Any more than the deep ocean bed.

Ewan Maccoll,
'Manchester Hiker's Song'

North West Water's predecessors' practice of building large impounding reservoirs with high rainfall catchment areas in open country has given it a legacy of magnificent land holdings. It owns 4,000 hectares of water and about 60,000 hectares of land, much of it in areas of outstanding scenery. Its holdings in the Lake District National Park include Ennerdale, Haweswater and Thirlmere; it has land in the forest of Bowland – an area of outstanding natural beauty – as well as the Dovestones, Longendale, Goyt and Macclesfield Forest areas of the Peak District National Park. The Haweswater estate alone is around 9,000 hectares.

The traditional approach to access onto this land has been straightforward – keep off! As late as 1953, Manchester Waterworks were saying, 'The moors form part of the gathering grounds ... and for this reason, general access may well prove to be contrary to the public interest'. A change in attitude came about partly as a result of public pressure and partly because water treatment became more widespread. The isolated catchment areas were chosen because they were just that; water would not be contaminated by humans and could be used without treatment. While the attitudes of most landowners in the north west and the Peak District can only be described as self-interested, the water undertakings seemed genuinely concerned for the public health, although one does feel that outdated traditions were sometimes seen as unquestionable law.

The mountains and moorlands of the north of England and Scotland were becoming less accessible. Grouse shooting and water catchment areas were forbidden territory, defended in some cases with considerable violence. A bill presented to Parliament in 1884 would have granted right of access to mountains and moorlands (in Scotland) and was supported by all parties, but all such bills invariably got lost in committees for many to years to come.

Rambling had become a popular recreation amongst all classes by the late nineteenth century. Manchester YMCA Rambling Club was founded in 1880 and was followed by many others, often with a co-operative or working man's theme. The industrial towns of the north were seldom more than a few kilometres from open country; they were often originally built around narrow valleys, whose streams had first given them the power for their factories, and the major arena in the battle for access was around the Peak District.

The interest in rambling and the open air was enormous by the 1920s and many of the various groups joined together in federations under a national council, the Ramblers Association, in 1935. Meetings of 5,000 people were coming together at demonstrations to listen to speakers like Professor Joad calling for public access. The *Manchester Guardian* wrote in 1925,

There is something wantonly perverse and profane in a society in which the rights of property can be used to defeat the emotions in which mankind has found its chief inspiration and comfort. If ever any truth lurked in the phrase 'the rights of man' those rights should surely include the right to climb the mountains, and the right to dream beside the sea.

Kinder reservoir with the Pennine Way crossing Kinder Scout in the background. (Photograph: Charles Hall)

The most celebrated mass trespass was on Kinder Scout in 1932 when nearly a thousand walkers deliberately made for the top. Police and stick-wielding gamekeepers were powerless against such numbers.

Arrests were made but the severity of the two- to six-month sentences, against non-violent protesters demanding their rights, probably did more to influence public opinion than the trespass. Such strong public feelings led to the introduction of the Access to Mountains Bill in 1938. After eighteen attempts since 1884, this one was actually passed, but in such an altered form that it was eventually being opposed by its sponsors. Never implemented, it was repealed by the National Parks and Access to the Countryside Act of 1949. This Act has finally brought access to those areas falling within the national park boundaries, although moors can still be closed for up to twelve days for grouse shooting. Improved filtration techniques and more enlightened attitudes have done as much as the law to open up water authority land. North West Water has been a leader in the movement by water authorities to open their land and their water to the public and has been resourceful in ensuring that the differing demands of recreation are sensitively matched to their surroundings.

Privatisation looks inevitable. If it does take place, North West Water is the area that will be looked at most carefully by open air enthusiasts and environmentalists. It is enormously rich in land holdings that bring in very little income, let alone profit, and it needs more money than any other area to bring its sewers and sewage works up to date. Since there is not much profit in sewage either, there will be a tremendous temptation to skimp on the capital spending or to cash in on the assets. A corporation that is to be run for business interests and shareholders may well make decisions that conflict with its public responsibilities.

Reservoirs Open to the Public

ADLINGTON, Wigan, Lancashire
2.2 hectares
Coarse Fishing
  Wigan Anglers, Mr W. Grattan, 66 Balcarres Road, Aspull, Wigan WN2 1SB
Country park, walking
Nature reserve
  Lancashire Trust for Nature Conservation, Cuerdon Pavillion, Cuerdon Hall, Bamber Bridge, Preston
Car park and toilets

ANGLEZARKE, Wigan, Lancashire
Birdwatching
  permits from North West Water R&CO

Climbing, fell-running, orienteering, walking, environmental trail
  enq. North West Water R&CO
Mixed Fishing
  Northern Anglers Assoc., Mr A.G.R. Brown, 10 Dale Road, Golbourne, Warrington WA3 3PN
Car park and picnic area

APPLETON, Warrington, Cheshire
7.7 hectares
Canoeing
Trout fishing
  Warrington Anglian Assoc., tel: Runcorn 716238
  Warrington B.C. Education Committee

ARLEY, Wigan, Gtr Manchester
7.7 hectares
Coarse fishing
  Wigan Anglers, see Adlington above
Country park, environmental trail, walking and **birdwatching**
  enq. North West Water R&CO
Car park, picnic area and toilets, educational facilities

ARNFIELD, High Peak, Gtr Manchester
15.8 hectares,
Birdwatching
  enq. North West Water RCO

AUDENSHAW, Thameside, Gtr Manchester
101.1 hectares
Birdwatching (hide available)
  permits from North West Water R&CO

BAYSTONE BANK, Copeland, Cumbria
Trout fishing
  Millom A.A., Mr O. Myers, 19 Market Street, Millom

BASSENTHWAITE LAKE, Cumbria
Canoeing and **Sailing** (free public access)

BELMONT RESERVOIR, Bolton
39.5 hectares
Sailing, (members only with open days for other clubs)
  Bolton Sailing Club, tel: Bolton 44897
Walking

BESOM HILL, Oldham, Gtr Manchester
0.9 hectares water, 51 hectares land
Mixed fishing
  enq. Oldham Central, Mr K. Hufton, 140 Main Road, Oldham
Walking

BLACKMOSS UPPER and LOWER, Pendle, Lancashire
Trout fishing enq. Blackmoss Fishing Assoc. Mr J.J.P. Smith, Great Hey, Hill Top, Foulridge, Colne, Lancs

BLACKSTONE EDGE, Rochdale, Lancashire
23.9 hectares water, 14 hectares land
Birdwatching
  Enq. North West Water, R&CO

BOLLINGHURST, Disley, Gtr Manchester
  5.8 hectares water, 5.5 hectares land
Trout fishing
  enq. Dystelegh FFC, Mr G. Heywood, 10 Martlett Avenue, Disley, Stockport

BORRANS, South Lakeland, Cumbria
Canoeing and **windsurfing, sailing, trout fishing**
  N. Tyneside Borough Education Dept., High Borrans Outdoor Pursuit Centre, Windermere, Cumbria

BOTTOMS RESERVOIR, Macclesfield, Cheshire
3.6 hectares water, 50 hectares land
Trout fishing, (5 permits issued per day)
  Prince Albert A.C., Mr J.A. Turner, 15 Pex Hill Drive, Macclesfield

BOUNDARY WATER PARK, Holmes Chapel
Windsurfing (day tickets, showers, hire, shop and tuition)
  Boundary Water Park, Knutsford Road, Cranage, Holmes Chapel, Chesire, tel: (0477) 33225

BUCKLEY WOOD, Rochdale, Gtr Manchester
2 hectares water, 18 hectares land
Mixed fishing
  Rochdale Walton A.S., D.R. Gent, 59 Croftshead Drive, Milnrow

BUDWORTH MERE, Great Budworth
Sailing and **windsurfing** (members only)
  enq. P. Gaskin, Budworth Sailing Club, tel: Arley 303

BUTTERMERE,
Canoeing and **rowing** (rowing boats for hire)
  Public access by permit from: Mrs T

Richardson, Gatesgarth Farm,
Buttermere, tel: Buttermere 256
Sailing and **windsurfing**

CALF HEY, Rossendale, Lancs
Environmental trail, orienteering
    enq. to North West Water. R&CO
Car park

CANT CLOUGH, Burnley, Lancs
Trout fishing
    Mitre A.C., R.D. Halstead, 32 Parrock
    Road, Nelson, Lancs.

CARR MILL DAM, St Helens
Power boats and **waterskiing** (Sat,
Sun and Wed evenings)
    enq. Lancashire Power Boat Club, tel:
    (074) 425 494

CHORLTON WATER PARK
Princess Park Way, Manchester
Sailing (free public access)
    enq. Wardens Office, tel: (061) 881
    4209

**CASTLESHAW LOWER and
UPPER**, Oldham, Gtr Manchester
10.5 hectares water (lower), 12.3 (upper),
226.5 hectares land
Birdwatching
Canoeing and **small dinghies**
    enq. to North West Water, R&CO
Mixed fishing
    Oldham United A.C., J.K. Lees, 22
    Epping Close, Firwood Park,
    Chadderton, Lancs.
Roman fort

CHELBURN UPPER, Rochdale, Gtr
Manchester
6.9 hectares water, 1.6 hectares land
Water skiing
    Pennine Water Ski Club, tel: (0204)
    88710

CHEW, Oldham, Gtr Manchester
15.8 hectares water, 336 hectares land
Fell running, orienteering
    enq. to North West Water, R&CO

CLOWBRIDGE RESERVOIR,
Dunnockshaw, Burnley

Sailing and **windsurfing** (for members
but visitors welcome)
    Rossendale Valley Sailing Club,
    S. Allen, 5 Sunnyside Close,
    Reedsholme, Rossendale BB4 8PE
Trout fishing
    Southbank Retirement Homes Ltd,
    tel: Burnley 35469

CONISTON
Cruising and **sailing**, (free access to all
non-powered craft)
    Coniston Tourist Information Centre,
    tel: (05394) 41533

COGRA MOSS, Copeland, Cumbria
Fishing
    Cockermouth Anglers, A. Ames, The
    Barn, High Lorton, Cockermouth,
    Cumbria CA13 9UQ

COLDWELL LOWER and UPPER,
Pendle, Lancs
Fishing
    Nelson A.A., tel: (0282) 68965
Nature reserve
    enq. to North West Water, R&CO

COMBS RESERVOIR, Chapel-on-le-
Frith
Sailing (members only)
    tel: N. Higgins, Combs Sailing Club
    (0457) 73714

COMPSTALL, Bredbury
Sailing and **windsurfing** (under
430 cm, Tue, Thur & weekends,
members only)
    Bredbury & Romiley Sailing Club, tel:
    061 483 8035

COTE LODGE, High Peak, Gtr
Manchester
0.8 hectares water, 13 hectares land
Mixed fishing (day tickets available)
    Walls Factory Sports & Social Club,
    Glossop

COWM RESERVOIR, Rossendale,
Lancs
Waterskiing (equipment hire available)
    enq. Cowm Valley Water Ski Centre,
    tel: (0706) 853565

CROMPTON LODGES, Bolton
Canoeing and **sailing** (free public access)
Windsurfing (except Sun)
Car park and toilets
    enq. The Warden, Moses Gate Country Park, tel: Bolton 71561

CROWTHORNE, Blackburn, Lancashire
Sub-aqua
    enq. to North West Water, R&CO

CRUMMOCK WATER
Canoeing and **rowing** (rowing boats for hire)
    Public access by permit from: Mrs R. Beard, Rannerdale Farm, Buttermere, nr Cockermouth, tel: Buttermere 232
Sailing and **windsurfing**

DEAN CLOUGH LOWER and UPPER, Hyndburn, Lancs
Fly fishing (day tickets available)
    Lancashire F.F.A., for permits tel: Accrington 34148
Orienteering
    enq. to North West Water, R&CO

DEEPLY VALE LODGE, Rossendale, Lancs
Birdwatching
    enq. to North West Water, R&CO

DEBDALE PARK, Gorton, Manchester
Sailing (public)
    Debdale Sailing Centre, tel: (061) 223 5182

DELPH RESERVOIR, Edgerton, Bolton
29.2 hectares water, 511.5 hectares land
Sailing (members only)
Birdwatching (SSSI), orienteering and **shooting**
    enq. to North West Water, R&CO
Windsurfing (Sat and Sun, weekday eves except Mon, members only)
    Mr G. Service, Delph Sailing Club, Buyukdere, Bolton Rd, Darwen

DERWENT WATER, Keswick
Motorised craft (no speed boats)

    enq. National Trust Regional Office, tel: (05394) 33883
Cruising, sailing and **windsurfing** (public access)

DINGLE, Blackburn, Lancs
6.1 hectares water, 19 hectares land
Birdwatching
    enq. to North West Water, R&CO
Trout fishing
    Dingle F.F.C., W.M. Ashton, 2 The Crescent, Westhoughton, Bolton

DODDINGTON LAKE, Nantwich, Cheshire
Sailing and **windsurfing** (members only)
    enq. Nantwich & Border Counties Sailing Club, tel: (0270) 214432

DOVESTONE, Oldham, Gtr Manchester
35.9 hectares water, 211.5 hectares land
Climbing, fell running and **orienteering**
    enq. to North West Water, R&CO
Sailing and **windsurfing**
    Dovestone Sailing Club, M. Freeman, Long Rigging Farm, Booth, Halifax, Yorks
Trail for the disabled
Car park, picnic area, information centre and toilets

EARNSDALE, Blackburn, Lancs
Trout fishing (day tickets available)
    Darwen A.A., tel: Darwen 72187

ELTON RESERVOIR, Elton, Bury
Sailing and windsurfing (weekends and evenings, for members but visitors welcome)
    enq. P. Tillett, Elton Sailing Club, tel: 061 764 2858

ENNERDALE, Copeland, Cumbria
Canoeing
    enq. to North West Water, R&CO
Trout fishing
    Ennerdale Fisheries, E. M. Wright, 43 Dale View Gardens, Green Dykes, Egremont, Cumbria CA22 2LM

ENTWISTLE, Blackburn, Lancashire
38.1 hectares water, 863 hectares land

Birdwatching (no permit required)
Climbing and **orienteering**
  enq. to North West Water, R&CO
Trout fishing
  Entwistle F.F., G.K. Thirkell, 87
  Higher Ashworth, Radcliffe
Car park, picnic area and toilets

ERRWOOD RESERVOIR, Buxton
31.6 hectares water, 1,878 hectares land
Birdwatching
  enq. to North West Water, R&CO
Sailing and windsurfing (Sat and Sun,
Wed evenings, members only)
  tel: C. Newman, Erwood Sailing Club
  (0625) 872631
Trout fishing (day tickets available)
  Errwood F.F.C., D. Hamnett, 30
  Kinross Ave, Woodsmore Park,
  Stockport SK2 7EL
Car park, picnic area and toilets

ESTHWAITE WATER, Nr
Hawkshead
Rowing (public)
  enq. Hawkshead Post Office, or
  Hawkshead Trout Farm, tel:
  Hawkshead 331

FERNILEE High Peak, Gtr.
Manchester
Birdwatching (also **SSSI**)
  enq. to North West Water, R&CO

FISHER TARN, South Lakeland,
Cumbria
Birdwatching
  Cumbria Trust for Nature
  Conservation, Mrs J. Ketchen,
  Church St, Ambleside, Cumbria
Trout fishing (day tickets available)
  Fisher Tarn Anglers, day tickets tel:
  (0539) 23433

FISHMOOR, Blackburn, Lancs
Sailing
  Lancashire Schools Sailing Assoc., tel:
  (0253) 810880
Trout Fishing (day tickets available)
  Oswaldtwistle A.A., for tickets tel:
  Accrington 34148 or Blackburn
  676977

FOULRIDGE RESERVOIR, Nelson
and Colne
Sailing and **windsurfing** (members
only)
  enq. Burwain Sailing Club, tel: (0282)
  62613

FRODSHAM LEISURE LAKES,
Manley, nr Frodsham
Boardsailing, leisure lakes, training,
shop and hire
  enq. Sail Sports, tel: (09284) 243

**GORTON LOWER and UPPER (a,b
and c)**, Manchester
Coarse fishing, (upper b Lawrence
Scott Arm)
  tickets available on site.
Coarse fishing (upper c Denton Arm)
Bulls Head A.C., Mr D. A. Plant,
Church Inn, 90 Audenshaw Road,
Audenshaw M34 5LP
Mixed fishing (lower, suitable for the
disabled)
  tickets available on site
Model boating (upper b Lawrence
Scott Arm with permission)
  Manchester C.C. Rec. Dept as below
Sailing, windsurfing and **canoeing**
(lower)
  courses by Manchester C.C. Ed. Dept
  (061) 223 5182, May-Sept,
  Manchester C.C. Rec. Dept, tel: (061)
  226 0131
Sailing (upper a only)
  Fairfield Golf & S.C., G.S. Barlow,
  Boothdale, Booth Road, Audenshaw
  M34 5GA
Sub-aqua (lower and upper a)
  permission from Rec. Dept above
Car park and toilets, educational facilities

GREENBOOTH, Rochdale, Gtr
Manchester
Coarse fishing
  Northern Anglers, tel: Wigan 726917

GREENFIELD, Oldham, Gtr
Manchester
Climbing, fell running and
orienteering
  enq. to North West Water, R&CO

GRIMARROW, Port Haverigg, Millom, Cumbria
Waterski club on man-made lake. Tournament courses, caravan park, hotel, holiday resort and tuition.
Port Haverigg Holiday Village, Haverigg, Millom, Cumbria, tel: (065) 72107

GRIMSARGH RESERVOIRS (1, 2 and 3) Preston, Lancs
Canoeing and **sailing** (2, for educational users)
Lancashire Schools Sailing Assoc., tel: (0253) 810880
Fly Fishing (3)
Red Scar A.A., tickets from Mrs D. Dewhurst, 140 Longridge Road, Ribbleton, Preston
Mixed fishing (1 & 2)

GRIZEDALE LEA, Wyre, Lancs
Birdwatching
enq. North West Water, R&CO
Trout fishing (day tickets available)
Kirkham F.F., A.W. Helme, 13–17 Freskleton St, Kirkham, Preston.

HARLOCK, South Lakeland, Cumbria
Trout fishing
Barrow A.A., D.M. Adams, The Old Post Office, Woodland, Broughton-in-Furness, Cumbria

HAWESWATER, Eden, Cumbria
Climbing and **walking**
Fishing (free to NWWA rod licence holders)
Nature reserve, SSSI
Sub-aqua
enq. to The Supply Officer, Lake District Supply, Mintsfeet Depot, Mintsfeet Ind. Est., Kendal
Car parks

HAYESWATER, Eden, Cumbria
Trout fishing
Penrith A.A., R.F. Allinson, 7 Scaws Drive, Penrith, Cumbria
No vehicle access, mountain tarn

HEATON, Bolton, Gtr Manchester
Birdwatching
North West Water, R&CO

Trout fishing
Heaton F.F., G. Forsyth, 6 Oakwood Drive, Heaton, Bolton

HIGH BULLOUGH, Chorley, Lancs
3.5 hectares water, 3,964 hectares land
Birdwatching
North West Water, R&CO
Environmental trail

HIGH NEWTON (1 and 2) South Lakeland, Cumbria
Trout fishing
Grange A.A., J. Gedye, The Ridge, 33 Kentsford Road, Grange

HODDLESTON, Blackburn, Lancs
Mixed fishing
Darwen Loyal Anglers, J. Thompson, 6 Tithebarn St, Darwen,

HOLLINGWORTH, High Peak, Gtr Manchester
Nature reserve
Manchester Education Committee environmental study area

HOLLINGWORTH LAKE (A and B), Littleborough, Rochdale, Gtr Manchester
Birdwatching and **nature reserve**
enq. Chief Warden, Information Centre, Hollingworth Lake Country Park, tel: Rochdale 73421
Mixed fishing (day permits available)
enq. to Chief Warden as above
Rowing (members only)
enq. Hollingworth Lake Rowing Club, tel: Rochdale (0706) 77154
Rowing and **canoeing** (public)
enq. to Chief Warden as above
Sailing (members only)
enq. Hollingworth Lake Sailing Club, tel: Rochdale 44427
Sailing and windsurfing (public access)
permits from Chief Warden as above
Sub-aqua
enq. to Chief Warden as above
Campsite and caravan site, country park and picnic area, information centre and educational facilities
Car parks and toilets

HORROBIN LODGE, Turton
Mixed fishing
Ramsey Angling Society

HORSECOPPICE, Macclesfield,
Cheshire
Trout fishing
Dystelegh F.F.C., G. Heywood, 10
Martlett Ave, Disley

HURSTWOOD, Burnley, Lancs
Orienteering
North West Water, R&CO

JUMBLES RESERVOIR, Turton, nr
Bolton
Canoeing (organised youth groups)
permits from the Recreation
Management Officer
Coarse fishing (free)
Nature reserve and **birdwatching**
enq. as above
Sailing and **windsurfing** (members
only, but available to youth groups)
Civil Service Sailing Assoc., tel: Bolton
852337
Sub-aqua
enq. as above
Country park and picnic area,
environmental trail, information centre
Car parks and toilets

KILLINGTON RESERVOIR,
Killington
Sailing (members only)
enq. J. Skellern, Killington Sailing
Assoc., tel: Kendal 23183

KITCLIFFE, Rochdale, Gtr
Manchester
Trout fishing
Oldham United A.C., J.K. Lees, 22
Epping Close, Firwood Park,
Chadderton, Lancs

LAMALOAD, Macclesfield, Cheshire
Trout fishing
Prince Albert A.C., day permits
available from Barlows,
Bond St, Macclesfield and Jones,
Altrincham Road, Wilmslow
Car park and toilets

LANESHAW, Pendle, Lancs
Trout fishing
Colne Water A.C., 2–5 tickets issued
daily, tel: 0282 864 016

LEA GREEN, Burnley, Lancs
Trout fishing
Burnley A.S., day permits from Macks,
33 Parliament Street, Burnley

LEADBETTERS, Macclesfield,
Cheshire
Trout fishing
Prince Albert A.C., J.A. Turner, 15
Pex Hill Dr, Macclesfield

LEG O'MUTTON, St Helens,
Merseyside
1.2 hectares water
Coarse fishing
St Helens Ramblers, D. Fishwick, 4
Sherwell Grove, Sutton Leach, St
Helens

LIGHT HAZZLES, Rochdale, Gtr
Manchester
Birdwatching
permits from North West Water,
R&CO

LITTLE SEA, Oldham, Gtr
Manchester
Coarse fishing
Oldham & District A.A.A., H.
Garside, 60 Queensway, Greenfield,
Saddleworth, Oldham OL3 7AH

LOWESWATER, Cumbria
Rowing (boats for hire)
Scale Hill Hotel, tel: (090085) 232

LUDWORTH (1 and 2), Stockport,
Gtr Manchester
Canoeing, sailing and **windsurfing**
enq. to North West Water, R&CO
Coarse fishing
H. Crosland A.C., tel 061 437 0935
some day tickets available on site
Trout fishing
Wath Brow & Ennerdale A.A., T.
Carty, 89 Mill Hill, Cleator Moor

MILLBROOK POOL, Macclesfield,
Cheshire

Trout fishing
Bollington A.C., T. Barber, 10 George St West, Macclesfield (3-day permits available from the warden)

MITCHELLS HOUSE (1 and 2), Rossendale, Lancs
Mixed fishing
Accrington & District A.C., tel: Accrington 33517

OGDEN, Rochdale, Gtr Manchester
Coarse fishing (disabled access)
Oldham United A.C., as Kitcliffe
Car park and toilets

OGDEN Lower and **Upper**, Pendle, Lancs
Orienteering
Pendle Countryside Management Scheme
Trout Fishing (lower)
Oswaldtwistle A.A., R. Hope, 3 Fielding Lane, Oswaldtwistle

PADDOCK DAM, St Helens, Merseyside
0.76 hectares water
Coarse fishing
St Helens Ramblers, as Leg o'Mutton

PARSONAGE, Hyndburn, Lancs
Trout fishing
Bowland Game F.A., tel: 0772 424018; day permits from Roe Lee Tackle Box, tel: Blackburn 676977

PENNINGTON, South Lakeland, Cumbria
Trout fishing
Barrow A.A., as for Harlock

PENNINGTON FLASH, Lowton, Leigh
Sailing and **windsurfing** (members only)
enq. Leigh & Loughton Sailing Club

PEX HILL, Knowsley, Merseyside
Information centre, picnic area, open space recreation area, viewpoint, **walking** and **climbing**, car park and toilets
warden service, tel: 051 423 5638 or 051 443 3627

PICKMERE
Canoeing, sailing and **windsurfing** (Easter–Oct)
Amusement park, cafe, toilets etc.
enq. Pickmere Boating Co. tel: Pickmere 3233

PIETHORNE, Oldham, Gtr Manchester
Nature reserve and **viewpoint**
Trout fishing
Oldham Game Fishing, M.J. Bishop, 17 Rivington Road, Springhead, Oldham, OL4 4RH
Sub-aqua (limited licence only)
enq. to North West Water, R&CO
Car park and toilets

PLANTATION MILL No 2, Hyndburn, Lancs
Trout fishing
Hyndburn & Blackburn A.A., K.G. Lambert, 79 Prospect Terrace, Whalley Road, Altham West, Accrington, Lancs

PINE LAKES (Holiday Centre), Carnforth
Tournament facilities, residential courses in **canoeing, sailing, waterskiing, windsurfing** and **parascending**
Hotel, s/c accommodation, swimming pool, gymnasium, shop and hire facilities
Pine Lakes, Carnforth, Lancs LA5 8ER, tel: (0524) 736191

POAKA BECK, South Lakeland, Cumbria
Trout fishing
Barrow A.A., as for Harlock

PRESCOT (3 and 4), Knowsley, Merseyside
11 and 16.1 hectares water
Birdwatching
enq. to North West Water, R&CO

RAKE BROOK, Chorley, Lancs
5.8 hectares water, 3,964 hectares land
Birdwatching and **orienteering**
Mixed fishing
Withnell Anglers, G. Braithwaite, 2 Edge Lane Terrace, Withnall, Chorley; permits from Anglers Den,

15 Railway Road, Brinscall; enq. to
North West Water, R&CO
Parking

RHODESWOOD, Macclesfield,
Cheshire
Birdwatching
  permits from North West Water,
  R&CO

RIDEGATE, Macclesfield, Cheshire
Trout fishing
  Macclesfield F.F.C., W.F. Williams,
  1 Westwood Drive, Brooklands, Sale
  M33 3QW; enq. to North West Water,
  R&CO. Car park

**RIVINGTON Lower (a and b),
RIVINGTON Upper**, Chorley, Lancs
85.4 hectares water (lower), 23.1 (upper),
3,964 hectares land
Birdwatching
  enq. to North West Water, R&CO
Canoeing, rowing and **sub-aqua** (b)
  St Thomas Centre, see below
Mixed fishing (a)
  permits from Gtr Manchester Youth
  Assoc., Anderton Hall, tel: 0257
  483304
Mixed fishing (upper)
  Bolton A.A., Mr McKee, 1 Lever Edge
  Lane, Bolton; permits from Leaches
  Tackle Shop, Lee Lane, Horwich
Nature reserve (upper, restricted
access)
  licensed to LTNC, viewing from
  public footpath only
Sailing (a)
  as below
Windsurfing (a)
  St Thomas Centre, tel: 061 273 7364
Information centre, viewpoint and picnic
area, educational facilities, refreshments,
car park and toilets

REDESMERE, Siddington
Sailing (members only)
  enq. Redesmere Sailing Club, tel:
  (0625) 877533

RISHTON RESERVOIR, Blackburn
Sailing (members only)
  East Lancs Sailing Club, tel:
  Blackburn 665329

RODDLESWORTH Lower and
Upper, Blackburn
6.4 hectares water (lower), 9.8 upper,
3,964 hectares land
Birdwatching, orienteering and **sub-
aqua**
  enq. to North West Water, R&CO
Environmental trail and **nature
reserve**
Coarse fishing
  Royal Ashton A. C., J. D. Nuttall, c/o
  Vulcan Hotel, Junction Road, Deane,
  Bolton
Mixed fishing (lower)
  Withnall Anglers, as Rake Brook above
Trout fishing (upper)
  Horwich F.F.C., C. Wilson, 10
  Ramswell Brow, Bromley Cross
Car park and toilets

SALE WATER PARK, Manchester
Canoeing
Fishing
  enq. Sale Water Park, tel: (061) 969
  7063
Waterskiing (only via the club)
  Sale Park Water Ski club, tel: (061) 748
  9620
Windsurfing, equipment hire, tel:
  Wilmslow 533122

SCOTSMANS FLASH, Wigan
Sailing and **windsurfing** (weekends
and evenings, members only)
  enq. Wigan Sailing Club, tel:
  Upholland 622323

STOCKS, Ribble Valley, Lancs
Birdwatching
  enq. to North West Water, R&CO
Trout fishing
  permits from the Trout Farm, tel: 0468
  61305 or the Fishermans Cabin, tel:
  Slaidburn (02006) 602
Area of natural beauty, picnic area and
fishing lodge, car park

STRINESDALE Lower and **Upper**,
Oldham, Gtr Manchester
Coarse fishing (upper)
  enq. to North West Water R&CO
Trout fishing (lower)

SUTTON RESERVOIR, Macclesfield
Sailing and **Windsurfing** (members
only)
 enq. Turks Head Sailing Club, tel:
 (0265) 613216

TALKIN TARN, Brampton
Rowing and **sailing** (public)
Windsurfing (all day Sun, Tue eves,
free public access)
 enq. The Warden, Talkin Tarn, tel:
 Brampton 3129

TARLETON LEISURE LAKES,
Tarleton, Preston
Fishing
Sailing and **windsurfing**
 marina, caravan and picnic park
 enq. Leisure Lakes, tel: (077473) 3446

TATTON MERE, Knutsford, Cheshire
Sailing (up to 490 cm, not Mon)
 Pay kiosk at park, tel: Knutsford 54822

TEGGNOSE, Macclesfield, Cheshire
Coarse fishing
 Macclesfield Waltonian A.C., tel:
 (0625) 34806, 5 day permits from The
 Cycle Shop, Sunderland St,
 Macclesfield

THIRLMERE, Allerdale, Cumbria
Climbing and **orienteering**
Deerwatching (hides available by
arrangement)
 enq. to the Deerwarden, tel: Keswick
 72334
Mixed fishing (free to NWW licence
holders)
Nature reserve and **environmental
trails (SSSI)**
Sailing, windsurfing and **canoeing**
 (free public access, life jackets must be
 worn) enq. North West Water R&CO,
 tel: (0772) 22200
Viewpoint and picnic area, car park and
toilets

TODDBROOK RESERVOIR,
Reservoir Road, Whaley Bridge,
Stockport
Sailing (members only)
 enq. Todd Brook Sailing Club

TORSIDE RESERVOIR, High Peak,
Glossop, Gtr Manchester
Birdwatching
 permits issued from North West
 Water, R&CO
Sailing (for members, with public access
from Apr-Sep, Sat only)
 enq. T.W. Flannagan, Glossop Sailing
 Club, tel: 061 368 5065; training
 courses available, tel: 061 338 4764
Windsurfing (weekends and Wed
evenings)
 enq. as sailing above

TRENTABANK, Macclesfield,
Cheshire
Birdwatching
Nature reserve and **environmental
trail**
Viewpoint, picnic area and information
centre, car park and toilets

ULLSWATER
Cruising, sailing and **windsurfing**
 Motorised craft (no speed boats)
 enq. National Trust Regional Office,
 tel: (0942) 33883

VALEHOUSE, High Peak, Gtr
Manchester
Birdwatching
Trout fishing
Car park and toilets

WATERGROVE RESERVOIR,
Wardle, Littleborough
Archaeological excavations and
historical trail
Fishing
 day permits from the warden, as above,
 or at Hollingworth Lake

WALKERWOOD, Tameside, Gtr
Manchester
Trout fishing
 tickets from Walkerwood Trout
 Fishery, tel: 061 368 3173

WALVERDEN, Pendle, Lancs
Coarse fishing
 Pendle B.C. Rec. Dept, Bank House,
 Albert Road, Colne
Conservation area
Car park

Windsurfing (clubhouse, facilities etc.
members only)
    enq. J. Forbes, West Pennine
    Sailboard Club, tel: Halifax 823427
Car park and toilets

WAYOH, Blackburn, Lancs
Fell running
Mixed fishing
Nature reserve and birdwatching
    enq. to North West Water, R&CO

WET SLEDDALE, Eden, Cumbria
Nature reserve
    Cumbria Trust for Nature
    Conservation, Miss J. Ketchen,
    Church Street, Ambleside, Cumbria
Car park

WHITE HOLME, Calderdale, Gtr
Manchester
Birdwatching
    enq. to North West Water, R&CO

WILTON QUARRIES (1, 2 and 3)
Bolton, Gtr Manchester
Climbing (at all times)
Shooting (2 and 3, time zoning
arrangement)
    Bolton Rifle & Pistol Club, N. Erlam,
    150 Bickershaw Lane, Abram, Bolton
    or Bolton Gun Club, C.E. Thompson,
    128 Deane Lane, Bolton

WOODHEAD, High Peak, Gtr
Manchester
Birdwatching
    enq. to North West Water, R&CO
SSSI
Car park and toilets

WORTHINGTON, Wigan, Gtr
Manchester
6.1 hectares water, 11.5 hectares land
Mixed fishing
    Wigan Anglers, W. Gratton, 66
    Balcarres Road, Aspull, Wigan
Country park and **environmental
trail**
Car park, toilets and picnic area

WINDERMERE
Cruising, sailing and **windsurfing**
Motorised craft and power boats (must
be registered)
    enq. The Lake Warden, tel:
    Windermere 2753, or South Lakeland
    District Council, tel: Kendal 33333

WINSFORD FLASH, Winsford
Sailing and **boardsailing** (members
only)
    enq. Winsford Flash Sailing Club, tel:
    Kingsley 88459

YARROW, Chorley, Lancs
26.3 hectares water, 3,964 hectares land
Birdwatching
Orienteering
    all enq. to North West Water, R&CO
Sub-squa
Windsurfing

YOEMAN HAY, Oldham, Gtr
Manchester
Climbing, fell running and
orienteering
    enq. to North West Water, R&CO
Viewpoint, car park

Northumbrian Water Authority

Northumbrian Water is geographically the smallest authority, being only about one-third of the size of Anglian Water. Since it has two of the larger companies within its boundary, it is actually supplying water to a relatively small region. It should be remembered, however, that as a water authority it is responsible for many other activities over the

Reservoirs with recreational facilities – Northumbrian Water Authority.

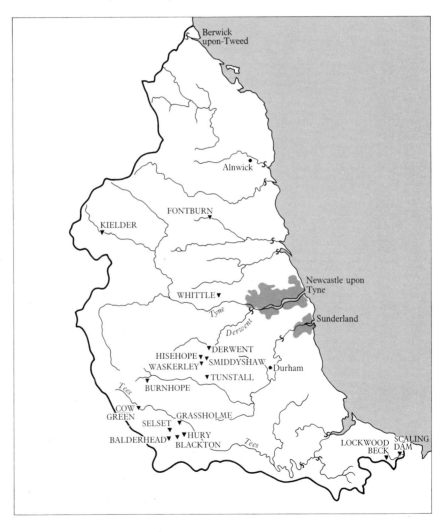

The interesting 'skew arched' bridge that crosses the Bakethin nature reserve at Kielder Water. The water level in this part is kept high all year round by a submerged embankment. (Photograph: Charles Hall)

whole region. In spite of the mountainous picture one holds of Northumberland, the authority's region includes the three great manufacturing rivers, the Tyne, Tees and Wear, and population is relatively high owing to the very heavy urban concentration around them. Away from these conurbations, on the high ground of the Pennines to the west, the Cheviots to the north and the Cleveland Hills in the south east, population is sparse.

The high ground is the principal source of Northumbrian's water and makes its position particularly favourable. The water naturally drains from west to east towards the urban areas and is clean, well oxygenated by its travel in the hills and fairly soft. Northumbrian Water's charges for water are the lowest in the UK. This plentiful supply has not been without problems, however, as abstraction direct

from the rivers in the nineteenth century was a recurrent source of disease; the water taken from too near the towns was badly polluted.

The west-east topography has been exploited as a water resource since the first of many impounding reservoirs was completed in 1848 at Whittle Dean by the Newcastle and Gateshead Company. It supplied water direct to the town, a distance of 19 km. Over the next decades more reservoirs were strategically placed in the head waters of the many small rivers, collecting surface water from their respective catchment areas. Nearer the coast, in a band stretching up from Darlington to Sunderland, smaller quantities of high quality water are taken from the magnesian limestone aquifer.

Kielder Water   In the second half of the nineteenth century demand continued to increase rapidly for both industrial and domestic use. More businesses attracted more people; houses more often had their own supply and, with water freely available, used more of it. With ports developing on all three rivers, the easy availability of coal as a source of power, and an increasingly skilled workforce in engineering, combined to make the north east a centre for heavy manufacturing. As demand for water rose, other reservoirs were added, both for direct supply by pipeline to the urban centres and also to regulate river flows in dry periods, so that abstraction could take place further downstream. In the twentieth century growth was less dramatic but the buoyant economy after the war, and particularly in the 1960s and 1970s, suggested that a really long-term source of supply would be more satisfactory than the (with hindsight) rather piecemeal addition of fairly small-scale developments – Cow Green reservoir at 316 hectares, built in 1970, was the largest in the authority's control so far. (Although Sunderland Water Company and Durham County Water Board constructed the Derwent reservoir in 1967, its 405 hectares making it one of the largest in England at that time, Kielder's capacity is four times greater.)

A two-part scheme was proposed. First, to build a really large 1,086-hectare reservoir in the Kielder valley, and second, to pipe this water south so that it would be available to supply any of the three major rivers, the Tyne, Wear or Tees. The tradition of west to east regulating reservoirs was not suitable for the scale of operation envisaged; six new reservoirs would have been needed if this pattern had been followed and they would not have given the flexibility to supply any changing demands of the industrial communities on the three rivers.

Two public enquiries were held concerning the proposed scheme. In 1974 the Secretary of State for the Environment made the Kielder Water Order and work began in 1976. Completed in 1982, Kielder is the largest manmade lake in Europe and has a number of features of special interest, but it is publicly admitted that so far it has not been necessary to use any of its water and it remains, at present, a very expensive recreation site. The current consumption of water in the region is 41 per cent of the available resources, leaving a massive surplus of 59 per cent. The reservoir's opening has coincided with a devastating decline in the traditional industries of the area. There were once more ships built on the Tyne than in all of the rest of the world put together; but shipbuilding is now almost a thing of the past. The coal mines have nearly all closed and the heavy iron and steel trade has been almost destroyed.

Unemployment here is now the highest in England and one might cynically suggest that the best prospect would be to make the whole area an industrial heritage theme park and multiple retail sales outlet, but it would not be fair to blame anyone for not forecasting the future correctly; between 1961 and 1971 demand rose from 640 Ml/d to 923 Ml/d and by 1981 the figure had reached 1,055 Ml. The consumption projected from these figures was 1,364 Ml for the year 2001 and the region's total resources before Kielder were 1,255 Ml. To put this in perspective, 1987's demand was for 1,018 Ml per day.

In addition to the problem of decline, many large consumers of water are finding ways of cutting their costs. In 1978, following rationalisation of the use of water in various departments, British Leyland (not in this region) is said to have saved £1 million over three years. Northumbrian Water supplies a greater proportion of its water to industry than any other authority – about 60 per cent, in comparison with 30 per cent by the others. Part of this is treated potable water, the rest raw or untreated. In fact, there are grounds for optimism, the bleak facts of declining large industry are not sharply reflected in the use of water; demand rose last year by 2 per cent for potable water and by 4.7 per cent for untreated, so what seems a very large surplus will eventually be reduced if that rate of increase continues. There are signs that the worst effects of the wholesale closures of heavy industry may now be offset by diversification into many smaller light industrial works.

Criticism has been, and still is, raised against the authority, not for getting it wrong but for getting it *so* wrong. There are other ways of increasing available resources without building large reservoirs but their mundane quality makes them less attractive to engineers. There is more glory in an impressive capital project (and it is probably easier to raise money for it) than in stopping up all the leaking pipes and making sure everyone uses water as economically as possible. Although if both of these had been done, the water saved would have been about the same, it is estimated that most authorities lose about 25 per cent of their water in leakage between the collection point and the customer.

Kielder has now been built and whatever its present usefulness may be for water storage, there are a number of interesting features about it; the recreational amenities go far beyond other reservoirs, the hydro-electric facility is the largest in England, and the regional distribution network is both large in scale and dramatically logical and simple.

Hydro-electric Power
The hydro-electric generators at Kielder are the joint venture of Northumbrian Water and the Central Electricity Generating Board. Water leaves the reservoir through a valve tower and is fed to the power station at the base of the dam. It is here that two water turbines generate electricity. One 5.5 megawatt 'Kaplan' generator is used when large

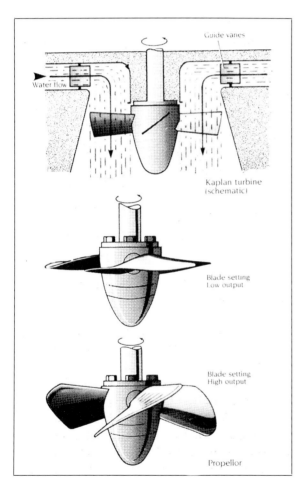

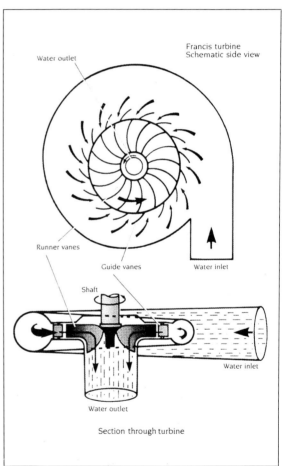

Kaplan turbine *Water enters through guide vanes and flows axially through the six-bladed 'propellor'. The turbo-generator rotates at 500 revolutions a minute. Output is 5.5 megawatts.* (CEGB)

Francis turbine *Water enters the turbine casing and flows through the guide vanes into the turbine runner. The turbo-generator rotates at 1,000 revolutions a minute and has an output of 0.5 megawatts.* (CEGB)

quantities of water are being discharged to regulate the river flows, a small 0.5 'Francis' generator is used when compensation water (water to compensate for the loss of normal river flow caused by the dam) is being released. Both generators can be run together and, to a certain extent, water can be released to coincide with periods of demand. The power produced can vary from 200 kilowatts to 6 megawatts, enough to supply a town of 10,000 people. It is estimated that 21.5 million kilowatt hours can be generated in an average year, a saving of 10,000 tonnes of coal. Revenue from this amounts to about £1 million shared equally between Northumbrian Water and the CEGB. The cost of constructing the hydro-electric facility was £6 million.

The Tyne Clean-up

Londoners may take pride in the fact that Newcastle is over 100 years behind them in making an attempt to clear its rivers of sewage and industrial waste. Samuel Johnson wrote,

No other river in Great Britain, and no river anywhere, has contributed more towards the characteristic development of the Century than the Tyne, while certainly no other has received greater benefits therefrom . . . everywhere from the dancing water of the harbour to the ebb and flow of the throbbing city, industry, resource and expansion, coal staiths, shipyards, engine shops, dry docks, chemical works, forges, electric lighting laboratories, warehouses, merchants offices, steamships, railway trains without number, without end . . . from Shields to Scotswood . . . there is not its like in any thirteen miles of river the world over. The traffic of the river is incessant. Night brings no rest to its throbbing waters. Steam colliers slip in and out of port with the regularity of the tides. The vessels are never a moment idle. They will load a cargo of 1,000 tons in four or five hours, hurry out to sea and up the coast to London . . . smoke ridden, grimy, noisy as it all is, what is it but the free expression of nineteenth century energy.

As with so many other free expressions of nineteenth-century energy, it had a dark side, and one of these was to throw all the waste and sewage straight into the river.

It was known in 1875 that such haphazard disposal was outdated and should not continue. In 1896 the Medical Officer of Health criticised the situation, but it was not until 1966 that the Tyneside Joint Sewerage Board was set up with the object of promoting the construction of a sewage collection and disposal scheme. Until October 1980 there were 200 major outfalls and discharges into the Tyne estuary. Almost all the crude sewage produced on Tyneside was still discharged directly into the river and its tributaries from as far back as Newburn and Ryton or onto the beaches at South Shields and Whitley Bay. This amounted to an average flow of about 3,000 litres a second, and only about 5 per cent of this received any form of treatment. The problem was further aggravated by the complex flow pattern in the river, which prevented the raw sewage from leaving the estuary when the tides changed. Raw sewage entering the river took up to ten days to leave the estuary. Flow patterns also encouraged solids to move upstream and settle on the river bed, or to arrive on the beaches around the mouth of the Tyne.

The proposed scheme is very similar in principle to that proposed by Sir Joseph Bazalgette for London in 1855. Large sewers, running parallel to the banks of the river, will intercept the old outfalls and carry all sewage, mostly by gravity, to a new treatment works at Howden on the north bank. Sewage from the south-east side is given preliminary treatment at Jarrow and then transferred through a tunnel under the river to Howden. Sewage from the south west will be collected at Derwenthaugh and transferred by a pipeline in the Scotswood Bridge to link up with the north-bank system. Provision has been made at Derwenthaugh to build another treatment works if demand rises.

The works at Howden are now giving primary treatment to 80 per cent of the effluent which previously entered the estuary, but Northumbrian Water's literature on the subject is a little misleading. They do not mention, nor do they show on an accompanying map, that the partially treated effluent is still discharged into the river. Local benefits are clear, however. In 1987 the Tyne had higher catches of salmon (over 1,000 fish) than any other river in England that year and all the beaches round the mouth of the Tyne, from Tynemouth to South Shields, now conform to EEC standards. This is obviously a result to be praised and one cannot help being impressed by the construction details and engineering feats. A nagging doubt remains, however, that since primary treatment removes only some 30 per cent of the organic waste (and the rest is still put in the river) and since the sludge removed is carried out to sea and dumped anyway, there is no less sewage entering the sea than before – only more of it is now carried away further, perhaps to become part of somebody else's problem.

Hartlepools Water Company

Population served: 93,000
Water supplied: 45 Ml/d
Length of mains: 572 km
Area: 90 sq km
Water is taken entirely from boreholes in Cleveland and south east Durham magnesian limestone.

The company was formed in 1846 as the Hartlepools Gas and Water Company and retained its joint interest in gas until 1949 when that industry was nationalised. Its source of water was prolific and of good quality and has allowed the company to expand successfully in line with the development of Hartlepool's docks and industries. A high proportion of this water has traditionally gone to manufacturing and the industry's late-nineteenth-century growth, together with another period in the 1950s and 1960s, created a company strong enough to withstand the leaner economy of the 1980s.

Hartlepools has recently installed an extremely interesting energy conservation scheme. Water from boreholes in south east Durham has to be pumped over a ridge of high ground and then has a 37-m drop into the service reservoir at Dalton Piercy. The energy in this fall, which previously caused a problem, has now been harnessed to a hydro-electric generator capable of producing 83 kilowatts of electricity. This can now be used for part of the pumping operation and has saved 33 per cent of the power costs. Turbines have a minimum working life of 25 years with very low maintenance costs; this one cost £80,000 and should save £20,000 per year.

Newcastle and Gateshead Water Company

Population served: 761,000
Water supplied: 65.2 Ml/d metered
138 Ml/d unmetered
Length of mains: 4,773 km
Area: 4,802 sq km
Water from 32 separate sources including ten upland impounding reservoirs, river intakes from the Tyne and Coquet rivers, deep bore-holes into the Fell sandstones in the Berwick upon Tweed area and several streams and springs.

Newcastle has to supply by far the largest area of all the water companies (double that of Bristol, the second largest) in spite of it being only the fifth largest company in size. Its area is even larger than that supplied by Northumbrian Water Authority, although serving fewer people.

The first public supply was made available in Newcastle as early as 1680, when water was pumped by Cuthbert Dykes, with a waterwheel, from the River Tyne at Sandgate to the east of the town. This proved unsatisfactorily dirty; it was taken from too near the town and contained large quantities of sewage. This was the start of a pattern which was to repeat itself many times in later years, at times with terrible consequences. Polluted water was taken from the river to feed the rapidly growing demands of the expanding town. Its poor or even dangerous quality forced a search for other supplies but ever-increasing needs tempted the suppliers back to the river again.

In 1697 William Yarnold, who had supplied water to Windsor, Deptford and Greenwich, obtained an Act of Parliament to bring water in by wooden pipes from springs south of the river, feeding some of the wealthier inhabitants with private supplies and also some public fountains, or 'pants' as they are known in the north. It is recorded that in about 1755 he was supplying only 227,000 litres per week to 161 individual properties. The Common Council was at this time also providing water to the pants at no charge and Yarnold's enterprise does not appear to have been prosperous. A number of reservoirs and cisterns were constructed and a new supply, pumped by steam, was brought in from the north in 1770, but these supplies were infrequent and one of the town's insurance companies, the Newcastle Fire Office, took over the works in 1797 in an attempt to improve matters.

At first sight it seems odd for an insurance company to take over the water supply, but the reason is obvious when one considers the rudimentary state of fire fighting at the time and the importance of a substantial and reliable supply of water. It was normal for the council to specify the number of fireplugs and their distance apart in negotiations with water companies, although with the older wooden pipes a hole could be made at any point and blocked up with a peg after the event. The new company's efforts to increase supplies included pumping by windmill from a disused coal working. Supplies were, in fact, increased to 340,000 litres per day but were still only available on two days of the week, a situation hard to imagine today. In 1831, problems with the sources of supply coincided with the arrival of cholera in Sunderland, from where it spread to Newcastle and Gateshead. Pumping from the river was almost certainly the source of infection and shortly afterwards new supplies replaced this source.

The situation was felt to be so unsatisfactory that another company was formed, the 'Newcastle Subscription Water Company' who obtained an Act to pump water again from the Tyne, although this time the scheme included filtering the water through sandbeds, a method recently invented by James Simpson and used by the Chelsea Waterworks Company to purify water from the Thames. The ensuing rivalry is clear from two different newspapers' reports of a fire in 1835. They both assured their readers that the fire was principally saved by plentiful supplies of water, but each credited different water companies with the supply; the partisan reporting was not unconnected with the ownership of shares in the water companies! The situation did not last long, however, as the old company sold out to the new company in 1836 for £15,000.

The new Subscription Company appeared to have inherited supply problems, as the following newspaper report makes clear:

... fire broke out in the coachworks of John Atkinson in Pilgrim Street and although discovered at 12.55 am it was only at 1.20 am that the company turncock went to turn on the main at the west end of Blackett Street. An attempt was made to utilise the Old Coxlodge main at Barras Bridge but the cock was found to be broken and the turncock then went to the reservoir at Arthur's Hill to ascertain the quantity of water in it. When it was found to be only half full he proceeded to Elswick to order the engineman to pump water to the reservoir, following which he returned to Pilgrim Street. Another turncock went to Barras Bridge to supervise the repair of the broken cock before going to Pilgrim Street to help the North British insurance company take water from the Blackett Street main and it would seem that no water was available until 1.45 am, a result of the water being turned off each night from 7 pm until 4 am.

Numerous complaints were received by the company in the following few years, principally about quantity, cost and quality, the latter often with regard to brackishness due to pumping from the river at unsuitable tides. The local brewer Addison Langhorn Potter was naturally particularly concerned about this, and engineers also reported damage to their boilers. Once again a new company was proposed by a group of leading citizens, including many, like Potter, who had a professional interest in improvements. Whittle Burn was chosen as a source of supply and the new company was formed in 1845 as the Whittle Dean Water Company. Once again the old company capitulated in the face of strong opposition and soon sold out to the new one. The Whittle Dean Company changed its name to the Newcastle and Gateshead Company in 1863.

The new Whittle Dean supply saved the town from the very severe 1849 outbreak of cholera which killed over 72,000 people in Britain. Newcastle escaped almost unscathed. Unfortunately the lesson had not been learned; supply difficulties in 1853 precipitated renewed abstraction from the river and, within months, 1,527 people had died of cholera. Water was immediately brought in from another source and pumping from the river stopped; the Town Council pronounced that 'no Tyne water should under any pretence whatsoever be supplied to the inhabitants of the Town'. Within a few years water was again taken from the river, although from further upstream.

The last impounding reservoir was built in 1905 at Catcleugh, about 70 km from Newcastle, and in 1940 water was again taken from the Tyne, this time at Barrasford, further upstream. In 1959 work was undertaken to take water from the River Coquet. The company's area expanded enormously in the reorganisations which took place in the 1950s and 1960s, growing from 104 to 2,217 sq km in 100 years.

Sunderland and South Shields Water Company

Population served: 550,000
Water supplied: 144 Ml/d
Length of mains: 2,671 km
Area: 342 sq km
Water from two upland impounding reservoirs, eleven deep wells and boreholes in the magnesian limestone and from the River Wear.

South Shields's first record of water supply is Roman – an elegant inscribed stone, possibly commemorating a conduit and dating from the third century AD. A number of medieval references imply problems with pollution; 'the whole village is ordered not to steep flax in the well at the Deans', for example (1370). There is no record of charges having been made for the water unless it was delivered. The South Shields Water Company was created by Act of Parliament in 1788 and used a small reservoir near a spring and wooden pipes to supply the town and ships. Supplies for most people must have changed little, as an old lady recalled in 1824 that 'many an hour I have sat there before I could get any water. You know it was very slow work, and without you got up early in the morning you had a long time to wait; the lasses came from all parts and sometimes got on larking or talking about their sweethearts and would not hurry, and everyone had to wait their turn.'

This carved stone was found at the site of the Roman station at Lawe, South Shields: 'The Emperor Caesar Marcus Aurelius Severus, pious, happy, august, high priest, with tribunitial power, father of his country, consul, grandson of the deified Severus, son of the deified Antonius the Great, led water into [the camp] for the use of the fifth cohort of Gauls under the direction of Marius Valerianus his legate, propraetor.' (South Shields Public Library)

The Ryhope pumping station of Sunderland and South Shields Water Company supplied water for 100 years with few modifications other than a new set of boilers in 1908. It could deliver 182,000 litres per hour from its 457 cm wide by 84 m deep main well. Designed in 1865 by Thomas Hawksley, it ceased commercial work in 1967, but remains open as a working museum. (Photograph: Charles Hall)

Sunderland is unlikely to be thought of as a spa nowadays but the medicinal water of its Spa Well was popular in the eighteenth century. This early source of prosperity was unfortunately washed away by the sea in the early nineteenth century. There are records of charges being made at wells in Sunderland. An interesting example is the Bodlewell, formally in Bodlewell Lane. (It is assumed that a 'bodle' was the price of a 'skeel', from the Icelandic 'skeola' or milk pail, holding 14–23 litres. A bodle was a Scottish half farthing and was not legal tender in England, although the large number of Scots in the town would explain its presence there.)

The first water company in Sunderland, formed in 1824, was the Bishopwearmouth Water Company. It raised water from a 49-m well with two beam engines; by 1845, 670 houses out of 6,086 had a supply, the highest proportion of any town in the north east at the time. In spite of this, the Health of Towns Commissioner felt that the supply was not sufficient for public health because it was intermittent and at a very low pressure. In consequence, a new company was formed, authorised by Act of Parliament to take over the Bishopwearmouth company, which it did very soon after its inauguration in 1846. The Sunderland Water Company obtained another Act to take over the South Shields Company in 1852 and became the Sunderland and South Shields Water Company in that year.

In terms of performance and profits, the company was remarkably successful. Sunderland itself was prosperous and forward looking; over 60 per cent of its houses had water-borne sewers by 1910, as opposed to 20 per cent on Tyneside generally, and the number of baths and WCs doubled in the first twenty years of the century. It was observed that the company was so favourably placed that it obtained water at half the cost of many other companies; the high profits benefited customers as well as shareholders as all statutory companies' dividends were restricted to 10 per cent.

A company of this strength was well able to resist any move by the town council towards municipalisation. The quality of the water was usually described as excellent – Mrs Ormiston Chant of the British Woman's Temperance Association said that 'in all her ten years' water drinking she had never tasted such delicious water as the water in Sunderland. Those who preferred intoxicants to it were simply idiotic'. The public did, however, force the company to shut down one of its wells in South Shields, which was polluted by salt.

Even though favoured by circumstances, the Sunderland and South Shields Water Company represents the best side of the statutory water companies, run from the start with a sense of social purpose inspired by William Mordey, its first chairman. He was a trained physician who worked with the cholera victims in Sunderland during the 1831 epidemic and subsequently campaigned for improved public health. When the Monopolies Commission looked at water supply there recently, they could not understand the motive for the company's performance in spite of restrictions to profits. They could not believe that doing a public service as well as possible might be more satisfying than status or financial gain.

Reservoirs Open to the Public

The three **BALDER VALLEY** reservoirs

BALDERHEAD, near Cotherstone
Built 1965, 233 hectares,
Bank fishing
  enq. to Northumbrian Water, tel: (091) 284 3151
Birdwatching and **walking**
Water skiing
  Balderhead Water Ski Club. tel: (0532) 812 732. Weekends, bank holidays and Wed only
Car park and toilets

BLACKTON, as above
Bank fishing
  Felling Fly Fishing Club (allows 10 permits a day for visitors, available at the fishing lodge)
Birdwatching and **walking**
Car park

HURY, as above
Built 1894, 83 hectares
Bank and **boat fishing**
  enq. to Northumbrian Water, tel: (091) 284 3151, permits from fishing lodge, special facilities for the disabled
Birdwatching and **walking**
Car parks and toilets

BURNHOPE, near Ireshopeburn, Weardale
Built 1936, 42 hectares
Bank fishing
  for details, tel: F. Graham (0498) 81263
Birdwatching and **walking**
Car park and toilet

COW GREEN, Upper Teesdale
Built 1970, 316 hectares
Bank fishing
  North Country Anglers, tel: (091) 386 0226
Birdwatching and **walking**
Nature reserve (restricted access)
  Widdybank Fell – alpine flora
Picnic area and nature trail, attractive woodland scenery, car park and toilet

DERWENT, Edmundbyers, Near Consett
Fishing and **sailing**
  enq. to Sunderland & South Shields Water Co., M. J. Jolly, tel: (091) 5101050
Picnic area, car parks and toilets

FONTBURN, 8 km south of Rothbury on the B6324
  Built 1904, 35 hectares
Bank fishing
  enq. to Northumbrian Water, tel: (091) 284 3151. Permits available from fishing lodge
Birdwatching and **walking**
Nature reserve (no public access)
Water skiing (members only)
  Fontburn Water Skiing Club, tel: (091) 252 5245 Wed, Sat and Sun only, 1 Apr–31 Oct
Car parks and toilets

2 **LUNEDALE** reservoirs

GRASSHOLME, near Middleton in Teesdale
Built 1915, 101 hectares

Bank and **boat fishing** (boat hire available)
Birdwatching and **walking**
Nature reserve (no public access)
Car park and toilet
SELSET, off the B6276 Middleton to Brough road
Built 1960, 253 hectares
Bank and **boat fishing** (fly only)
   permits from lodge on site, enq. to Northumbrian Water, tel: (091) 284 3151
Canoing
   organised groups by prior arrangement only, tel: Teesdale 40504
Nature Reserve (no public access)
Sailing
   Club only: Apr–Oct; public: May–Sept Selset Sailing Club (**dinghy** and **windsurfing**), tel: Teeside 40504
Windsurfing
   Club only Apr–Oct; public May–Sept. To hire boards, tel: Teesdale 40504
Car parks and toilets

DURHAM MOOR RESERVOIRS

HISEHOPE, nr Consett
Fishing (club only)

SMIDDYSHAW, nr Consett
Birdwatching and **walking**
Fishing (club only)

WASKERLEY, 10 km south west of Consett on Muggleswick Common
Built 1872, 25 hectares
Bank fishing
   North West Durham Angling Assoc. (allows 10 permits per day for visitors, available at the fishing lodge)
Birdwatching and **walking**
Car parks and toilet

KIELDER, 3 km from the Scottish border on the edge of the Northumberland National Park (72 km from Tyneside) Northern Europe's largest man-made lake set in Europe's largest man-made forest.
Opened 1982, 1,086 hectares, 200,000 Ml, max depth 52 m

Kielder offers more recreational facilities than any other site in Britain. Those listed below are intended as an only as an indication of the possibilities. Anyone contemplating activities on the water at Kielder should contact the Kielder Controller, tel: (0660) 40398

Canoeing
   Access as sailing. Flat water, exploratory and canoe camping available to all. Canoes may be hired, tel: (0660) 50203
Cruising boats
   up to 10 m, day visits, access as sailing, seasonal moorings available
Fishing
   Bank and motor boat.
   Rods may be hired from the fishing centre, tel: (0660) 50271
   For fishing boat hire, tel: (0660) 40398, or enq. at the visitor centre.
   Fishing from own boat if over 460 cm long and 152 cm wide
Motor boats
   Access as sailing, tel: (0660) 50241. Boats must be over 3 m in length and not exceed the 6 knots speed limit. 25 boats for hire, tel: (0660) 50203 or 50271
Rowing
   Access as above. Boats can be hired, tel: (0660) 50203
Sailing and **windsurfing**
   Access to all on registration with the warden at Leaplish.
   Dinghies and boards available for hire, tel. (0660) 50203
Sub-aqua
   Kielder Water Club, tel: (0660) 50241
Water skiing (members only, guests by arrangement)
   Kielder Water Club, tel: (0660) 50241
Self-guided trails, information centre, holiday cabins, caravan site etc., cycle hire, unlimited walking in the Border Forest Park

BAKETHIN, at the tail of Kielder Water.
Built 1979, 56 hectares
Bank and **boat fishing** (fly only, for boats tel: (0660) 40398)

Birdwatching and **walking**
Nature reserve (limited access)
There is an unusual 'skew arch' viaduct
on the site
Car park and toilet

LOCKWOOD BECK, off A171
Guisborough to Whitby road
Built 1887, 24 hectares water
Bank and **boat fishing** (fly only, rowing
boats may be hired)
    enq. to the Fishing Lodge Warden, tel:
    (0287) 51383 or 40540
Birdwatching and **walking**
Car park and toilets

SCALING DAM in North Yorkshire
Moors National Park, off A171 –
Guisborough to Whitby road
Built 1957, 42 hectares,
Bank fishing
    permits from fishing lodge. Special
    facilities for the handicapped
Birdwatching and **walking** (public
access to 2 hides)
Canoeing
    enq. to Selset Sailing Club, tel: Teeside
    40504
Nature reserve (no public access)

Sailing
    Scaling Sailing Club (Dinghy and
    Windsurfing), tel: (0947) 600 2971
    Club only: Mar–Oct; public 1 Jul–14
    Sept, 12–7.30, Mon–Fri
Windsurfing (club members only)
Picnic area, car park and toilets
To minimise disturbance to birds, access
in winter is limited to the sailing club
area only.

TUNSTALL, 5 km north of
Wolsingham in Weardale
An attractive reservoir in mature
woodland.
Built 1879, 45 hectares
Bank and **boat fishing** (fly only, boats
may be hired)
    enq. to the reservoir superintendent,
    tel: Woolsingham 527293
Birdwatching and **walking**
Nature reserve (no public access)
Picnic area, car park and toilet

WHITTLE DENE, on the B6318,
13 km west of Newcastle
Game fishing
    enq. to Newcastle & Gateshead Water
    Company, tel: (091) 265 4144
Car park

Severn Trent Water Authority

The Severn, the Trent and their tributaries effectively divide England, gathering in the huge Midland industrial and manufacturing area that lies between the Humber estuary and the Bristol Channel. Reaching out to cut Wales almost in half to take in the headwaters of the Severn in the Cambrian mountains, it contrasts the unacceptable face of industry with such classic British institutions as Stratford-on-Avon and Cheltenham, and includes the dramatic beauty of Dovedale and Wenlock Edge together with the urban nightmare of Birmingham and Stoke-on-Trent. The source of the River Swift, feeding the Avon (the largest tributary of the Severn), and the source of the Soar, feeding the Trent, are within a few kilometres of one another and several important canals make it a simple matter to cross England by water, using the two rivers for most of the journey.

It is the second largest authority after Thames, but with a considerably larger area, needing, for instance, nearly 10,000 km more water main than Thames. The average rainfall exceeds the needs of the area and water is exported to Bristol, Sheffield and Liverpool, although, unfortunately, this rain does not necessarily fall where it is most wanted. In the Welsh uplands, where the population is lowest, the average annual rainfall is 240 cm, while in the Vale of Evesham and parts of Nottingham the effective rainfall is only 60 cm since about 45 cm is lost through evaporation. It is easy to see why large reservoirs have been built in the uplands and why water is carried great distances across the region. Water from the Elan valley reservoir in Wales is taken 116 km by gravity to Birmingham; water from the Derwent valley goes to Sheffield, Derby, Nottingham and Leicester, the latter a distance of 90 km. These, with Lake Vyrnwy, are the region's main impounding reservoirs. They are filled by the natural run-off of water from the surrounding land and contribute about 33 per cent of the supply. The water enters and leaves by gravity, which keeps down costs, and is generally soft and clean, but the reliability of these sources tends to be low because the gathering ground and storage available are limited and therefore vulnerable to drought.

A further 30 per cent is taken from groundwater sources, the bunter and keuper sandstones of the area being the main aquifers, holding

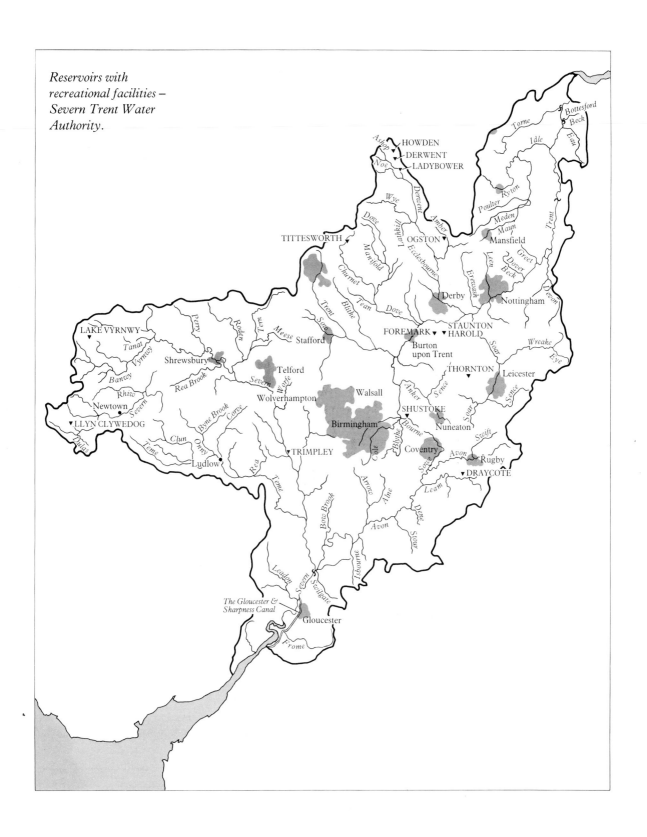

Reservoirs with
recreational facilities –
Severn Trent Water
Authority.

Craig Goch Dam – part of the Elan Valley complex. (Photograph: Severn Trent Water)

great quantities of water rather like a sponge. They are reliable and the quality is good, needing little treatment. Apart from minor local sources, the remaining 30 per cent is drawn from the rivers, either directly into supply or into reservoirs. They, in their turn, either feed the supply directly or are used to maintain water levels in the rivers at times of low flow, enabling extraction to continue further downstream.

The River Severn

The River Severn is 354 km in length – the longest river in Great Britain. It is said to have been named after Sabrina, a tragic water nymph reputed to have drowned in its waters. In its upper reaches of Powys it is known by its Welsh name, Afon Hafren. It rises on the north-east slopes of Bryn Cras in the south west of Powys at a height of 610 m, a clean fast-flowing river that travels through pastoral country-side and rolling hills all the way to the sea. Its large drainage area of 11,420 sq km has the relatively low population, for England, of 2 million. Before the Ice Age the Severn was thought to have joined the Trent until the River Dee started to drain its upper reaches. The retreating ice created a barrier to the north, forming the lost 'Lake Lapworth', which covered what is now the Shropshire Plain. The rising waters of the lake overspilled the range of hills at Ironbridge, cut the gorge and so established the present course of the Severn. The rush of water also laid bare the coal, limestone, clay and ironstone in the rocks, exposing all the ingredients that were to make industrialisation in the valley possible. The district became a centre for the iron industry from Tudor times onward, and it was here that Abraham Darby first successfully smelted iron, using coke in a blast furnace and, later, following designs by a Shrewsbury architect, cast the famous 'Iron Bridge', the first of its kind in the world.

The bridge was completed in 1780 and has a span of 30 m. It was originally a private toll bridge – charges ranged from 2s. (10p) for a coach and six horses to a farthing for a pedestrian. Many other fine eighteenth- and nineteenth-century bridges survive, including six by the famous Victorian engineer Thomas Telford. Telford's origins as a stone mason and his training as an architect combined to make his work both practical and aesthetically pleasing, although his bridge at Over near Gloucester came closer than any of his others to structural failure. When the centering that supported the masonry during construction was removed, the arch sank 25 cm in the middle. He made the following comment in his diary:

Upon the whole, although the sinking of the large arch is small in comparison with what took place in M. Perronet's Neuilly Bridge, yet I much regret it, as I never have had occasion to state any thing of the sort in any other of the numerous bridges described in this volume; and I more especially take blame to myself for having suffered an ill-judged parsimony to prevail in the foundations of the wing walls, leaving them unsupported by piles and platforms – because if so secured, I am convinced that the sinking of the arch would not have exceeded three inches.

The bridge remains in use to this day and the flaw can still be seen in the line of the parapet. The Severn has always been subject to flooding and has therefore presented something of a challenge to bridge builders – the bad floods of 1795 demolished sixteen bridges in Shropshire alone. The main cause of flooding in the lower reaches is an enormous tidal variation; the maximum, at Avonmouth, can be 14.5 m – far greater than any other river in the British Isles. The flooding is not all bad news, however – Worcestershire County Cricket ground is claimed to be one of the finest in the country because it is flooded by the Severn every winter. Many riverside fields, known as flood meadows or hams, are deliberately allowed to flood, both because it has been thought to increase fertility and because they act as overspill reservoirs for the floods, holding back water from greater flooding downstream. The Severn Bore is a famous tidal wave which occurs in the lower reaches of the River Severn during unusually-high tides. For a bore to form, a considerable rise in tide and a converging channel with a rising bed are needed; under the most favourable conditions the Severn Bore can reach a height of 2 m. The average speed of the bore is 16 kmph and a high bore may reverse the flow of the tide as far up as Tewkesbury Lock, 21 km above Gloucester.

The river has always been important for transport and trade. By the seventeenth century it was navigable, for 250 km below Welshpool, to barges and trows carrying passengers and goods. The barges were about 15 m long, single-masted with a square sail, and could carry 50 tonnes. The trows were shallow, with rounded bilges, flat bottoms and masts that could be lowered at bridges, making them particularly suitable for the special conditions on the Severn. In length they went up to 18 m and they could carry 80 tonnes. Both types of boat were dragged by men known as bow-hauliers when the sails could not be used. In 1756 there were 376 vessels owned by traders living between Welshpool and Gloucester. They charged about 10s. (50p) a ton from Shrewsbury to Bristol and 15s. (75p) in the other direction, against the tide.

Commercial fishing has a long tradition on the Severn, lamprey and salmon being much sought after in the past. Nowadays about 3,000 salmon are usually caught between Gloucester and Avonmouth, many of them in the old-style basket traps, and up to 80 tonnes of young eels, or elvers, are taken on their return migration from the Sargasso Sea on the spring tides. The huge numbers can be imagined as there are 3 million to the tonne. Most fishing now is recreational and the Severn is extremely popular.

Stoke Bardolph Estate   Stoke Bardolph is a 627-hectare farm created to make use of the liquid digested sludge from one of the largest sewage treatment works in the country. It has been used for the treatment and disposal of sewage and sludge for well over 100 years. Approximately 455 Ml of the digested sludge are disposed of each year on the estate. Tractor-drawn machines inject the sludge into the soil at the rate of 136 Ml per 10,480 sq km on grassland and up to 205 Ml on arable land. Sludge is continuously fed to the injection machines through a permanent system of pumping mains delivering to hoses dragged along behind each machine. The injecters are designed to cause minimum damage when injecting into grass. In order to keep the land in good heart following such heavy and repeated applications of sludge, it is essential for the soil to be cropped intensively to break down the organic matter and to utilise the high level of nutrients.

The farm is run commercially and forms an integral part of the sludge-disposal system. Its two main enterprises are cereals and milk production. Cereal cropping concentrates on winter wheat and no further fertiliser dressings are required apart from the sludge – yields are slightly higher than average for the locality. There are two herds of pedigree Friesian cattle, totalling 430 milking cows plus their offspring. These animals have the use of 202 hectares of grass and 77 hectares of forage maize. Although the Trent valley is not a traditional grass-producing area because of its gravels and low annual rainfall, very high yields are achieved. Store lambs are grazed during the winter months to clean off the surplus autumn grass growth and improve the sward condition. The maize was introduced to the farm in 1977, proving a suitable crop for many reasons; it can utilise large quantities of nitrogen to give high yields of dry matter for silage; late sowing leaves arable land available for injecting well into April and it is an excellent winter stock feed.

One disadvantage to the method is that the long history of applying sludge containing trace metals, such as zinc, cadmium and copper, has resulted in the accumulation of these metals in the soil. To reduce their uptake by crops, the soil is maintained at a near neutral pH and soil samples are regularly analysed to determine the lime application required to maintain pH 6.5 or above. Milk samples are no different in terms of metal concentration from those from other sources, but the cereals are sold for animal feed rather than for human consumption.

Carsington Civil engineers flinch and quail at the mention of Carsington. It is a large reservoir in the Midlands, begun in 1980 after three public enquiries had questioned its rationale. It was famous then for the acrimonious debate which took place about the need to build it – it is now notorious for what should have been impossible in the twentieth century – part of its embankment subsided.

After heavy rain at the beginning of June 1984, a crack appeared in the crest of the dam. This grew in width and was followed by others. At the end of three days the crest had dropped, at one point by 10 m, there were wide cracks and 'disruption' of the upstream slope and the foot of the embankment had moved 13 m. Work was stopped and two enquiries were immediately commissioned, one by Severn Trent and another by the DOE. The Secretary of State gave permission in 1987 for the dam to be rebuilt and work on the project has been resumed, it is expected to be complete and full by 1994.

The reasons for the failure are extremely complex technically and centre around the physical properties of the yellow clay used in the dam's core. Severn Trent say that, 'The causes of the collapse are now well understood'. If this is true, they have not been made public. An out-of-court settlement of £3.25 million awarded to them against the contractors was thought by a trade journal likely to bury the chance of finding out exactly why it happened. In the past you employed an engineer and he built a dam for you; nowadays specialists from many disciplines work together on the geological and physical calculations and analyses. Such work is no longer even carried out by one team, dozens of sub-contractors may be involved. It must be very difficult to 'blame' anybody.

It is thought that the fault would not have endangered life had the dam been full but this is speculative and not much comfort to those living in its shadow. The fact that the slip took place has stimulated the most intense investigation and the possibility that the problem has not been put right must be discounted – but the awkward thing with such situations is that experts would have assured one that there was no possible problem in the first place.

Carsington is a river-regulating reservoir designed to take high flows from the River Derwent and release water in dry weather for abstracting downstream. Planning permission was turned down at the first public enquiry in 1973 on the grounds that the impact on the very beautiful Derwent valley would be too great and that alternatives should be sought. A second enquiry was ordered in 1976 and this time the Secretary of State for the Environment gave his approval in 1978.

Projections of future demands for anything are notoriously unreliable. The water industry is as fallible as any of us but there are aspects of long-term planning at Carsington which are disheartening. At the original enquiry the water was said to be needed for the towns on the Trent north of Nottingham; while at the second enquiry, water for Leicester was given as the essential need – a town that had not been mentioned the first time round. Since Anglian Water's Rutland reservoir is near Leicester and had spare capacity, it was suggested, with Anglian's agreement, that water could be taken from there instead of building a new reservoir. Unfortunately, Severn Trent and Anglian could not agree the terms; their negotiations were described as 'like getting two elephants to tango' by the Council for the Protection of Rural England, and nothing came of this suggestion. It is disappointing that greater flexibility does not seem to be a strong aspect of long-term planning objectives.

East Worcestershire Waterworks Company

Population served: 226,000
Length of mains: 1,744 km
Area: 785 sq km
Water from boreholes in red and keuper sandstone

> The necessity for waterworks or other means by which a supply of pure water in Bromsgrove could be ensured was strongly shown by the opening of a well in the Institute yard during the past week. The water from this well has been found to be very impure for some time past and on opening the well to discover the cause of the impurity it was seen that through a defect, the drainage from a water closet and other filth was running into it
>
> Local press report, March 1866

In 1832, 50 local inhabitants died of cholera and there were epidemics of smallpox in 1835 and 1838. All the water in Redditch and Bromsgrove, where East Worcestershire began its operations, came from shallow wells or the local Spadesbourne Brook. Both sources appear to have been heavily polluted – a farmer at that time was observed manuring his fields with mud from the brook! There were demands for a clean supply, but a proposal put forward in 1868 was turned down and it was not until the Local Government Board declared the authority 'a defaulting authority' under the Public Health Act of 1875, in view of the fact that a public sewerage and water-supply scheme had not been implemented, that the Local Health Board encouraged the incorporation of the company. The first water flowed in 1882, at a cost to the company of £24,880 for the construction of a pumping station and machinery, three reservoirs, a water tower and the entire mains distribution system. Unusually, the company increased the area of its supplies very little over the years, although it naturally grew in size as demand increased, until it widened its area of supply by 389 sq km in the 1960–61 regrouping.

South Staffordshire Waterworks Company

Population supplied: 1,203,800
Water supplied: 350 Ml/d
Length of mains: 5,345 km
Area: 1,507 sq km
Water from wells and boreholes in the new red sandstone and pebble beds, the Severn and the Blithe rivers.

The area covered by South Staffordshire was another in which the pressure of industry and its accompanying dense population created too great a demand on traditional water supplies from shallow wells and local rivers. At best, the water supplies, often from the pumped drains of coalmines or canals, were unpleasant in character; often they were responsible for rampant disease, including a decimating outbreak of cholera in 1848. An Act of Parliament was secured in 1853, and the first water was supplied from springs and streams to the west of Lichfield.

The company seems immediately to have reflected the energy and industry of one of its founders, John Robinson McClean, a civil engineer born in Ireland in 1815. His many interests included the South Staffordshire Railway, for which he acquired the lease in 1849, becoming the first individual ever to lease a railway. The railway's profits were over £1,000 a week by 1869, when he was compensated by £110,000 on its takeover by others, and he was apparently making even more money from his coalmining interests in the Cannock Chase coalfield. He worked on several other railways in the Midlands and north west; sat on royal commissions studying the Thames embankment, cattle plague and railways; was Government engineer to the harbours of Aldeney, Dover and Plymouth; was director of two telegraph companies; formed part of the international commission on the practicability of the Suez Canal, and was a fellow of at least two eminent societies and president of the Institute of Civil Engineers. He was elected as a Liberal MP in 1868 but does not appear to have been active, which was perhaps not surprising in view of his outside interests.

The company's approach was professional and thorough. By 1863 reservoirs at Lichfield, Walsall, Wednesbury and Tipton were in commission, two pumping stations were in action, Dudley and Burton waterworks companies had been taken over, and all these were connected by mains with a 117-km distribution and service network. These gave a revenue of £7,000 per annum, an exceptionally high amount for a water company at that time. Other areas were added in the late nineteenth century but the greatest expansion took place in the 1920s with twelve new sources and thirteen reservoirs being constructed, making the company one of the largest and most progressive in England.

The company has preserved one of its steam pumping stations at Brindley Bank as a museum, together with early documents and photographs.

Reservoirs Open to the Public

CLYWEDOG, nr Llanidloes, Powys
248 hectares, 50,000 Ml
Fishing
Bryn-tail **mine trail**

(way marked trail through old lead mines and woods)
Sailing

THE DERWENT GROUP
3 reservoirs totalling 203 hectares

DERWENT RESERVOIR
9,500 Ml
Game fishing

LADYBOWER RESERVOIR, North
Derbyshire
204 hectares, 28,000 Ml
Game fishing
Fishery Office, Ladybower, tel: (0433)
51254
Sub-aqua
Fairholmes visitors' centre

DRAYCOTE WATER, Kites
Hardwick, nr Rugby
243 hectares, 22,700 Ml, max.
depth 18 m
Game fishing
Fishing Lodge, Draycote Reservoir,
tel: (0788) 811107
Sailing
Sub-aqua
Windsurfing
Picnic area

Warwickshire County Council's Country
Park adjoins the south side of Draycote
Water.

FOREMARK RESERVOIR, nr
Burton-on-Trent
93 hectares, 13,400 Ml
Game fishing
tel: (0283) 702352 or (0533) 352011
Sailing
Windsurfing

LINACRE RESERVOIR, nr
Chesterfield
10 hectares
Game fishing
Linacre Fy Fishing Assoc., tel: (0246)
473290

OGSTON RESERVOIR, nr
Chesterfield
83.5 hectares, 5,900 Ml
Game fishing
tel: (0629) 55051 or (0246) 590413

Sailing
Windsurfing
Picnic facilities

SHUSTOKE, nr Coleshill
40 hectares
Game fishing
Shustoke Fly Fishers, tel: (0675) 81702
or (0675) 52370

STAUNTON HAROLD, nr
Melbourne
85 hectares, 6,365 Ml
Coarse fishing
tel: (0533) 352011 or (0331) 62091
Sailing

THORNTON RESERVOIR, nr
Leicester
30 hectares
Game fishing
Cambrian Fisheries, tel: (0530) 230807
or (0533) 352011

TITTESWORTH RESERVOIR, nr
Leek, Staffs
74 hectares, 6,750 Ml
Game fishing
Fishing Lodge, Tittesworth reservoir,
tel: (053 834 389)
Visitors' centre, information on the
natural history of the area

TRIMPLEY RESERVOIR, nr
Kidderminster
12 hectares, 955 Ml
Game and coarse fishing
Trimpley A.A., tel: (0562) 68568
Sailing

VYRNWY
454 hectares, 59,500 Ml
Forest walks
Game fishing
Nature reserve
RSPB, c/o the Estate Office, tel:
Llanwddyn 246
Nature trails
Shooting
Visitors' centre, history and description
of the estate.
Car parks and toilets

South West Water Authority

South West Water covers the counties of Devon and Cornwall, with just a corner of Somerset and Dorset taken in to include the headwaters of the Rivers Exe and Axe. Associated for so many of us with summer seaside holidays and cream teas, Devon and Cornwall's summer holiday trade grew up with the increased mobility and affluence of the last hundred years, and is now one of the principal sources of revenue for these counties. There are 1.5 million permanent residents in the South West, but there are also now regularly about 6 million annual visitors – 500,000 a week in the peak summer holiday period – so water supplies

Reservoirs with recreational facilities – South West Water Authority.

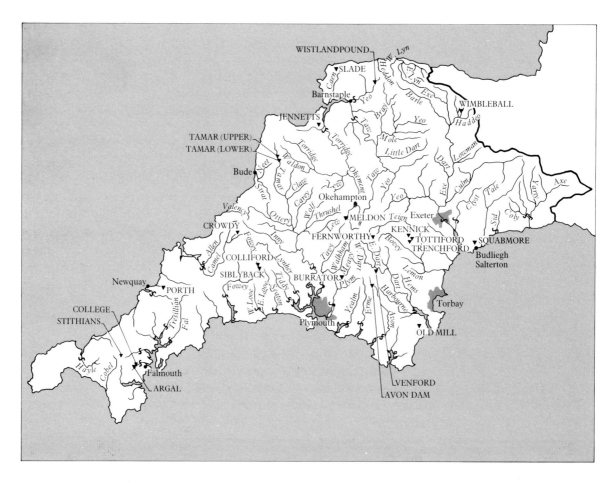

must allow for this large influx. Cornwall, in particular, has a long history of proud independence and isolation still reflected in its small but vocal desire for self-determination.

The whole area has been inhabited since prehistoric times and many dolmens and stone circles still stand as witness to the activity of this period. Mining, fishing and farming have been the traditional strengths of the economy but only the last of these now continues on anything like its former scale. The population continues to grow as it does in most regions in the south, and new roads into the area have benefited the many small businesses which have grown up. They replace some of the lost jobs in the traditional large industries, but unemployment remains high.

A backbone of granite runs up from Land's End almost to Exeter, with good quality agricultural soil on the lower land used mostly for dairy and beef production – Cornish and Devonshire cream and butter are almost a national institution. There is some arable farming and sheep are kept on the higher and less hospitable ground which is often moorland in character. An offshoot of this in the past was the production, in Devon, of serge from the long-woolled Dartmoor sheep. In the lowlands agriculture benefits from the mild climate which comes with the Gulf Stream, winter temperatures are the mildest on mainland Britain, snow is rare and summers are warm. On the high moorlands of Dartmoor, however, the winters are harsh and farms and villages are often cut off by snow.

Mining of copper and tin, from the ore deposits that follow the line of the granite, has taken place since pre-Roman times; it is thought that the Phoenicians came to trade in tin in the fifth century BC. The Romans make many references in their writings to Britain's mineral wealth and a block of tin was found in Plymouth harbour, which exactly fitted descriptions given by Roman historians. In the twelfth and thirteenth centuries, the Cornish tin trade was mostly in the hands of Jews who may have been the descendants of Phoenician settlers. Old smelting hearths are still sometimes known here as 'Jews' houses'. The banishment of the Jews in 1290 temporarily halted the industry, but it was revived in the fourteenth century with the passing of the Stannary Laws (from the Latin *stannum* meaning tin).

For four centuries the stannaries had their own parliaments, one of the roots of Cornish nationalism. (The word 'coinage' comes from the marking of tin bars for taxation purposes.) The tinners used water power to drive their machinery in the Middle Ages and it was a Dartmoor tin-streamer called Forsland who advised the Plymouth city corporation on carrying water over long distances to supply Plymouth. Cornwall remained one of the world's only sources of tin until the early nineteenth century. Lead, silver and zinc have also been important, but the only mineral now mined in any quantity is china clay.

The Dartmoor Leats

The tinminers controlled water for their operations by diverting streams along 'leats', shallow channels 1.5–3 m wide and 30–60 cm deep, constructed of earth and stone and often carrying water several kilometres along the contours of the moors. Their experience must have provided both the inspiration and expertise to construct one of the most remarkable early water supplies in England. Plymouth city corporation had taken an interest in supplies at least since 1495 when it was recorded that the sum of 17 pence was given to repair a conduit. There are frequent references to expenditure on wells, conduits and pumps in subsequent years. In the sixteenth century the town's population grew very fast, in line with its increasing prosperity from world trading and its importance as a naval base. In 1569 a nearby stream was diverted and the conduits and pumps repaired, but this was not enough to satisfy the demands of the town, let alone the needs of the many ships anchored there, who often had to be supplied by carts carrying barrels over considerable distances.

A team of surveyers was commissioned in 1576 to examine the feasibility of constructing a leat to bring water into the town from the prolific catchment area of the River Meavy on Dartmoor, a distance of about 27 km. The results must have been favourable because a Bill was put before Parliament in 1584, which received the royal assent in 1585. The Bill authorised the corporation to

... digge and myne a Diche or Trench conteynenge in bredthe betweene sixe or seven foote over in all places throughe and over all landes and groundes lyeing betweene the saide towne of Plymouth and anye parte of the saide ryver of Mewe als Mevye, cast upp all and all mener of rockes, stones, grevel, ande and all other lets for the convenyent or necessarie conveyenge of the same river to the saide towne ...

It is interesting that the water was seen as a valuable resource, apart from its domestic use to the town and shipping. It was an important source of power for milling (and a source of much litigation in this respect); it provided water for fire-fighting; it could improve the poor land over which it ran; it could help to scour the harbour, which was becoming silted up due to the activities of the tin streamers.

The war with Spain took away all the local able-bodied men and work did not start until 1589, when Sir Francis Drake was contracted to oversee the job. His prestige and ability as a leader must have been important in negotiations with local landowners and probably contributed significantly to the scheme's success, but his involvement

Opposite: *The Devonport leat in the Meavy Valley above Burrator reservoir.* (Photograph: Charles Hall)

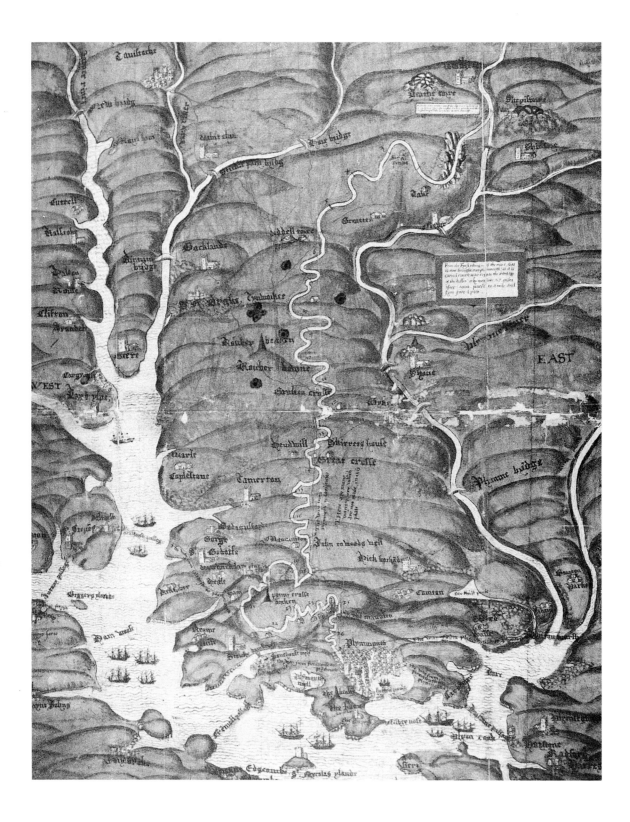

was not entirely altruistic and he appears to have made a large profit from the venture. He was paid £300 to execute the work, and is thought to have made a direct profit of about £140; the surveyors' fees, by contrast, amounted to £1 9s. 6d. among them. Other deals struck included five hogsheads of claret to Sir Thomas Wise, in compensation for the leat running through his orchard, and 100 deal boards (left over from construction work) to Sir Walter Elford for the use of his land.

Drake, with astute business sense, had demanded rights to the milling leases on the leat and these brought him an additional income of £200 per year. Milling was big business. Accounts survive for three mills working from the leat at about this time; their weekly expenses were high at £9 for labour, rent, upkeep and materials, but they could grind 800 bushels of grain a week, with an end profit of £6. Leases continued to be granted into the nineteenth century, to run machinery for several trades. It is known that eleven factories were authorised to take water in 1854 for washing wool, tanning, canvas making, malting, and making cement and paper among other things.

As a source the Meavy was capable of giving an adequate supply of water well into the nineteenth century, but the open nature of the leat made it particularly liable to pollution and leaks. Repairs were made regularly, but by the 1850s there was a general feeling that it was outdated. Thomas Hawksley, the celebrated water engineer, reported in 1864 that as a supply, it was 'amongst the most imperfect I have ever met with' and suggested several improvements. It is only fair to point out, however, that he said something like this about every scheme he was appointed to look at. As he was hoping to be engaged as engineer, one imagines he was a little biased.

The borough water engineer, Edward Sandeman, said in 1891 that 'It is a matter of regret that cattle are allowed to drink from the Leat along its course'. He made a number of improvements to prevent polluted water from running into the leat and to reduce leakage along its course. These were really only stopgap measures and by the end of the century the demands of a modern distribution network of reservoirs and pipes needed more reliable supplies to satisfy the still-increasing population. This brought a final end to the Plymouth leat. The Burrator reservoir was built at its head in 1898 and a 64-cm diameter pipeline replaced the open channel.

Left: *The map, known as 'Spry's Plot', which was presented to the Privy Council in 1584 with Plymouth Corporation's Water Bill.* (The British Library)

The growth of Plymouth as a maritime and trading base was so great that its expansion into new areas eventually resulted in the formation of three quite separate towns: Plymouth, Stonehouse and Devonport. Each needed its own water supply and the success of Plymouth's leat encouraged the others to take it as a model. The Stonehouse leat was given parliamentary approval in 1593. It was considered by a committee headed by Drake, who added the proviso that no mills should be constructed in, upon or near it which might damage the interests of any mill in, upon or near 'the ryver or streame of water latelie brought to the saide Towne of Plymouth' with severe penalties spelt out! Sir Francis was clearly not one to miss an opportunity to protect his own interests.

This leat was very short at 2 km long, and did not benefit from the high rainfall on Dartmoor; its source was a small stream which could never give an adequate supply. In spite of minor improvements which allowed it to remain in use, it was never satisfactory and was abandoned at the end of the nineteenth century when supplies could be taken from Plymouth and Devonport.

The Devonport leat has the greatest attraction today as it not only survives and still brings 11 Ml of water from the moor every day, but its very concept is so ambitious and romantic. It is 64 km long and for most of that length seems to wander in random loops and curves about the open moorland. Only the fact that its water is always running fluently downhill reveals that its apparently aimless meandering is slowly taking it higher and higher. Eventually, several kilometres inland, it extracts water from three streams: the Blackabrook, the Cowsic and the West Dart.

There are many other names to give pleasure; the leat travels through the parishes of Lidford, Walkhampton, Meavy, Buckland Monachorum, Tamerton Foliot, Egg Buckland, St Budeaux, Pennycross, Stoke Damerel and Stonehouse – it is hard not to believe that one is in the world of Grimpen Mire. The strongest memory one has after the great openness of unending moor is the constant and subtle variation in the sound of the water as its gradient changes on the long journey, from a gentle soft whispering when almost on the level, to a thrilling, excited shouting where it crashes down a cascade at Raddick Hill before crossing the River Meavy on a rickety cast-iron aqueduct.

The leat ends at Burrator now, although its water can be taken further by pipe to the Dousland reservoir in an emergency. A proposal which would have substantially altered much of its route was defeated by vigorous public opposition on the grounds that it was an important amenity. Could a leat be scheduled as an ancient monument? It would be nice to feel that such interesting and special works could carry on without interference for several more hundred years.

Water Supply

Perhaps more than any other region, the South West has suffered from water-supply problems – dry taps in the summer were once a familiar part of the holidays. One finds, in fact, that the region has a good supply of rain – rather higher than the average for England, although it is rather uneven, geographically and seasonally. The lowest rainfall is in east Devon where some parts receive 750 mm; the highest place, on the tops of the moors, receives 1,800 mm. Unfortunately, the rainfall is lowest from April to September, a period when the population rises by several hundred thousand and garden and horticultural needs are greatest.

Water is taken from 57 boreholes and 41 river abstractions, but most of these sources are small-scale and insufficient to cope with the large summer demand, making the region dependent on impounding reservoirs to bridge the gap. There are over 37 reservoirs, many dating back to the nineteenth century, but they do not now have sufficient capacity for contemporary demands.

South West Water Authority calculated the amount of extra water needed and made the decision to build three large new reservoirs, spaced strategically across the region. Colliford on Bodmin Moor and Wimbleball on Exmoor have now been completed; Roadford in west Devon will be finished in 1990. The combined capacity will then be 114,000 Ml, more than four times the amount that the authority inherited in 1974. It is interesting to note that a public enquiry, held in 1983, only approved a reservoir at Roadford which was two-thirds of the size estimated as necessary by South West Water, but the severe drought of 1984 was enough to turn public opinion and the larger reservoir and dam which are now being constructed were approved in 1985.

Roadford Roadford is the only large reservoir being built in England at the time of writing and is a most impressive site – soil and rock being carried around in dozens of enormous machines with the ease of children playing on a sand heap. Most of this activity results from the type of dam chosen for the site. A huge mound of rock is piled up in a shallow inverted V-shape, 200 m across at the bottom, with a 12-m wide road running along the top. The length along the crest is 430 m and its height is 40 m above the valley floor, an area requiring nearly 1,000,000 cu m of material to fill it, hence the endless stream of trucks carrying material from a site further down the valley, within the future reservoir, and the continual rolling of the rock to create a firm base. It will take two and a half years to construct the dam, although some of this time will be spent on constructing the reinforced concrete culverts, overflows and access gallery underneath, and on making the dam waterproof. The rock infilling is not in itself waterproof, so an asphaltic concrete facing is put onto the upstream side to ensure a watertight structure. Some seepage will occur, but this, and any stress, will be constantly monitored by gauges inserted into all parts of the dam during construction.

The draw-off tower and 'bellmouth spillway' overflow of the new Roadford reservoir, still under construction. The height of the overflow will be 39.7 m. (Photograph: South West Water)

When complete, the reservoir will hold back 37,000 Ml of the water that at present flows down the River Wolf and into the Tamar. It will have a surface area of 300 hectares, and be capable of supplying over 200 Ml/d. This water can be released into the Wolf for abstraction at Gunnislake, or pumped into the Northlew stream, which feeds the Torridge, for abstraction at the Torrington treatment works. Water from Torrington will supply Bideford and Barnstaple, while water from Gunnislake will go to Plymouth, supplementing supplies from the Burrator reservoir. This will allow Burrator to feed water to the River

Dart to supply the Torbay area. This entire supply network will cost approximately £50 million and will be carried out in several phases; the cost of the dam at Roadford alone is £16.1 million.

The three big new reservoirs in the South West all incorporate nature reserves which had been planned from the start of the project in conjunction with conservation groups. Bats have been rehoused where their colonies were disturbed, dormice have been trapped and moved to new sites and efforts generally have been made to cause the minimum disruption to affected wildlife. Archaeological projects, by Exeter City Museum and others, to investigate historic buildings and early settlements in the reservoir basin, have been recognised as rescue work of national importance and gained the support of English Heritage, Devon County Council, the Royal Commission for Historic Monuments and the Manpower Services Commission. Field studies of hedges, trees and soils of the valley have helped to trace the history of the valley back over 5,000 years.

Bathing Water Quality and Long Sea Outfalls

There are a number of problems peculiar to the region, which make improvements to its supply and sewage systems expensive. The resident population has the lowest density of all the authorities; 132 persons per sq km compared with a national average of 328. For this reason South West Water has the longest length of water main of any region and the second longest length of sewer per head, while the number of customers served by each sewage works is by far the lowest in the country. A very large proportion of people are resident near the coast and for years their sewage has been piped into the sea through outfalls falling on beaches which are used regularly by large numbers of holiday-makers. At present there are 615 sewage treatment works and 230 sea outfalls in the region. The importance of tourism to the South West naturally makes it particularly sensitive about bathing water quality.

In 1976, the EEC issued a Directive on this subject (see page 70) asking members to list important beaches. After some notorious backsliding, the UK Government designated 392 beaches and admitted that 40 per cent of these failed to meet EEC requirements. Of those designated, 109 are in South West Water's region, a far higher number than in any other, and about 20 per cent of these fail to meet the necessary standards at present. South West Water states in its corporate plan that it sees pollution of the marine environment as its largest single problem and the most important area for improvement is to raise the standard of effluent discharged into rivers and estuaries by the many small and old works.

The method chosen by South West Water for most of its coastal

One of George Cruikshank's engravings for Smollet's The Expedition of Humphry Clinker: '... I could not help sobbing and bawling out from the effects of the cold. Clinker, who heard my cry, and saw me indistinctly a good way without the guide, buffeting the waves, took it for granted I was drowning ...'.

sewage disposal is the long sea outfall. In spite of some misgivings (see page 71), it has to be said that this method is recognised as an acceptable option by many, including the Coastal Anti-Pollution League and the Royal Commissiom on Environmental Pollution. The latter said in its 1984 report that,

... it is becoming possible to design outfalls which reliably ensure rapid dilution of the sewage. With well-designed sewage outfalls we believe that discharge of sewage to the sea is not only acceptable but, in many cases, environmentally preferable to alternative methods of disposal.

It is refreshing that South West Water admits that it needs 'much more information' on its river, estuarine and coastal water quality and one hopes that it will be able to obtain this before committing huge capital sums towards improvements. Some of the problems faced can be seen on the River Torridge. Here, out of 431 licensed discharges into the river, only 76 are from South West Water's own works, and there is a potential agricultural discharge equivalent to the sewage production of a city three times the size of Plymouth. It is thought that changes in land use and agricultural practice, together with an associated rapid rise in the numbers of farm animals, have been principally responsible for the deterioration of river water quality over the last few years; a trend which may now be reversed as figures at the time of writing do show a small improvement. An intensive campaign aimed at farmers, called 'Pollution – Together We Can Beat It', must take some of the credit for a 20 per cent drop in farm pollution incidents during 1988.

Taw-Torridge Estuary Environmental Study

The Taw-Torridge estuary is at present the subject of a wide-ranging environmental study aimed at identifying 'environmental quality objectives' (EQOs) designed to ensure that the 'best practical environmental option' (BPEO) is chosen for the disposal of effluent from local communities. They are:

- The protection of the tidal water's ecosystem (fish, shellfish and other plants and animals, including dependent organisms).
- The protection of designated bathing waters.
- The avoidance of public nuisance.

The study follows the Secretary of State for the Environment's decision to allow the marine discharge of sewage through a long sea outfall in the area, provided that South West Water produces, by the end of 1989, a comprehensive plan for water quality throughout the estuary, supported by adequate monitoring, both of water quality and effluent discharge. The area is a sensitive one for both recreation and conservation and includes a nature conservation zone and Site of Special Scientific Interest (SSSI), with flora and fauna of local and national importance, while for a few species of birds the area is of international importance. Sampling and monitoring were carried out at three-monthly intervals from 1987 to 1989, and computer models will be set up to simulate the effect of variable inputs under changing environmental conditions. It is to be hoped that the results of the study will form a useful base for planning a structured approach for future conservation and overall water management of the area.

The environmental quality objective (EQO) and the environmental quality standard (EQS) are terms that have been taken to typify the different approaches of Britain and the other European countries to environmental pollution. Generally, an EQO is the overall quality to be aimed for and an EQS is a specific standard, often backed by legislation. Britain, for example, feels that if predetermined environmental objectives are met, pollution levels can be flexible; the other Europeans favour very specific limits to pollution to achieve good environmental quality. The argument has generated more heat than light but it is probably now generally accepted that both approaches have a role to play in achieving the desired results.

The best practical environmental option (BPEO), now used in many areas of environmental debate, was, in fact, a concept first put forward by a 1972 royal commission concerned with coastal waters. They said, 'control of pollution in estuaries must be part of *a national integrated policy* for waste disposal, which determines that waste shall be put where it will do least harm, not just where it is under least control' (my italics). BPEO tries to look at any specific environmental problem in terms of its widest implications. The Government seems sympathetic to the approach but cannot yet be said to have shown any determination to carry out such a policy nationally.

One feels that the Taw/Torridge EQOs are a little negative in their use of 'protection' and 'avoidance', which imply a rather British leaning towards the status quo – a more positive approach might have emphasised the authority's duty to *further* conservation and, by implication, the environment. One hopes that the final report will encourage the highest aims and not just the minimum standard that will be acceptable.

Reservoirs Open to the Public

ARGAL AND COLLEGE WATER PARK, nr Penryn, Cornwall. 3 km west of Falmouth
Argal: 1940, raised 1961, 28 hectares, 1,350 Ml
College: 1906, 17 hectares, 332 Ml
Birdwatching and **walking**
Game and **coarse fishing**
  fly only for game, boats for hire
Picnic area, car park and toilets
  enq. on all the above to the ranger, tel: (0326) 72544

AVON DAM, 5 km north west of South Brent
built 1956, 20 hectares, 1,286 Ml
A reservoir in open moorland with no vehicular access, 2.5 km riverside walk from the car park to picnic area
Game fishing
Walking
Car park
  enq. the Ranger, tel: (06473) 2440

BURRATOR, 18 km north east of Plymouth.
A beautiful setting in the Meavy valley, surrounded by mature forest and open moorland. No formal picnic sites.
built 1898, enlarged 1928, 60 hectares, 4,664 Ml
Birdwatching
  by permit from the Recreation Office, tel: (0392) 219666

Fishing (natural trout)
Footpaths
Parking and toilets
    enq. the Ranger, tel: (06473) 2440
Colliford & Siblyback Water Park
Active sports on the high ground of
Bodmin's peat and heather moor, less
extrovert pleasures at Colliford.
Colliford: 1983, 364 hectares, 29,000 Ml
Siblyback: 1969, 56 hectares, 3,200 Ml
Birdwatching hide (Siblyback)
    permit from the Recreation Office, tel:
    (0392) 219666
Game fishing, (fly only, boats for hire
at Siblyback)
    permits available on site.
Nature reserve (Colliford, limited
access)
    Cornwall Trust for Nature
    Conservation, Cornwall Birdwatching
    and Preservation Society.
Sailing, Windsurfing, Canoeing and
Rowing (Siblyback)
    Water Sports Assoc., tel: (0822) 3547
Walking (waymarked walks over the
moors at Colliford)
Windsurfing training (Siblyback)
    Cornwall Windsurfing, tel: (0579)
    46522
Visitors' centre (Siblyback)
    History of Bodmin Moor, local wildlife
    information, facilities and attractions,
    etc. open Easter–end Sept.
Lakeview cafeteria, (Siblyback)
    open daily Easter–end Sept. and Sun
    all the year.
Picnic & play areas (Siblyback), car parks
and toilets

CRAFTHOLE
A small reservoir only reached by
footpath from the village. 0.8 hectares.
Coarse fishing (limited day permits
only)
    tel: (0503) 30225

CROWDY, 5 km east of Camelford
1973; 46 hectares water, 1,036 Ml
Birdwatching
    permit from the Recreation Office, tel:
    (0392) 219666

Canoeing and **Windsurfing**
Game fishing
Nature reserve (restricted entry)
Outdoor adventure
    tel: (0288) 85312
Car park and toilets
    enq. to the Ranger, tel: (0579) 42366
FERNWORTHY, 6 km south west of
Chagford
In a scenic part of the Dartmoor National
Park
1942; 30 hectares water, 1636 Ml
Birdwatching (no access to special
protection zone)
    Devon Birdwatching Society
Footpaths and **forest walks**
Game Fishing (fly only, permits on site,
boats for hire)
Nature trail (provided by the Forestry
Commission)
Picnic area, car park and toilets
    enq. to the Ranger, tel: (06473) 2440

JENNETTS, 1.5 km south of Bideford,
Devon
1927; 3 hectares water
Coarse fishing (limited day permits
only)
    tel: (023 72) 70043

KENNICK, Tottiford and Trenchford,
19 km south west of Exeter
3 reservoirs in the Dartmoor National
Park where mixed farming, forestry and
moorland make a varied habitat rich in
wildlife, Tottiford is the oldest reservoir
on the moor.
Kennick: 1884, 21 hectares, 886 Ml, max.
depth 9 m; Tottiford: 1861, 12 hectares,
468 Ml, max. depth 7 m; Trenchford:
1907, 13 hectares, 777 Ml, max. depth
15 m
Course fishing (Trenchford)
Game fishing (Kennick and Tottiford,
fly only, permits on site)
    Kennick F.F., tel (0626) 865739
Marked forest walks and
birdwatching
    A leaflet describes the interesting
    history of the reservoirs.
Picnic area, car park and toilets at
Trenchford.

MELDON, 5 km south west of Okehampton
Surrounded by open moorland suitable for walking.
22 hectares; 3018 Ml
Birdwatching
Game fishing
Sailing and **canoeing**
  tel: (0837) 82421
Windsurfing
  Windsurfing Mid Devon, tel: (0837) 840258
Picnic area, car park and toilets
  other enq. to the Ranger, tel: (064 73) 2440

OLD MILL, 2.5 km west of Dartmouth
1900; 2 hectares.
Coarse fishing (limited daily permits)
  tel: 'Sportsman's Rendezvous' (080 43) 3509

PORTH, 5 km east of Newquay
1960; 15 hectares, 514 Ml
Birdwatching
  permit from the Recreation Office, tel: (0392) 219666
Coarse fishing (day permits on site)
  enq. to the Ranger, tel: (0326) 72544

SLADE UPPER AND LOWER, 1.5 km south west of Ilfracombe
Upper 1866, 1.6 hectares; lower 1889, 2.4 hectares; 218 Ml
Coarse fishing (both)
  permits from Slade PO, tel: (0271) 62257

SQUABMOOR, Knowle, Budleigh Salterton
1985; 1.7 hectares
Coarse fishing
  permits from Knowle Post Office and Exmouth Tackle Shop
Walking on surrounding common land.
General access

STITHIANS, 11 km north west of Falmouth
1965; 110 hectacres, 4,584 Ml
Birdwatching
  permits from the Recreation Office, tel: (0392) 219666

Canoeing
  The Canoeing Club, tel: (0209) 714187
Fishing
  permits from Golden Lion Inn, Menherion, tel: (0209) 860332
Nature reserve (members only)
  Cornwall Birdwatching and Preservation Soc., tel: (0326) 74865
Sailing
  The Sailing Club tel: (0326) 319795
Water skiing
  The Waterskiing Club, tel: (0326) 574679
Windsurfing
  The Boardsailing Club, tel: (0209) 712310
Windsurfing school
  Falmouth Windsurfing Centre, tel: (0209) 861083
Water Sports at Stithians are controlled by the Stithians Water Sports Assoc.
Visitors should telephone (0209) 215897
Car park and toilets

TAMAR LAKES WATER PARK, 11 km north east of Bude
The lower lake was originally a feeder to the Bude canal. Nearby is a newly opened walk along the Bude aqueduct.
Upper, 1975, 33 hectares, 1,331 Ml; lower, 1820, 20 hectares, 186 Ml
Coarse fishing (lower)
Game fishing (upper, fly only, boats for hire, permits on site)
  Upper Tamar F.C., tel: (040 922) 485
Nature reserve and **birdwatching**
(some restrictions on access)
  permits from the Recreation Office, tel: (0392) 219666
Sailing, windsurfing and **canoeing**
  Upper Tamar Lake Sailing Club, tel: (0237) 277702
Windsurfing and **canoeing courses**
(equipment provided)
  adventure days, tel: (0288) 2493
Picnic and recreation area, with cafe, car park and toilets

VENFORD, 6.5 km north west of Buckfastleigh
13 hectares

Natural trout fishing
General access to the surrounding
moorland
Picnic area, car park

**WIMBLEBALL LAKE WATER
PARK**, 8 km north east of Dulverton
An attractive and isolated lake in the
Exmoor National Park.
1978; 151 hectares water, 19,320 Ml, 200
hectares land
Game fishing (fly only, boats for hire,
permits on site)
   Wimbleball F.F.C., tel: (0823) 23699
Nature reserve and **nature trail**
   Somerset Trust for Nature
   Conservation, tel: (082 345) 587
Rowing
   Rowing Club, tel: (03987) 316
Sailing, windsurfing and **canoeing**
(day visits possible)
   Wimbleball Sailing Club, tel: day
   (0278) 422261 eve (0823 47) 3223
Walking (several miles of waymarked
paths)
Picnic areas and adventure playground
Refreshments
   open Easter-end Oct and weekends to
   Christmas (weather permitting)

Camp site (no caravans)
   open 1 May – 31 Oct, car parks and
   toilets

WISTLANDPOUND, 13 km north of
Barnstaple
1956; 16 hectares, 1,546 Ml
Game fishing (fly only, permits on site,
boats for hire)
Nature reserve
   enq. to honorary warden, tel: (076 95)
   2449
Picnic area, and marked walk, car park
and toilets

'Picnic area' means that tables are
provided, 'general access' means access
to the banks where picnicking and
walking are welcome.

A guide to South West Water Fisheries
is produced, called *Guide to Angling &
Recreation*, The price for 1989 is £1.50
inc. p&p. Available from the Recreation
Office, Peninsular House, Rydon Lane,
Exeter EX2 7HR.

Southern Water Authority

Southern Water roughly covers the area of the counties of Hampshire, Sussex and Kent; the boundaries are not exact because the authorities conform to the river basins rather than the traditional county boundaries. In fact, there seems something fairly arbitrary in the boundaries between all the authorities on the south coast. There are no obvious large natural divisions and each authority is fairly small, ruling over a diverse group of short rivers. The Western Yar, on the Isle of Wight, must surely be one of England's shortest rivers, being officially listed at 5 km long. The Medway is the area's longest. Its 113 km drain the ground between the Weald and the North Downs, gaining this length by cutting through the North Downs to the Thames estuary.

The proximity of the region to the coast of France makes its placenames read like a history of England, and all its larger harbours have an important naval tradition. The smaller harbours and ports were once famous for their fish – many are reflected by the names of their catch, like Dover sole and Whitstable oysters – but the local fishing industry struggles to survive now against the competition of larger vessels

Reservoirs with recreational facilities – Southern Water Authority.

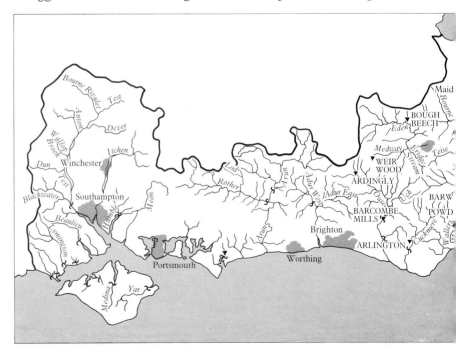

working deeper waters. Naval docks now only remain at Portsmouth and Chatham, and the latter has recently come under the Government's financial axe. In the past Gravesend, Dover and Southampton, the latter the deepest harbour in Britain, were actively engaged in ship-building and repairs. The busiest sea trade now is ferrying tourists, but that too will soon be cut back when the Channel Tunnel is opened.

Compost from Sewage

Two increasingly important problems facing us are the disposal of society's wastes and the provision of fertiliser to maintain intensively cultivated soils in a state of adequate fertility. That the recycling of such waste materials would be beneficial is self-evident, but the economics of such recycling has not encouraged its widespread use or even much research. The high cost of energy and a growing ecological awareness have created a new interest in such approaches and, about five years ago, Dr Joseph Lopez-Real, a lecturer in microbiology at Wye College near Canterbury, approached Southern Water to ask if one of his students could do some work on the subject of composting sewage. Trials proved so successful that by 1985 the Canterbury Sewage Works went over to composting all 30 tonnes of sewage sludge which the works produce every day. All good gardeners know the value of a compost heap; it is one of the oldest methods of providing material to improve and enrich the soil. The process which has been developed at Canterbury is really garden composting on a huge scale with the added ingredient of mechanical aeration.

Composting is the decomposition of organic wastes by microbes in a warm, moist, oxygen-rich environment. The wastes are gathered into a large heap. This raises their temperature and accelerates the process of decomposition which, under natural conditions, occurs slowly on the surface of the ground. The basic requirements for successful composting are a suitable vehicle for microbial growth, insulation in order to conserve heat, moisture, and a supply of air to give oxygen. Most organic wastes are susceptible to this decomposition although not all allow the rapid microbial growth needed to generate the heat to do it quickly. Enough insulation is usually provided by the waste material itself, but, in the case of sewage-sludge composting, extra insulation is provided by covering the piles with finished compost. It is essential that all the material reaches temperatures of 50–60°C in order to destroy any disease-carrying germs.

Moisture is essential for microbial growth and the more the better, provided it does not inhibit an adequate supply of oxygen. In practice this means a moisture content of 55–65 per cent. As the temperature rises during the first week of composting, the oxygen initially present in the pile is rapidly used up, and the process would be inhibited unless fresh air is introduced. This is done by turning the pile and blowing air through it. After about a month the rapid microbial action has done its work and the pile will start to cool. It now enters a phase of slower decomposition, during which micro-organisms, earthworms and insects play an important role. This phase may take several months to a year, until the material attains the familiar compost texture, colour and smell.

At Canterbury, straw and sewage sludge are thoroughly mixed by tractor-operated machinery and then built into a huge heap on top of a series of specially designed plastic pipes drilled with many holes. The pipes are coupled to an air-blower which can raise the temperature to 60–70°C within a few days. After four weeks the forced air ceases and the material is left to cool in stacks for six to nine months. Weight losses during composting are very high. This is important as it reduces further handling and transport costs. Dry solid losses and water losses are both around 35–45 per cent, so a pile with an initial weight of 10 tonnes will produce about 4 tonnes of compost.

The finished compost finds a whole range of applications: in land reclamation where it may take the place of topsoil; on golfcourses and landscaping schemes; in public and private gardens. In contrast to all other forms of treated sewage sludge, composting provides an income for the treatment plant and offsets some of the running costs. The work received national recognition when it was awarded first prize in the general section of the Pollution Abatement Technology Awards for 1986. A contract worth £100,000 has been signed with Adco for the supply of mushroom compost, which will account for about one-third of the plant's output, so the scheme seems already to have a firm commercial base.

Aquifer Management

Opposite: *Southern Water is the only water authority to manage a harbour, the good deep-water channel being essential for the drainage of the River Rother's catchment area of 30,900 hectares. There are small commercial docks and a fishing fleet, but it is mainly used by yachts touring the south coast.* (Photograph: Charles Hall)

Chalk is the principal aquifer, or water-bearing rock, in England where its characteristic landscapes dominate much of the south east. From Dorset it widens out to form the Salisbury Plain, then divides, its northern part forming the Chiltern Hills, the Berkshire Downs, the Norfolk and Suffolk Downs and the Lincolnshire and Yorkshire Wolds. Its southern branch forms the North and South Downs. The grand scale of its landscapes, with their soft, rolling forms, gives the south some of its most characteristically English country scenery.

The South Downs chalk outcrop extends from Eastbourne to the Hampshire-Sussex border, a distance of over 80 km and forms the main aquifer in Sussex. 'Water bearing' chalk is, in fact, virtually impermeable and the water movement takes place through joints and fissures within the rock, allowing it to be pumped out through boreholes and wells. A well was sunk to the north of Brighton in 1825, the first public source of its type in the area, and this was followed by so

many others that today the South Downs chalk aquifer is almost fully exploited.

If you pump too much water from an aquifer which reaches the sea, there is a tendency to draw saltwater back into it. With so much pumping taking place, it was found that many sources were becoming brackish and four major nineteenth-century sources out of seven became unusable, although abstraction has recommenced at one of these after a break of 50 years. Unfortunately, if you do not pump from the coastal zone, much of the available freshwater leaks into the sea. By 1957, increasing salinity in several of its sources led Brighton Corporation, which was the main water undertaker in the region and the predecessor of Southern Water, to introduce an abstraction policy. This sought to conserve inland aquifer storage and place greater emphasis on intercepting the coastal outflows which would otherwise be lost to the sea.

This policy, at first sight contradictory, means pumping as little as possible inland so that the water gravitates towards the coast, keeping the aquifer there full of water, which is both available for pumping and also holds back the seawater. This has proved so successful in controlling salinity that, despite an increase in abstraction of approximately one-third, groundwater levels in the aquifer are as high now as they were nearly 30 years ago. The plan has been reinforced by a long-term programme, launched in 1971 by Brighton and Worthing Corporations, Sussex River Authority and the Water Resources Board, to investigate coastal salinities and resources. It was taken over by Southern Water in 1974 and largely completed by 1983. Hydrometric monitoring was seen as very important and special boreholes, mostly near the coast but some inland, have been used to chart resistivity, gamma, flow, temperature, differential temperature and conductivity. Near the coast, this logging has to be phased to coincide with the tides and a programme of tide-cycle logging has been carried out for ten years. In particular, this has revealed a cyclic pattern when groundwater levels are low: pumping at Balsdean, for example, is usually stopped in the summer for two hours on each side of high water.

Inevitably, computers are involved in this work and it is thought that Brighton was the first undertaking in Britain to use telemetry. Abstraction can now be controlled electronically from the divisional centre to respond to fluctuating demand, varying electrical tariffs, water levels and salinity. A computer model was constructed in 1972, and has been updated since, to assess the overall groundwater levels. It is admitted that the complexity of the Brighton distribution system, with fourteen separate sources and sixteen booster stations feeding, via 33 service reservoirs, to six separate pressure zones under four different electrical tariffs, was defying attempts at mathematical simulation, but no doubt that is only a matter of time. Estimates suggest that the operation of this abstraction policy accounts for an additional 5 per cent on power costs compared with those that would be incurred if the cheapest sources were used to their fullest extent, but this is considered an acceptable price to pay for the security of having larger resources.

In the old days, when questions to geologists usually elicited vague replies, aquifers in particular were thought to be unpredictable. It is a tribute to the advance in the specialised areas of this science that such an extraordinary degree of management control is now possible.

The Seaford Sea Defence Scheme

There is nothing under heaven more soft and yielding than water.
Yet for attacking the solid and strong, nothing can surpass it.
That weakness can overcome strength,
And the submissive overcomes the hard,
Everyone under heaven knows –
Yet no one puts it into practice.

Lao Tzu, *Tao Te Ching* (*c.* 604BC)

The sea is powerful. It is constantly changing our coastline, taking material from one place and depositing it in another. Much of the area around Seaford and Newhaven on the Sussex coast is low-lying and would be liable to flooding if the sea was allowed to eat away at the shingle beaches that make up the shore. There are two approaches to preventing this: build a barrier stronger than the sea, or dissipate the strength of the sea in a natural way by building a better beach. Southern Water chose the latter option.

Littoral drift, as at many other places on the south coast, is the force that constantly moves the shingle bank at Seaford along the coast and tends to block the mouth of Newhaven harbour to the west. Attempts were first made to protect the channel into the harbour with piers in 1644 but never proved satisfactory until, in 1890, a 914-m breakwater was constructed. Unfortunately, these efforts made matters worse at Seaford, 'There can be little doubt but that . . . the increasing difficulties . . . in the maintenance of the foreshore are mainly attributable to the creation and improvement of Newhaven harbour,' wrote a surveyor in 1876.

The Newhaven and Seaford Sea Defence Act was passed in 1898 to allow a Board of Commissioners to construct and maintain the necessary works. Groynes were built at 76-m intervals and a concrete wall along the top of the beach. Erosion continued to take place, however; between 1900 and 1945 the beach levels fell by an average of 3 m and the low water mark moved about 60 m nearer the wall, exposing it to storm

Waves breaking over Seaford prior to the scheme. (Photograph: Water Authorities Association)

waves. The surveyor previously quoted had said that, '. . . the immediate effect of such . . . a wall would be to cause the erosion and wasting away of the shingle banks in front . . . ' and a royal commission reporting in 1911 said, '. . . sea walls unless properly constructed are . . . agents of their own destruction inasmuch as . . . the waves breaking against it, when recoiling, tend to scoop out the beach material . . . and cause undermining of the structure which not infrequently leads to the destruction of the wall'.

Shingle was artificially replaced in 1936 but neglect during the last war allowed the wall to collapse in many places. Subsequent remedial work concentrated on improving and strengthening the wall, but in 1981 a 60-m section subsided and the sea broke through under the wall at another point in 1985. Research by Southern Water concluded that either a stronger wall must be built or the beach in front of it restored. A restored beach (technically 'renourished') could be cheaper and more environmentally acceptable, so a hydraulic study was commissioned to assess the effectiveness of such a scheme. Three solutions were proposed:

New shingle being pumped onto the beach at Seaford. (Photograph: Water Authorities Association)

1. An open beach, rebuilt of imported shingle, contained by two groynes at either end. It could be maintained by regularly picking up the shingle drifting east and replacing it.
2. A beach with groynes at 250-m or 80-m widths, with recycling as in option 1 but less for the narrower groyne.
3. Constructing offshore breakwaters parallel to the shoreline to reduce wave energy.

Solution 3 was very expensive and might not work, and 2 was more expensive than 1 while giving little advantage. Solution 1 was therefore adopted but in a slightly modified form; only one groyne was thought to be necessary and the old wall would be given an additional protection of rocks to ensure its long-term stability, particularly against a prolonged (several days') storm.

Five thousand granite blocks, of a total weight of 55,000 tonnes, were imported from Galicia in north-west Spain and placed in front of the old wall, and 2.5 km of foreshore were replenished with 3 million tonnes of new shingle dredged and carried in by boat from the seabed off

Littlehampton. The material was pumped ashore through a pipeline submerged in the sea. This operation carried on 24 hours a day and took six months to complete.

The new beach successfully defended Seaford from the hurricane in October 1987, although a low tide also helped matters. It has been found that little movement of shingle takes place in the summer, but about 1,180 tonnes had to be recycled over the winter of 1987–88. Southern Water say that it is too early to draw definite conclusions but the scheme appears a success. An environmentally acceptable, relatively low-cost and quickly constructed defence has been built with the added advantage of a new beach.

The Eastbourne Waterworks Company

Population served: 202,000 (240,000 summer season)
Length of mains: 1,405 km
Area: 826 sq km
Water from the chalk downs and Weald sandstones, and from the Rivers Cuckmere, Wallers Haven and Rother

The Weald is an area of outstanding natural beauty, its sandstone is rich in iron ore and was in the past extensively mined. These facts have directly influenced the look of the company's borehole pumping stations. The water has to be treated on site (by dissolved air flotation) to remove an excessive iron content so the buildings need to be about the size of a barn. The company has shown great sensitivity in the design and siting of these stations. Their vernacular style, chosen in consultation with local councils and residents, makes them almost indistinguishable from traditional old Sussex barns. The pumping stations release water from the boreholes into local streams which carry it south for abstraction lower down. This has saved disruptive and expensive pipe laying and farmers are able to benefit by using some of it as it passes through their land.

Folkestone and District Water Company

Population served: 142,000
Water supplied: 53 Ml
Length of mains: 919 km
Area: 420 sq km
Water from wells and boreholes in the chalk, the Dungeness shingle and the Folkestone and Hythe lower greensand beds.

The Folkestone Waterworks Company was formed in 1848 to take advantage of natural springs feeding the pond at a neolithic fort, Castle Hill. The neighbouring Cherry Garden Hill, the burial site of the fort's chieftain, gave its name to the firm's steam pumping station built in 1865. A supply suitable for a prehistoric tribe proved inadequate for the growing nineteenth-century Folkestone and wells were later sunk in the greensand beds near the town to supplement it. The company took over a number of other undertakings in the twentieth century, partly in a seach for more resources, and took its present name when it incorporated the Hythe and Sandgate areas in 1955. It later added Dover Corporation's supply and the old East Kent Water Company in 1970.

The company has an unusual supply at Dungeness, where wave action is depositing a shingle bank, growing at the rate of about 1 m a year. Fine sand and silt under the bank holds back freshwater which is pumped from 28 very shallow wells near the beach. Nearby sand and gravel excavations are threatening this source of supply, but the company may have the necessary legal powers to prevent this.

The demand for water is still increasing in the area and the company may, in future, have to look for a river source outside its boundaries when the underground sources have been fully exploited.

Mid Kent Water Company

Population served: 504,800
Water supplied: 148 Ml/d (1985)
Length of mains: 3,687 km
Area: 2,956 sq km
Water mostly taken from a large number of small boreholes in the chalk, lower greensand and Hastings beds, the remainder from the Medway and its tributaries.

Established in 1888 as a small company to supply twelve parishes to the west of Maidstone, Mid Kent's area of supply has changed since then 42 times – amalgamations and takeovers of similar small companies making it one of the larger private water undertakings. The Canterbury and District Water Company, with which it amalgamated in 1968, was particularly old, formed as a result of the Canterbury Gas Light and Coke Company's decision to add a water supply to its activities in 1823. The company commissioned a steam engine in 1829, under the direction of George Stephenson, to pump water from the Great Stour River.

Although most of Mid Kent's water is taken from boreholes, the company has a 25 per cent share in the Bewl Bridge reservoir, part of a scheme to extract water from the Medway. This is a river-regulating reservoir created to store water in the Bewl valley to provide a top-up facility, via the River Teise, for the Medway. Water can be drawn by Mid Kent from the Medway at Springfield or, in much smaller quantities, directly from the reservoir. Water is released from the reservoir in sufficient amounts to maintain an adequate level in the river for extraction or, if the reservoir level falls, water can be pumped back into it from the Teise at Smallbridge.

The Chilham Mill pumping station is a Victorian mill converted to house the treatment and standby alternator equipment for use with boreholes on the site. The building was derelict when the company bought it and the renovation is a successful example of using redundant buildings for modern technology. The site has been sympathetically landscaped and now includes a nature walk, fishing, rambling and birdwatching facilities.

Mid Sussex Water Company

Population served: 248,000
Length of mains: 2,189 km
Area: 1,041 sq km
Water from boreholes and the River Ouse.

This company has developed from the Newhaven & Seaford Water Company, formed in 1881 to amalgamate several small private works serving local estates. Its first source was a well at East Blatchington, equipped with a steam pump and an auxiliary windmill, later wrecked in a storm. This source became contaminated with seawater as a result of overpumping and a new site was developed at Poverty Bottom, Bishopstone using two compound condensing steam engines. In 1923 a new pump house was built, equipped with a Crossley oil engine with turbine pumps, capable of working at half the cost of the steam plant.

The company retains records of many other details, like complaints that the town crier had not announced an interruption of the water supply, or the agreed charge for water at a Boer War volunteer camp – one farthing per man per day, one halfpenny per horse. An amalgamation with East Grinstead Water was delayed for six months by a resident in Newhaven who felt she would be less well served. Exercising her rights, she petitioned Parliament and appeared in person to plead her case before a joint committee of the Lords and Commons. Her objection was given a courteous and patient hearing but overruled.

Portsmouth Water Company

Population served: 630,000
Water supplied: 220 Ml/d
Length of mains: 3,150 km
Area: 868 sq km
Water from boreholes in the chalk, springs and the River Itchen.

The history of Portsmouth's water supply is unusually well documented, having detailed and interesting records which go back as far as 1540 when a map was drawn showing a pond at Four House Green where The Dragon, The Rose, The Lyon and The Wight Hart engaged in brewing beer for the Royal Navy, using the local water. Other early records tell us:

Also where as many undiscret persons not considering the quenes mats affayres nor ther owne helthes nor ye comodity of the hole towns, hath usid and yet do use to wash both bucks [foul underclothing] and upr clothes in the diche and springs of the iiij [four] howses. We geve in charge yt none hereaftr prsume to do the lyk in paine of xs [10 s.] for evry offence.

7 Dec 1562

We give a paine against Barty Drake Chamberlain of this towne that he cause the Towne wells where the pumps stand to be clensed and digged deeper and from time to tyme to keep them sufficiently repaired uppon paine to loose. . . . .vjs. viijd. [6 s. 8 p.]

Oct 1636

. . . noe Water Carte-man or Seller of Well Water . . . shall . . . carry above foure caskes or halfe hogsheads in one cart upon paine that every person offending herein shall forfeite and loose for every offence th sume of Three shillings and foure pence . . .

16 May 1690

(In order to prevent damage to the roads, a cask held about 123 litres.)

A grant from the corporation for supplying the town was given to Benjamin Oakshott in 1665 for a term of 1,000 years and a map, dated 1668, shows his two 'fresh water mils', suggesting that he used a waterwheel of some sort to pump water into tanks for distribution by cart. His name does not appear again after that date, so the 1,000 years seems to have been a rather optimistic figure. A new grant was made to Richard Barry and the famous water engineer George Surracold in 1694, which included 'lieve to digg through the streetes . . . for layeing pipes . . . ', but this also appears to have foundered, as there is no further mention of it in the records.

The first Act of Parliament relating to Portsmouth's water supply was obtained by Thomas Smith, Lord of the Manor of Farlington, in 1740, to convey water from his estate to 'every street, lane and alley' of Portsmouth and to The Common, later known as Portsea. Unfortunately, he died a year later, but the Act could be assigned to another and was sold by his trustees to one Peter Taylor, later to become MP for Portsmouth (1774–77). He initiated a rather extravagant scheme which involved an 800-m tunnel through chalk, which produced no water at all, and he also died before gaining any benefit from the Act.

By 1801, the population had reached 33,000 and Portsmouth was a thriving town with a busy naval dockyard but with no piped water supply, the inhabitants still relying on shallow wells and water carts. When the 'new' borough gaol was built, one of the items of equipment was a treadmill, worked by ten men, for pumping water to supply the establishment. Many of England's larger towns had some sort of piped supply by this time and it was natural that schemes should be put forward by enterprising groups hoping to make a profit from public works. Two rival proposers were considered by the town in 1808. The first, the Company of Proprietors of the Portsea Island Waterworks, was backed by local finance and adopted by public meeting. The second, the Portsea Island Water-Works Company, backed by London finance, decided to proceed anyway and purchased the old Act of Parliament for £5,000. The local company managed to obtain its own Act and the subsequent rivalry between the two was largely responsible for the eventual failure of both companies.

The London company seems to have had the more professional approach; it used a more reliable source, which gave cleaner water, and a service reservoir to give gravity pressure to the supply. The local company did, in fact, produce the first water in the town, but its colour was bad, there were complaints about its taste and it contained a good deal of sand. Some idea of the crude nature of early supplies can be gained from the fact that pumping only took place two or three times a week for a few hours and when this stopped the supply stopped, making it essential for customers to have their own storage tanks.

Another difficulty was experienced in obtaining parts for the mechanical side of the operations. The pumping engine for the London group was made by the famous firm of Boulton and Watt in Birmingham. It was carried in sections by canal to London and brought round by sail to Portsmouth. The cast-iron pipes were made in Derby, carried to Lincolnshire by canal and the River Trent, taken by sloop to the Humber and then shipped round the east coast. Difficulties were also made by the Commissioners for Paving over digging up the streets; the local company in particular tried to exploit this further with an unsuccessful court injunction. A letter, dated 10 August 1810, from the local agent of the London company to his superiors reads:

... I this morning went down to Portsmouth with a gang of men and set them to work in laying down pipes on the High Street; they had not been at work long before several of the Commissioners came and in very angry and peremptory language desired us to desist, but I of course kept the men at their work. However, in about an hour afterwards, they brought four men with shovels who, as fast as we opened the trench, filled it up again and put an entire stop to our progress. I immediately went in search of Mr. Spicer [the mayor] to request his interference, but he refused to act in the business, not knowing how far he was justified in so doing ...

More unexpected difficulties may be imagined from the postscript to another letter sent in April 1812:

P.S. The new Engine Man had scarce got off the Coach the other day and got him something to eat before the Press Gang said grace and walked him off to the Guard House, where he spent the Night with many others. I knew nothing of this till he came here the next Morning, soon after he had his liberty.

At the end of the Napoleonic War there was a series of heavy redundancies in the shipyards, bringing serious unemployment to Portsmouth. Neither company could find new customers and a large proportion of the old ones were in arrears. Cutting off supplies was not the deterrent it is today, as public pumps and wells were still in regular use. Each company tried to undercut the other, making their precarious financial situation still worse. The local company raised mortgages but could not save itself when the mortgagees foreclosed and this company was auctioned in 1828, on the instructions of the Court of Chancery. The London company made an unsuccessful bid at that time, but did, in fact, take over the local company in 1840.

It seems, however, to have been too late; the united companies had not the financial resources to recover, demand for water remained low, equipment was out of date and a serious storm put the best water source out of action for over a year. Out of a population which, by 1851, had reached 72,000 in Portsmouth and Portsea, only 4,500 had a piped supply and the equipment was barely able to cope with that. A committee was set up by local worthies to inaugurate a new company from the two old ones, and a civil engineer engaged to advise on improvements; the necessary finance was raised and the new venture became the Borough of Portsmouth Waterworks Company in 1858. The improvements made by the new company to the pipework, and the development of a new source, meant that, by 1869, five-sixths of the population had a piped supply, the quantity supplied increasing fivefold in ten years. By enforcing improvements on consumers' fittings to prevent the wastage that resulted from higher pressures, the whole area had a permanant constant supply by 1880.

The new source of supply was at Havant, where a remarkable series of 25 springs break out along the north shore of Langstone harbour, fed by percolation of rainfall through the chalk of the South Downs. They form the largest spring supply in the country, yielding up to 136 Ml a day in wet periods and never falling below 54 Ml even in drought. They continue to give 40 per cent of Portsmouth's supply.

The company subsequently took over a number of other local undertakings. It now draws water from the Itchen and various boreholes to keep up with the general growth and development of the south Hampshire area. Its managers are now more concerned with updating its computer networks than with its engineers being press-ganged.

West Kent Water Company

Population served: 142,000
Water supplied: 31.5 Ml
Length of mains: 924 km
Area: 241 sq km
Water drawn entirely from underground sources in the Hythe, Ashdown and Tunbridge Wells sandstone beds and from shallow gravels near the River Medway.

The earliest supply in the area followed the discovery of a mineral spring near Eridge in 1606 by Dudley, Lord North. This led directly to the establishment of the spa at Tunbridge Wells (taking its name from nearby Tonbridge) and the development of a limited supply system for the town in the 1790s. The Tunbridge Wells Waterworks Company was formed in the 1850s. A company at Sevenoaks, later to become part of West Kent, was another that resulted from the accidental discovery of unwanted water when the Sevenoaks to Tonbridge railway was being constructed in 1864; a well was sunk to draw it off and it was pumped from there into the supply.

Reservoirs Open to the Public

ARDINGLY, College Road, Ardingly, Haywards Heath, West Sussex
1979, 73 hectares, 4,773 Ml, max depth 14 m
Coarse fishing
Sailing and **canoeing** for schools
Public footpaths, picnic area, car park and toilets
    enq. Mr C. Kinsman, tel: Ardingly 892549

ARLINGTON, Berwick, Eastbourne, Sussex
49 hectares
Birdwatching and **walking**
Trout fishing (day tickets sometimes available)
    fishing lodge facilities
Picnic area, car park and toilets
    enq. Recreation Officer, tel: (0320) 870815

BARCOMBE MILLS, nr Lewes, East Sussex
16 hectares, 545 Ml, max depth 3.5 m
Birdwatching
  permits from Mid Sussex Water Co., tel: Haywards Heath 457711
Trout fishing
  Ouse Angling Preservation Soc., D.J. Drummond, Whistlefield, Lewes Road, Ringmer

BEWL WATER, Lamberhurst, Kent
1975, 312 hectares, 31,367 Ml, max depth 29.5 m
Canoeing
  Mrs D. Grounds, Bewl Bridge Canoe Club, Robindale, The Common, Cranbrook, Kent
Nature reserve 50 hectares (restricted access)
  P. Bance, Sussex Wildlife Trust, Littlecote
Trout fishing (fly only, boat and bank, fly fishing courses)
  The Fishing Lodge, Bewl Water, Lamberhurst, Kent, tel: Lamberhurst 890352
Riding
  M. Pearsons, Burnt Ash, Sheep Street Lane, Etchingham, East Sussex
Rowing
  C. Wynne, Bewl Bridge Rowing Club, Down Farmhouse, Lamberhurst Down, Lamberhurst, Kent
Sailing
  The administrator, Bewl Valley Sailing Club, Sailing Club Office, Bewl Water, Lamberhurst, Kent, or tel: Lamberhurst 890930, also Bewl Sailing School, tel: Wadhurst 3670
Schools and **youth canoeing, rowing** and **sailing**
  Schools Sailing Centre, tel: Lamberhurst 890716
Sub-aqua
  E. Burrows, Bewl Valley Diving Club, 67 Robinhood Road, Knaphill, Woking, Surrey
Walks (up to 21 km)
Windsurfing (day permit, weekdays only)

The Manager, Bewl Water, Lamberhurst, Kent, tel: Lamberhurst 890661. Tuition provided by LDC Sailsports, weekdays during summer, tel: Tunbridge Wells 28019
Visitor centre, history, local interest, displays etc. Crowborough Hill, Crowborough, East Sussex
  light refreshments. open daily Apr–Oct, weekends Nov–Mar tel: Lamberhurst 890389 or 890661
Pleasure Cruiser, *Francis Mary*
  enq. to visitor centre as above.
Picnic area, adventure playground, refreshments and toilets
  enq. to the Recreation Office, tel: Lamberhurst 890661

BOUGH BEECH
130 hectares
Birdwatching (permit required)
Sailing and **windsurfing**
Trout fishing
Walking
  enq to East Surrey Water Co., tel: Redhill 66333

CHILHAM MILL, details from Mid Kent

DARWELL
1938–50, 73 hectares
Birdwatching (permit required)
(**SSSI**)
Trout fishing (day tickets available)
  Hastings F.F.C., tel: Cooden 3957
Walking
  enq. to SWA, Sussex Div., tel: Brighton 606766

PAGHAM HARBOUR, West Sussex
283 hectares of saltmarsh, part of SW's land drainage operations, **SSSI**, Ramsar Wetland of International Importance and a Special Protection Area

POWDERMILL
1932, 21 hectares
Birdwatching (permit required)
Trout fishing (day tickets available)
  Hastings F.F.C., tel: Cooden 3957

Walking
enq. to SWA, Sussex Div., tel: Brighton 606766

ROYAL MILITARY CANAL, Kent
Coarse fishing
Ashford & District Angling Club. Listed ancient monument, built as a Napoleonic defence (includes **SSSI**)

RYE HARBOUR, East Sussex
Historic and picturesque harbour, the only one administered by a water authority (part **SSSI** and **nature reserve**)

WEIR WOOD, East Grinstead, West Sussex
1950s, 113 hectares, max. depth 11 m
Coarse fishing (1 Nov–14 Mar) enq. Mr D. Reilly, Weir Wood office, tel: Forest Row 2731
Trout fishing (1 Apr–31 Oct)

Nature reserve (28 hectares, formal recognition expected shortly)
Sailing and **wind surfing**
Mrs J. Davies, Weir Wood Sailing Club, 5 Shepherds Walk, Hassocks, West Sussex
Schools and **youth canoeing**
enq. to Weir Wood Office as above
Bird Sanctuary, SSSI
enq. to Weir Wood Office

The fishing opportunities above only cover the larger reservoirs. Angling enthusiasts are advised to get Southern Water's guide *Fishing in the South* which lists all the lakes, rivers and clubs in the area as well as other useful information. It is available from Southern Water Authority, Guildbourne House, Chelsworth Road, Worthing, West Sussex BN11 1LD.

Thames Water Authority

Ev'n like two little bank-dividing brookes,
That wash the pebles with their wanton streames,
And having rang'd and search'd a thousand nookes,
Meet both at lengthe in silver-brested *Thames*,
Where in a greater Current they conjoyne:
So I my Best-Beloveds am: so He is mine.

Francis Quarles, *Canticles* II. xvi (*c*. 1640)

Reservoirs with recreational facilities – Thames Water Authority.

The regions of the water authorities were conceived as areas forming natural river basins, but Thames is the only one to fit this concept clearly and elegantly. It is, quite simply, the area drained by the River Thames and its tributaries – a very large area. The Thames itself

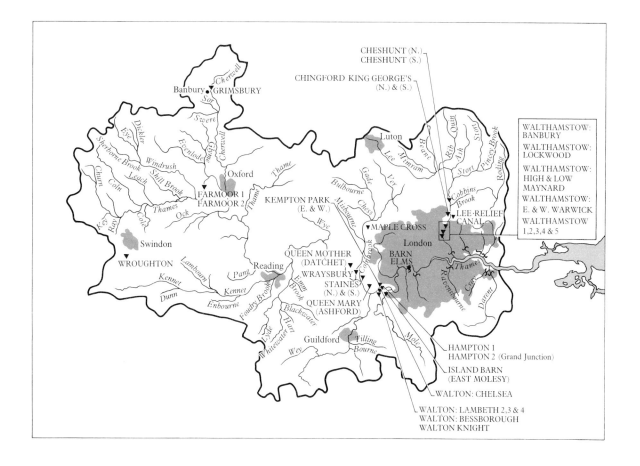

reaches well into Gloucestershire; the Cherwell stretches north beyond Banbury; the Stort, not surprisingly, goes through Bishop's Stortford; the Mole cuts through the North Downs to Crawley; the Wey and its many tributaries drain a large part of Hampshire and the Kennet descends from the Marlborough downs before crossing Wiltshire.

It seems quite characteristically English that one river should flow through both urban and suburban London and the classic countryside of the Cotswolds, the Chilterns and the Marlborough downs, all directly connected, geographically, through this one river system. It is nice to be nostalgic sometimes, to forget all that people have done to the region and to try to imagine London even in the nineteenth century, when sheep grazed at Shepherd's Bush and Covent Garden *was* a garden.

The river is navigable for cruising and transport as far as Cricklade near Cirencester. Fourty-four locks maintain the correct height of water, although very little commercial traffic uses the non-tidal reaches now. It is possible to reach the Midlands and the north via the Oxford and Grand Union Canals; Peterborough and Kings Lynn via the River Nene; Guildford along the River Wey; Hertford and Bishop's Stortford through the Lee Navigation and the Stort river. It must once have been true that one could go anywhere in the world from the Thames estuary. Now the only passenger traffic is the tourist trade.

Thames Water is the largest water undertaking in the world; it is one of the ten largest companies in Britain and provides services to almost a quarter of the population of England. London has always formed a magnetic attraction for the people of Britain as a whole and the pressure of growth has been responsible for many of its problems. It is a city which has been overcrowded for hundreds of years but always manages to keep one step ahead by expanding in area. Only very recently has industry felt that the disadvantages of transport difficulties, high costs and a deteriorating environment make it worth while for some companies to move away. Huge and growing numbers still remain, however, and the region contains more commerce within its boundaries than any other in the country.

Pollution and the Thames

If I would drink water, I must quaff the maukish of an open aqueduct, exposed to all manner of defilement, or swallow that which comes from the river Thames, impregnated with all the filth of London and Westminster. Human excrement is the least offensive part of the concrete, which is composed of all the drugs, minerals, and poisons, used in mechanics and manufacture, enriched with the putrifying carcasses of beasts and men, mixed with the scourings of all the wash tubs, kennels and common sewers within the bills of mortality.

Tobias Smollett, *The Expedition of Humphrey Clinker* (1771)

DIPHTHERIA   SCROFULA   CHOLERA

Father Thames introduces his offspring to the fair City of London.

Perhaps London's greatest recent success has been getting rid of its own human waste, a much more complicated job than the demanding but straightforward task of delivering water in a pipe to people's homes. The simple expedient of throwing such waste into the nearest river, either the Thames or one of its larger tributaries like the Fleet or Walbrook, was perhaps workable for a small population, but even by 1288 it was 'determined that the watercouse of Walebrook should be made free of dung and other nuisances', and in 1383 the same river was 'stopped up by divers filth and dung thrown therein by persons who have houses along the said course, to the great nuisence and damage of all the city'. By the end of the sixteenth century the population numbered 300,000, and contamination of the wells and small tributaries was so great that in 1531 eight regional Boards of Commissioners of Sewers were established to recommend improvements. Unfortunately, their approach was to improve the flow of sewage rather than to attend to the source of the problem, and disease, most noticeably cholera, remained endemic.

After the Great Plague of 1665, and the rebuilding that followed the Great Fire of London in 1666, more attention was given to the disposal of rubbish. The smaller rivers, which had virtually become open sewers, were gradually enclosed and London became the city of hidden water-ways with which we are familiar today. The river, however, continued to be the main drain until the mid-1850s, when the stench from it was so foul that the windows of the Houses of Parliament had to be draped with curtains soaked in chloride of lime to enable the members to breathe; sittings were suspended on more than one occasion!

The Victorians were very capable sanitary engineers. The intro-duction of the WC greatly improved conditions in the household, although it caused worse pollution problems outside the house until the sewage was efficiently carried away and treated. The connection between disease and contamination of the water supply by sewage was not conclusively proved until 1854, when Dr John Snow demonstrated that bad water had been responsible for the many outbreaks of cholera.

In 1856 the Metropolitan Board of Works was formed, with Sir Joseph Bazalgette as chief engineer. He devised and carried out the scheme which still forms the base of London's sewage disposal system today. Five large new sewers were run parallel to the Thames and these intercepted the old sewers running from north to south into the river. These carried all the sewage to treatment works and outfalls several kilometres downriver and were completed in 1874. The beneficial effects of these improvements were dramatic, but they were, unfor-tunately, eroded by subsequent massive increases in London's popu-lation and larger releases of industrial effluent.

London's sewage is carried east across the city to be treated at Beckton on the north bank and Crossness on the south. These are the largest sewage works in Britain, the Beckton works possibly being the largest in Europe. It has received sewage since 1864 as part of Bazal-gette's sewerage scheme, although at that time the entire London output was released on the ebb tide without treatment. By 1889, the solids were separated from the effluent and disposed of by a sludge vessel in the North Sea, though still without treatment. Treatment to about a third of the effluent began in the 1930s and was gradually extended to cover all the effluent and sludge by the 1960s. Today, this amounts to an average flow of 1,136 Ml/d, reaching 2,727 Ml/d in storm conditions. The digested wet sludge, with a solids content not exceeding 4.5 per cent, is still disposed of at sea; four ships collect 11–12,000 tonnes of it every day from Beckton and Crossness for dumping in the Barrow Deep area of the Thames estuary. (This is discussed further in the section on pollution, page 71.)

The releases of industrial effluent, combined with the use of non-biodegradable detergents, eventually caused such heavy pollution of the river that in 1951 a committee was set up to investigate all discharges into the estuary. The committee recommended that the Port of London

Authority (Thames Water's predecessor in this field) should be given full statutory pollution control powers, and these were granted in 1964. Working in conjunction with the Water Pollution Research Laboratory, the authority established water quality objectives which have now substantially been met; the Thames is now the cleanest metropolitan estuary in the world.

No fish were recorded for about 40 years after 1920, but now over 100 species live there, an encouraging example of what can be achieved. In addition to the fish, all other forms of wildlife have increased, from invertebrates such as crabs and sea anemones, to birds and plantlife.

The London Water Ring Main

A unique technical development in the Thames area is the construction of the London Water Ring Main. Traditionally, water trunk mains leave the service reservoirs or treatment works and run along main roads, usually only a metre or so below ground, before dividing and branching off to consumers along the way. They are vulnerable to heavy traffic, bad weather and disturbance from other services; any leaks or repairs entail digging up the roads, which is a serious inconvenience to everybody, particularly in urban areas. In large towns they often have to run very long distances from the reservoirs and require elaborate pumping en route to maintain the pressure necessary to reach so many customers. These pumps are, in many cases, expensive to run and also, particularly in London, out of date.

The ring main, claimed to be the most advanced water system in the world, is a 2.5-m diameter tunnel that will eventually extend for 140 km round London at an average depth of 40 m. The tunnel will be filled and kept under pressure by the weight of water alone, a high head of water only being necessary at the treatment works which fill it. This means that no pumping is necessary to circulate the water, it always finds its own level and will flow under its own weight to any point in the tunnel where there is demand. Eventually, eighteen shafts containing heavy-duty pumps will bring water to the surface for local distribution and, because the water can flow in both directions round the ring, it can approach any shaft from two directions, thus allowing any section of tunnel to be isolated for servicing without disrupting supply.

The power consumed in pumping water is enormous. It is estimated that the gravity feed on the ring main will save over £4 million a year. Further savings will come from rationalising water treatment works; instead of having several small works serving local areas, a few large works can feed into the main. Any of these works could be shut down leaving the others to cover supplies, an option not possible before. There are nine large water treatment works now serving London, six in the Thames valley and three in the Lee valley. The more efficient distribution will allow this number to be reduced to six, although the output from these will have to be increased.

Comparative trials at Ashford Common waterworks are underway to increase the output from the slow sand filters, a reliable filtering technique used in London for over 150 years. Experiments with sand handling, pre-treatment and alternative media on the beds have doubled the output on trial runs without affecting quality. When these techniques are fully applied they will save nearly £2 million annually.

Another £1 million should be saved by modern computer systems. High technology monitoring and control are important features of the ring; ultrasound, a kind of underwater radar, will be used to measure flow; sensors will detect vibration in working parts and monitor the behaviour of pumps; water quality will be continually checked; and all this information will be carried in fibre optic cables inside the tunnel. The possibility of having an unmanned mini submarine is being investigated; remotely controlled and equipped with video cameras, it could tour the tunnel relaying pictures to the surface.

London is fortunate in having a stable and benign clay subsoil. Most of the tunnel can be cut through this London clay which will form an effective and safe support. In parts of north London, however, the large number of other service tunnels has forced it to go deeper into the underlying beds of sand, which do not offer the same support. These sections have had to use special lining methods capable of withstanding the full internal water pressure. The first 80-km section of the ring should be fully operational in 1994 and be capable of supplying 1,300 Ml of water a day to some 5 million people.

The Thames Barrier

There was last night the greatest tide that ever was remembered in England to have been in this River, all Whitehall having been drowned.

Samuel Pepys, diary for 7 December 1663

The Thames Barrier has become a symbol; its distinctive shell roofs, clearly functional but looking dramatically organic, are now seen as a confident sign that we can still control our environment. The strength of their shape modestly, but firmly, tells us that we are safe and they take their place alongside the Tower of London and Nelson's Column as part of our mental picture of London. It is indeed very gratifying that we not only feel this, but believe it too, at least for the near future.

The risk of flooding is not new to London and many records before Pepys speak of widespread problems. In 1236 'in the great Palace of Westminster men did row with wherries in the midst of the Hall'.

Ironically, the 'taming' of the river for extra space and commercial use by constructing embankments, wharves and docks increased the chances of flood by narrowing the channel and thereby raising the water level. These floods were likely to be from a high river flow coming against the tide. Today the greatest risk comes from the surge tides of the North Sea, although the banks have also been raised upstream in case of river flooding.

Tide records show that water levels have been rising in the Thames and the North Sea for as long as records have been kept; the average has been about 300 mm a century. Tidal surges, or freak high tides, can occur under certain weather conditions. They can be particularly dangerous for any low-lying land on the east coast when deep

The Thames barrier. (Photograph: Thames Water)

depressions travel east across the Atlantic, pass to the north of Scotland and then run south down the North Sea pushing a mass of water into a shallower and narrowing channel. These surges are usually brief, but when combined with seasonal high tides they can add 2 m or even more to the level and can be the cause of disastrous flooding and damage.

The worst British sea flooding in living memory was in 1953 when gales and huge tides drove the sea over defences along the Anglian coast and up the Thames. It was a major disaster made particularly frightening for those involved because it happened in the middle of the night with all communications and services like electricity cut off by the storm. About 25,000 people had to be rescued, many of them by boat; thousands of homes were wrecked; the food and stock in shops and businesses were ruined. A third of the 300 people drowned in England lived on the lower reaches of the Thames, although to put this in a wider context, the same storm surge in Holland killed nearly 2,000 people.

This flood concentrated the minds of local and national government to examine the existing flood defences and consider their suitability against predicted surge tides. It was realised that London was not adequately protected and large areas of the metropolis could be devastated by the slowly rising tides – 116 sq km of densely populated land where one and quarter million people were living, plus thousands of offices and factories. This led to Parliament passing the Thames Barrier and Flood Protection Act authorising the construction of an extensive battery of defences that include the Thames Barrier. In addition to this, sea defences were raised and strengthened all round the Anglian coast.

The 'Thames Barrier' is, in fact, only the most visible and well-known part of a defence scheme that extends for many kilometres down both sides of the estuary. Other large barriers have been built at Barking, Benfleet and Pitsea, in addition to a special gate at Tilbury and raised concrete walls as far as Shoeburyness. The height of the defences was based on the one in a thousand probability of a flood by the year 2030. This must be a realistic assessment for the short term but, quite apart from any other factors, the global warming resulting from the 'greenhouse effect' is certain to make still greater demands on protection in the future.

Colne Valley Water Company

Population served: 760,000
Water supplied: 200 Ml/d
Length of mains: 2,682 km
Area: 386 sq km
Water obtained from the wells and boreholes in the chalk and from the Thames via the Three Valleys scheme.

It comes as a surprise to find that the Colne Valley Company, supplying such densely populated areas as Edgware, Stanmore and Hendon, was formed as late as 1873. It is hard to imagine that they were then only small villages surrounded by fields. Their first source of supply, from boreholes in the chalk along the River Colne, was discovered near Watford Junction by Robert Stevenson in 1837 when he needed water for the men and machines working on the London to Birmingham railway line.

The company was one of those formed by 'public spirited gentlemen' for the good of the community. The local wells were inadequate for the area's needs and there had been a number of typhoid outbreaks. Opposition to the scheme came from local millers and landowners on the banks of the river who felt their interests would be affected, but a local magistrate and headmaster was a keen supporter, saying, 'one sees an enormous amount of immorality and uncleanliness, simply on account of the entire absence of water ... the other day I had to send five men to prison for theft'.

The company expanded its area of supply, both in the nineteenth century and by taking over the St Albans area in the 1960s. Its increasing need for water could not be met by the local aquifers and the company, in conjunction with the Rickmansworth Water Company and the Lee Valley Water Company, promoted the Three Valleys Water scheme in 1970 (see under Rickmansworth Water Company on page 198).

East Surrey Water Company

Population served: 320,000
Water supplied: 109 Ml/d
Length of mains: 17,279 km
Area: 681 sq km
66 per cent of the water comes from boreholes in the chalk and greensand; 33 per cent from the River Eden.

The company was founded in 1862, growing and acquiring other undertakings to reach its present area of supply in the 1950s. A major recent growth in demand is associated with Gatwick Airport which is one of its largest customers. The water from the chalk is hard. Local authorities, when asked if the company should continue its water softening policy, replied that it should and that customers would be prepared to pay extra for this service, so all underground supplies are softened to within limits acceptable to the EEC.

East Surrey is one of the few statutory companies with large reservoirs. Its pumped storage reservoir at Bough Beech was particularly designed to blend with the local countryside and is one of many landscaped by Dame Sylvia Crowe, a landscape artist described recently by the BBC as one of the great women of the century. The intake works, built like a Kentish barn, has won an environmental award. The reservoir is used for fishing and sailing and has a nature trail, study pond and flora and fauna displays in a restored oast house, set up in conjunction with the Kent Trust for Nature Conservancy.

Lee Valley Water Company

Population served: 1,014,000
Water supplied: 283 Ml/d
Length of mains: 5,270 km
Area: 2,226 sq km
Water from boreholes in the chalk, bulk supplies from the Great Ouse via Grafham Water and from the Thames via the Three Valleys scheme.

This must be the youngest statutory water company, set up by Act of Parliament in 1960 as a direct result of the Government's regrouping policy. It amalgamated sixteen different water undertakings in the upper Lee catchment area; the largest of these were the Barnet District Water Company, formed in 1872, and the Herts and Essex Water Company, formed in 1883. The latter appears to have been the only statutory company among them and only became one in 1953; the remainder were mostly local council undertakings.

Three more local council supplies were added in 1963 and the first years of the company concentrated on building up an effective infrastructure between the areas taken over. The area now had such a dense population that the water resources within its boundaries could not meet local needs, so the company jointly promoted the Great Ouse Water Bill to construct Grafham Water as a pumped storage reservoir. This was passed in 1961 and up to 73 Ml can now be taken through an 86-km pipeline into the area every day. Further water was made available when the company joined the Three Valleys Water scheme.

The many small towns in the region and its undulating terrain make the company dependent on 57 water towers; several of these date from the nineteenth century and many are of architectural interest.

Mid Southern Water Company

Population served: 654,000
Water supplied: 210 Ml/d
Length of mains: 4,240 km
Area: 1,502 sq km
Water from boreholes in chalk, lower greensand and gravels and a bulk supply of river water from the North Surrey Water Company.

The company was incorporated by Act of Parliament in 1893 as the Frimley and Farnborough District Water Company, but a number of the other companies they took over had older origins. Most water suppliers formed a company and then looked for a water supply; Frimley must be unique in the accidental discovery of a water supply proving a reason to start a company. When the engineers building the main railway line cut through a deep cutting near Frimley Green, they were seriously hampered by exposed springs flooding the work. Enterprising locals, however, were pleased to pipe the water and supply it to Frimley and Farnborough. This remarkable source remained in use until 1986.

The earliest undertaking in the region was the Aldershot Gas, Water and District Lighting Co., started by Frederick Eggar in 1866, hoping to fulfil the needs of the army training camp set up there after the Crimean War. His approach does not appear to have been very professional – a well digger, John Dibbs, was instructed to dig a large number of shallow wells around the town. Those in the water industry complaining of the extra work involved in preparing for privatisation should reflect on the Victorian values of Dibbs. He walked 16 km to work, did a twelve-hour day and then walked home. He is reported to have said, 'Once I walked four miles in my sleep; I found a man walking by my side, so I said, "Good morning, I don't know where I be".

"No" he answered, "you be asleep all the way!"'

Dibbs's industry (or perhaps he was too tired to dig a decent well?) was not rewarded with any useful outcome and a pump was finally set up in gravel beds which produced reasonable results. Deeper boreholes were eventually sunk in 1870, the first, 126 cm wide by 73 m deep took five years to complete. A contract to supply the army was not signed until 1888. They also had failed to find a satisfactory well and had dug open channels to collect rainwater. These are said still to exist and be capable of giving up to 0.36 Ml per year.

The present company took its name in 1970 when it amalgamated with the Wey Valley Water Company but it still has its head office and central control room at Frimley Green.

North Surrey Water Company

Population served: 466,000
Water supplied: 165 Ml/d
Length of mains: 2,230 km
Area: 526 sq km
Water from the Thames with some wells in gravel.

Rickmansworth Water Company

Population served: 552,000
Water supplied: est. 200 Ml/d
Length of mains: 2,847 km
Area: 601 sq km
Water from 23 groundwater sources and the Thames via the Three
Valleys Water scheme.

The company was formed by Parliamentary Act in 1884:

Whereas the Parish of Rickmansworth in the County of Hertford is
imperfectly supplied with water: and whereas the persons in this Act named
are willing with others to provide a better supply of water to that parish and
it is expedient that they be incorporated into a company with the necessary
powers for that purpose and be empowered to make and maintain the works
herein-after described.

About £24,000 was raised in £10 shares to finance a well and pumping
station but it was realised that the area of supply was too small to give
a sufficient return on this sum and another Act was passed the next
year, authorising supplies to a larger area. A 100-m borehole was sunk,
steam engines installed, 11 km of mains laid and the first water reached
the public in 1889. The reluctance of the public to buy what they had
previously had for nothing was eventually overcome when they saw the
advantages, and the company soon expanded by buying a mill at
Batchworth, which had a well that could be put straight into supply.

Batchworth Mills is an interesting site which the company still owns
today. Its history can be traced back to 1666 when it was a corn and
fulling mill; subsequently there was a paper mill, a hose and cotton
manufactury, a silk spinning mill and a bone button works. Other wells
and boreholes were sunk until, in 1965, the Thames Conservancy
announced that there was clear evidence that groundwater abstraction
was depleting river flows in the Misbourne and Colne valleys. An
alternative source had to be found for the three undertakers pumping in
this area: the Rickmansworth, Lee Valley and Colne Valley Companies.

A meeting between the Ministry of Housing and local government,
the Water Resources Board, the Thames Conservancy and the three
companies decided that the only alternative was to take water from the
Thames and the joint Three Valleys scheme was promoted. Raw water
is taken from the river through a tunnel to the shared Iver treatment
works and from there by pipes to the companies' respective areas. The
Iver works can supply up to 160 Ml, but a second tunnel is being built
to connect it to Thames Water's reservoir system to give flexibility.

Rickmansworth water goes all over the world – they supply London
Airport with 4.55 Ml a day.

Reservoirs Open to the Public

BARN ELMS no. 5, Merthyr Terrace, Barnes SW13

10 hectares

Birdwatching

Permit required from TW, tel: (01) 833 6639

Trout fishing (fly only, boat and bank)

enq. and permits to the gatehouse, tel: (01) 748 3423

Car park and toilets

BARN ELMS no. 6

8 hectares

Birdwatching

as no. 5 above

Trout fishing (bank only)

as no. 5 above

Car park and toilets

BARN ELMS no. 7

9 hectares

Birdwatching

as no. 5 above.

BARN ELMS no. 8

7 hectares

Water sports training (advance booking only)

enq. to the gatehouse, as no. 5 above

CHESHUNT NORTH

Birdwatching (no permit required)

Coarse fishing (bank only)

Kings Arms Angling Club, tel: (01) 805 8233

Cheshunt Carp Club, tel: Cuffley 874765

Picnic area

CHESHUNT SOUTH

Coarse fishing (bank only)

Red Spinner Angling Soc., tel: (0707) 874705

CHINGFORD KING GEORGE NORTH

Coarse fishing (bank only)

enq. and permits from Walthamstow gatehouse, tel: (01) 808 1527

Sub-aqua

enq. to R. Nugent, Beckton Sewage Treatment Works, tel: (01) 594 9474 (home) or (01) 591 3911 (office)

Windsurfing

Essex Sailboard Club, tel: (01) 367 5369

CHINGFORD KING GEORGE SOUTH

Coarse fishing (bank only)

as north above

Sailing and **windsurfing**

King George Sailing Club, 49 Drysdale Avenue, Chingford E4 7NL

FARMOOR no. 1, Cumnor Road, Farmoor, nr Oxford

Birdwatching

enq. to Senior Warden, tel: Oxford 863033 or 862166

Trout fishing (bank only)

enq. to Farmoor F.F.C. 27 Manor Road, Ducklington, Nr Witney, Oxon OX8 7YD

Sailing (facilities)

Oxford Sailing Club, tel: Oxford 863201

School sailing

Oxford & District Sailing Assoc., tel: Oxford 863201

Clubhouse, car park and toilets

FARMOOR no. 2

97 hectares

Birdwatching

permits from the Senior Warden as above

Sailing and **windsurfing** (facilities)
Oxford Sailing Club as above
School sailing
Oxford & District Sailing Assoc. as above
Trout fishing (fly only, bank & boat)
day permits available from the Senior Warden as above
Walking
Fishing tackle shop, picnic area, clubhouse, car park and toilets

GRIMSBURY, Banbury, Oxon
Birdwatching
no permit required
Coarse fishing
Banbury & District A.A., tel: (0295) 710488
Sailing (also for schools)
Banbury Cross Sailing Club, tel: (0869) 38020

ISLAND BARN, East Molesey
Sailing
Walton on Thames Sailing Club, tel: (0932) 841514

KEMPTON PARK WEST, Hanworth
Birdwatching
permit required from TW, tel: (01) 833 6639

LEE RELIEF CHANNEL FISHERY, between Waltham Abbey and Fishers Green. The River Lee flood relief channel is run as a stocked mixed coarse fishery open to the public. Facilities for matches and competitions.
enq. and permits from TW, tel: Waltham Cross 23611
Facilities and car parking at Fishers Green only

MAPLE LODGE NATURE RESERVE, Maple Lodge Close, Maple Cross, nr Rickmansworth
16-hectare site on former sewage works managed as a reserve for birds, mammals, moths, butterflies and plants. Access restricted to members of the Maple Lodge Conservation Society. Visits by non-members and groups can be arranged in advance.

enq. to the Secretary, Mr D. Edmunds, 20 Dickinson Square, Croxley Green, Herts WD3 3HA
Car parking and toilet

QUEEN MARY, Ashford Road, Ashford, Middx
Birdwatching
permit as Kempton Park above
Sailing and **windsurfing** (training available)
enq. to Queen Mary Sailing Club, tel: (0784) 243219

QUEEN MOTHER, Horton Road, Horton, Slough
192 hectares
Birdwatching
permit as Kempton Park above
Trout fishing (fly only, boat and bank)
Queen Mother Trout Fishery, tel: Slough 683605
Sailing and **windsurfing** (training available)
enq. to Datchet Water Sailing Club, tel: Slough 683872
Sailing for the disabled
enq. tel: Ascot 25326
Tackle shop, refreshments, clubhouse, car park and toilets

STAINES NORTH and SOUTH
Birdwatching
no permit required

RIVER THAMES
Thames Water have provided 3 sites on the Thames for free public coarse fishing for the disabled. There are no special facilities.
a) Upstream of Sunbury Lock, nr Walton-on-Thames, Surrey
b) Upstream of Penton Hook Lock, Staines, Middx
c) Poplar Island to Bucks Eyot, Tilehurst, nr Reading, Berks

WALTHAMSTOW no. 1, Ferry Lane, Tottenham N17
8 hectares
Coarse fishing (bank only)
enq. and permits, telephone the gatehouse, (01) 808 1527
Car park and toilets

WALTHAMSTOW nos. 2 and 3
13 and 12 acres
Coarse fishing (bank only)
  permits as no. 1 above
Car park and toilets

WALTHAMSTOW no. 4
Canoeing, sailing and **windsurfing**
(training only)
  Dir. of Leisure Services, Lee Valley
  Regional Park Authority, PO Box 88,
  Enfield, Middx
Trout fishing (fly only from the bank)
  as Walthamstow no. 1 above
Tackle shop, car park and toilets
Walthamstow nos. 4 and 5 offer pike
fishing in winter, enq. as no. 1.

WALTHAMSTOW: Banbury
Water skiing
  as sailing above
Car park and toilets

WALTHAMSTOW no. 5
Trout fishing (mixed method from the
bank)
  as Walthamstow 1 above

WALTHAMSTOW: East Warwick
17 hectares
Coarse fishing (bank only)
  as Walthamstow 1 above
Tackle shop, car park and toilets

WALTHAMSTOW: High Maynard
15 hectares
Coarse fishing (bank only)
  enq. and permits as Walthamstow
  no. 1
Car park and toilets

WALTHAMSTOW: Lockwood
Coarse fishing (bank only)
  enq. to Eastern Metropolitan Water
  Assoc., tel: (01) 531 4752
Car park and toilets

WALTHAMSTOW: Low Maynard
10 hectares
Coarse fishing (bank only)
  enq. and permits as Walthamstow
  no. 1
Car park and toilets

WALTHAMSTOW: West Warwick
14 hectares
Coarse fishing (season permits only,
bank only)
  enq. as Walthamstow no. 1
Car park and toilets

The Walthamstow reservoirs offer
canal/river fishing in the Coppermill
Stream, New Cut and Lee Navigation.
Details as for no 1.
Birdwatching is permitted on all the
Walthamstow reservoirs, a permit is
required from the gatehouse, tel: (01) 808
1527

WALTON: Bessborough, Chelsea (4
reservoirs) and Knight,
Birdwatching
  enq. and permits to TW, tel: (01) 833
  6639

WALTON: Lambeth nos. 2 and 3
Birdwatching
  as Bessborough above
Scout sailing
  Molesey Scout Group, 11 Church
  Walk, Thames Ditton, Surrey KT7
  0EY

WALTON: Lambeth no. 4
Birdwatching
  as Beesborough above
Club coarse fishing (bank only)
  enq. to London Anglers Assoc., tel:
  (01) 520 7477

WRAYSBURY
Public **horse riding**
  season permits from TW, tel: (01) 837
  3300 ext. 778423

WROUGHTON, Overtown Hill,
Wroughton, Swindon
1.2 hectares
Trout fishing (fly only, bank or punt)
  enq. to 'Pebley Beach', tel: (0793)
  812235
Car park and toilet

Welsh Water Authority

One could almost say that the greater part of England is now spoilt, and that one has to look carefully into the odd corners to find landscapes unadulterated by development or traffic. In Wales it is the industry and urban population that have to be hunted for among huge areas of beautiful scenery. An oversimplification perhaps, but it is a fact that about one-quarter of Wales is designated a national park or area of outstanding natural beauty, and it also, perhaps, underlines the hard truth that the great industries of Wales, coal and steel, are now sadly inconspicuous and most of the region is a declared development area. The old traditions of hard work and intelligence are now more likely to be made use of in lighter engineering and manufacturing, with diversification into chemicals, pharmaceuticals, textiles and manmade fibres. There are two nuclear power stations at Trawsfynydd and Wylfa, and the large oil refinery at Milford Haven is a big employer. Most commerce is still along the southern seaboard and 75 per cent of Wales's 2.7 million inhabitants live in the industrial areas of either the south or the north east, although these only amount to 25 per cent of the land area.

Much of the best land lies within the south-east Wales and Wrexham areas, with a few other highly productive parts. Sheep farming has for many years been the mainstay of Welsh agriculture and the south east has a higher concentration of sheep than anywhere else in the world. A less-dignified pursuit is people farming, in the form of retirement homes and 'B and B', but tourism is one of the largest revenue earners; a recent survey estimated that about 12.5 million tourist trips are made to Wales annually, bringing in about £510 million. Wales takes third place after Austria and Switzerland in the value of tourist income per head of population and is the second most popular region in the United Kingdom (after south-west England) for British tourists. Another noticeable crop, although not one that employs very large numbers, is forestry. Nine per cent of Wales's surface area is covered by economically productive forest and woodland, most of it owned by the Forestry Commission.

The topography and meteorology of Wales makes it such an effective water resource that, since the nineteenth century, England has taken Welsh water for many of its larger cities – a source of some bitterness to the Welsh. Much of the land is on high ground. Craggy mountains,

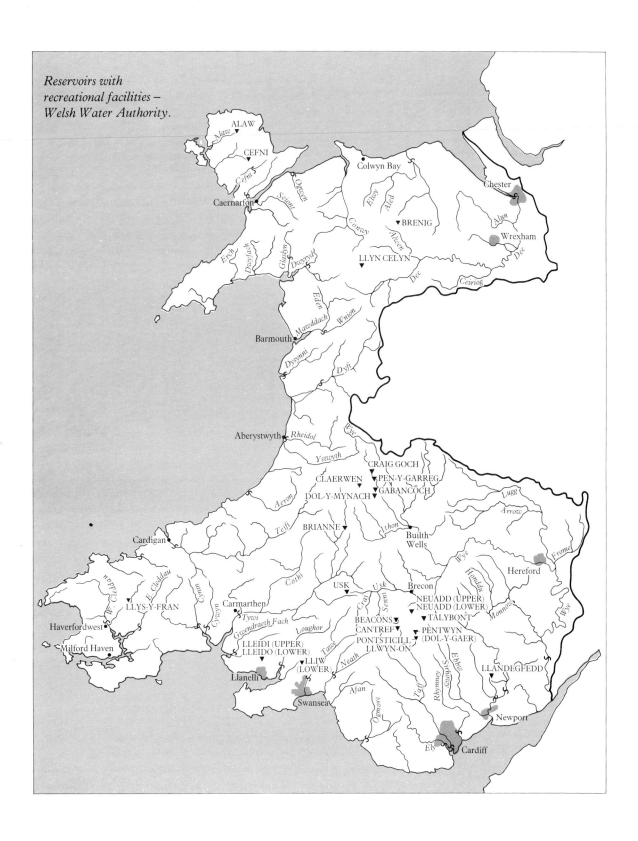

Reservoirs with recreational facilities – Welsh Water Authority.

'No sound is here.
Save of the stream that
* shrills, and now and*
* then*
A cry as of faint wailing,
* when a kite*
Comes sailing o'er the
* crags, or straggling lamb*
Bleats for its mother.'
*   Thomas Grove*
*   'Cwm Elan'*
(Photograph: Charles
Hall)

rising to over 900 m, dominate the landscape of the north west, and most of mid-Wales consists of a high plateau 300–600 m above sea level, the Brecon Beacons and Black Mountains forming a similar range in the south. The greater part of North and mid-Wales consists of ancient impervious rocks which, together with the widespread mantle of boulder clay on the valley sides, allows little or no loss of water through downward percolation. A sponge-like layer of peat covers the slopes and plateaux above 460 m. Sandstone and carboniferous limestone in the north east, and carboniferous limestone in the South Wales coalfield, are aquifers which provide local supplies of water.

More than two-thirds of the total land area of Wales has an average rainfall of over 127 cm; low temperature, high humidity and cloud cover keep evaporation in the uplands fairly low. Cloud cover in the upper catchment areas, like the Elan Valley, is responsible for them receiving between 200 and 300 fewer hours of sunshine than the coastal localities. The highest rainfall is in Snowdonia (437 cm) and the driest area is around Hereford (64 cm). The 30 per cent lost through evaporation compares with Anglian's 45 per cent. The average daily run-off of water amounts to 50,000 Ml and accounts for the many fine rivers, the largest of which is the Wye. Wales is an exceptional place for fishing.

Politics *Welsh* Water Authority is a title that raises the emotions. Nationalism leaves the dry scientific principles of integrated river basin management in second place. The catchment areas of the Dee, Wye and Severn Rivers have disobligingly not conformed to national boundaries and this gives rise to considerable feelings of injustice – Welsh water is perceived by many of the Welsh as rightfully belonging to Wales.

Half the rainfall collected in Wales is directly taken by the English and considerably more is abstracted indirectly from the major rivers. It is quite possible that nobody would be greatly worried by this if it were not for the fact that the charges for water in Wales have been the highest in Britain. It is easy to denigrate Plaid Cymru's emotional lack of understanding of the hydrographic principles involved; but would anyone be happy to have their neighbour purchase the water from their backyard at half the price they had to pay for it? Nobody pays more for electricity, the telephone, the post or roads because they live in an area that, by geographical and administrative accident, makes these services more expensive.

In a hung Parliament in 1976, the Labour Party, under pressure from Plaid Cymru, passed the Water Charges Equalisation Act which made payments from those areas with cheap rates to those with more expensive ones. Under this scheme the Welsh received an extra £3 million annually from other authorities, a small amount in terms of the overall budgets but at least a recognition of the problem. The Act was repealed by the present Government in 1980; partly because it was felt to be unfair by the water authorities, as it only equalised water and not the many other services they perform; and partly because it was not felt to be a positive step towards promoting a fairer system. This seems ironic in view of the privatisation moves that followed, which are likely to increase such differences and make inter-regional arrangements more expensive.

In 1974 Welsh Water took over a large fragmented region containing numerous sewage works neglected by local councils. They were also the agents of an English Parliament and it has been said that resentment about this resulted in considerable difficulties in establishing efficient management. The practical problems are well documented; one division which thought it was taking over 85 sewage works found, after nearly two years, that there were 190 of them, mostly undocumented. By the early 1980s, Welsh Water had regularly lost money, and financial support, which had previously come from central Government and local councils, had been withdrawn, as the new authorities were meant to be self-financing. Bitter accusations were exchanged between the chairman of Welsh Water and the Welsh Office. The headquarters of Severn Trent Water were bombed by Welsh activists in 1982 and a water rate non-payment campaign was launched by Plaid Cymru.

The other water authorities' rates have risen and there now seems to be less feeling over the cost of water in Wales but the old bitterness about taking Welsh water remains – encouraged by the traditonal insensitivity of a central Parliament towards the regions. The English are, however, very nervous now of taking more Welsh water; a scheme to enlarge the Elan Valley reservoirs was dropped recently, although there seems no hope of coming to more equitable national arrangements in the present climate of profit making.

Acid Rain   One result of the area's high rainfall is to increase the effects of 'acid rain' in the water supply, and Welsh Water, with grants from the Department of the Environment and the Welsh Office, are co-ordinating a programme to investigate this complex problem. The Institutes of Hydrology and Terrestrial Ecology, four Welsh university colleges, the University of Wales and the Forestry Commission are all involved. Welsh rain is, in fact, among the least acidic in the British Isles, but, because of the quantity of it, the deposited acidity in the upland areas is higher than in many parts receiving a more acidic rain but less rainfall. It is usual to hear about the effects on trees, but a number of factors can combine to alter water quality significantly and one obvious result of this is the damage to wildlife, particularly fish stocks. The principal factors emerging from the study are wind direction, geology and land use.

Acid precipitation results principally from the emission of sulphur and nitrogen compounds from the combustion of coal and oil. These compounds can be transported in the atmosphere over long distances, according to wind speed and direction, before being deposited either as 'acid rain' or as a dry deposition. In upland areas there are also likely to be significant inputs of acidity from 'occult' deposition (via fog, mist and cloud). Analysing the pH (the standard acid/alkali measure) by wind direction showed that easterly and southerly winds were, on average, the greatest acid-rain bearers.

The areas that are most vulnerable to acid precipitation are those where the bedrock is hard and resistant to weathering and the soils are thin and poor and often naturally acidic. Such areas are low in natural calcium and magnesium, which might neutralise any acid in the rain, and stream, lake and river waters may, consequently, become acidic and contain high levels of toxic aluminium leached from the soil. Preliminary studies, based on soil and geology studies of Wales, have shown that the upland areas of Dyfed and Gwynedd are likely to be the most vulnerable, as the soils are thin and poor in the upland areas. Some soils also tend to acidify surface waters by releasing organic and inorganic acids.

Variations in land use are important in determining the impact that acid rain will have on drainage waters. In particular, comparisons of adjacent moorland and afforested catchments have shown that waters draining conifer plantations are more acidic and have higher concentrations of toxic dissolved aluminium than is the case with moorlands. Consequently, the fishing conditions of the streams and lakes draining forestry plantations are impoverished. Results suggest that conifer forests can adversely affect water quality in such areas by:

- Concentrating pollutants in water run-off as a result of increased transpiration by trees.
- More efficient scavenging of 'dry' and 'occult' deposition of atmospheric pollutants.
- Removal by tree uptake of free ions that would otherwise be beneficial to water quality.
- Leaching of aluminium instead of calcium and magnesium surface run-off as a result of improved drainage and consequent reduction of contact time with soils.
- Increased oxidation of sulphur and nitrogen to sulphate and nitrate within the soils as a result of improved drainage.

The area of productive forests has almost trebled in the past 60 years and the 1.6 million hectares currently afforested in England and Wales represents 22 per cent of the total upland area. Recently published reports have suggested that the proportion of uplands under forestry could be doubled over the next 40 years, although the Forestry Commission do not now envisage increased planting on this scale in Wales.

On remaining moorland areas there has been a substantial reduction in the application of lime by farmers since the changes in the lime subsidy in 1964 and its subsequent abolition. Before that, they had been given substantial grants to lime their land and this had been a useful neutralising agent for acid rain in the past.

Initial surveys of a number of streams on the Upper Tywi catchment, and several lakes in mid and North Wales, were undertaken in the early 1980s. The results showed that many upland streams, rivers and lakes draining afforested catchments in Dyfed and Gwynedd could not support natural fish populations and had depleted populations of aquatic plants and animals. Attempts to restock the River Tywi above Llyn Brianne, with trout and salmon, proved unsuccessful and fish-survival tests showed that the native brown trout cannot survive the combined effects of the acidity and the raised aluminium concentration found in water draining from conifer forests in the area.

Lakes in conifer-afforested catchments, such as Llyn Berwyn and Llyn Blaenmelindwr, have been recognised as marginal fisheries for some years, and in recent years they have had to be operated as 'put and take' fisheries using American brook charr (this species is more tolerant of acidic conditions than indigenous ones like the brown trout). This solution to the problem was not, however, found to be generally applicable. Llyn Berwyn, for example, was found to be too acidic even to support the hardy brook charr. In the fisheries' survey, trout abundance was found to be inversely correlated with soluble aluminium concentration, and the latter, in turn, correlated with the amount of forest cover. Although some stocked fish are surviving and reproducing at Blaenmelindwr, the implications of introducing exotic species have to be carefully monitored. Furthermore, stocked marginal fisheries, with hatchery-reared fish of low acid tolerance, may reduce the resistance of natural stocks to further acidification.

In September 1984 there was a significant fish kill on the Afon Glaslyn in North Wales, involving over 100 sea trout, seven salmon and many other fish. An analysis of blood taken from the fish revealed that they had died from the effects of acidity and/or aluminium following a high flow event. In addition to the implication for fisheries described above, failure to neutralise acidic waters can result in excessive corrosion of mains, with, in some areas, unacceptable high lead levels and consumer complaints about coloured water. Increased acidity is also linked with higher levels of manganese and iron, as well as aluminium, in natural upland waters. If they become any more acidic, additional treatment costs will be inevitable.

The acidity of several upland lakes is such that they are only marginal fisheries and a few cannot now maintain a salmonid fishery. In Scandinavia and Canada acidic lakes have been neutralised successfully by adding lime.

After discussing these techniques with experts from these countries, and carrying out laboratory tests on several limestones, liming trials were carried out at the small lake of Llyn Pendam near Aberystwyth. These proved successful and treatment was extended to two larger lakes. Pre-liming surveys of the water quality were undertaken and the effects of liming on this and the ecology of the lakes is currently being monitored. All three lakes are low viable fisheries and have been stocked by local angling clubs with brown and rainbow trout.

Two related studies are being carried out on the wider implications of acidification on conservation. The Nature Conservancy Council is monitoring lichen and sulphur dioxide – lichens have been used as indicators of air pollution for many years. The RSPB is also surveying how the dipper population is affected at the sites monitored by Welsh Water. The results suggest that breeding abundance correlates with stream acidity and that in at least one catchment, where run-off had become more acidic, the dipper population had declined.

When all the investigations are complete, the data will be used to develop mathematical models which should help to predict the effects of changes in land-use and acid rain on stream water quality and ecology. This should provide a greater understanding of the complex process leading to the acidification of streams and enable remedial action to be taken in the future.

Virology Welsh Water's virologist, Dr Janice Tyler, was the first scientist in the UK to prove that potentially harmful viruses could get into treated mains supplies, and her work has led to improvements at several Welsh waterworks. She has also made studies of viruses in seawater. It is not generally accepted that a virus can survive the processes used in water treatment to kill bacteria, or that they could be a potential source of infection if they did, but in addition to Welsh Water, Thames, Severn Trent and Yorkshire Water Authorities have all thought it worth while to set up virological units. Once treated, water can still be at risk if the level of chlorine cannot cope with seepage from the ground into old or damaged distribution systems, or from 'foreign bodies' entering service reservoirs. When worn out water mains in Gwent became polluted while standing empty during replacement work, Dr Tyler was still finding viruses in the water after all bacteria had been killed. They survived in deposits on the old iron pipes, despite normal flushing and sterilisation.

It takes quite a large count of bacteria to infect a healthy person but viruses can infect in very small numbers, so it is an important area of research. Dr Tyler puts it in perspective by saying:

... these viruses are mostly passed on by direct physical contact with an infected person in the family, at work or in school. Your chances of picking up this type of infection from water, by bathing say, are extremely remote as viruses die off rapidly when exposed to sunlight, extreme heat or cold, and other factors. However, it is important that we know enough about natural waters to give any advice that may be needed.

Chester Waterworks Company

Population served: 112,500
Water supplied: 26.4 Ml/d (1982)
Length of mains: 527 km
Area: 132 sq km
Water from the River Dee at Chester and a borehole at Plemstall.

Chester Waterworks Company is probably the oldest surviving water company in Britain and the history of the town's supply encapsulates the history of water supply in this country. The town was the head-quarters of the XXth Roman legion and a number of Roman lead water pipes have been found, one of which can be dated to AD 78–86 when Agricola was Governor of Britain. The inscription reads,

This lead pipe was made when Vespasian and Titus were Consuls for the ninth and seventh times respectively and when Cnaeus Julius Agricola was Governor of Britain.

Two monasteries brought water into the town in earthenware pipes at the end of the thirteenth century. This supply came from springs and was only for the monks' own use, although, like many similar ecclesiastical supplies, it was taken over by the town after the dissolution of the monasteries. By the end of the sixteenth century, public supplies came by water carrier from the River Dee or from two conduits that had been constructed; the carriers in Chester were a strong enough body to petition the Crown for a charter in 1587.

The present company traces its origins back to the year 1600 when the mayor and citizens granted John Tyrer the right to install a water-wheel in the river. This pumped water to a cistern on a tower at Bridge Gate and then through pipes in the streets for the use of the town. A waterworks was later built at Spital, in 1622, which is still the site of the company's treatment works. These schemes may have been too ambitious for the time as they fell into such a decline that, by 1692, the rights were transferred to others to build new works. Although these were more successful, the rights were again passed on to a new company, this time formed by an Act of Parliament in 1826. The company took its final name and form from another Act passed in 1857.

Wrexham and East Denbighshire Water Company

Population served: 148,000
Water supplied: 45 Ml/d
Length of mains: 1,338 km
Area: 689 sq km
Water mainly from the River Dee, but also from several impounding reservoirs and boreholes.

The company was formed in 1867 to supply the town of Wrexham and it subsequently took over a number of local authority undertakings in the area. Its geographical position makes it one of the few companies able to use impounding reservoirs from an early date; it makes use of twelve at present, the earliest of which dates from 1867, although it did not belong to the company at that time. The complexity of its area necessitates the use of 40 different water towers. The company is unusual in sending out a full chemical analysis of its various water supplies, a welcome example of open communications.

Reservoirs Open to the Public

LLYN ALAW, Llantrisant, nr Holyhead, Gwynedd
1966, 314 hectares, 7,455 Ml, max. depth 4.5 m
This shallow reservoir, formed from flooded marshland, has a rich inflow of nutrients from the surrounding land making it a very productive fishery and an important site for wildfowl and waders.
Birdwatching (hide available)
Game fishing (open to the public)
Nature reserve
Visitors' centre tells the story of the reservoir's history and functions.
   enq. tel: Llanfeathlu 730762
Picnic sites, outdoor sculpture – Relief Map of Wales – car parks and toilets

LLYN BRENIG, Cerrig-y-Drudion, nr Corwen, Clwyd
1976, 372 hectares, 61,400 Ml, max. depth 45 m
Set in a 987-hectare estate of unspoilt heather moorland rising to 434 m, Llyn Brenig is rich both in its archaeological history and its wildlife. One part has been designated an SSSI because of its plants. Outstanding views. Wales's premier boat fishery.
Archaeological and **Nature trails** (choice of 4)
Game fishing (fly only, open to the public, special facilities)
   boats for hire

Sailing, windsurfing and **canoeing** (open to the public)
   1 Apr–31 Oct (special facilities). Sailing school, equipment shop and hire facilities. Use of own boat on purchase of a permit. Enq. to Llyn Brenig Watersports Club, c/o the visitors' centre
Sub-aqua
Adventure playground and picnic areas, craft shop and cafe (with local specialities and fishing tackle)
Round the lake walk (16 km)
Visitors' centre explains the local archaeology, history, wildlife, geology and engineering of the estate. Audio-visual theatre.
Car park and toilets
   enq. on all the above to Canol fan Llyn Brenig Centre, tel: Cerrig-y-Drudion 463

LLYN BRIANNE
1972, 210 hectares, 61,000 Ml
Llyn Brianne is a place of solitude and peace. The whole area is very rich in birdlife and surrounded by beautiful countryside.
Car park, viewpoint and toilets
The RSPB Dinas **reserve** is nearby
   Access to RSBP reserve (no permit needed) mid-Apr–Aug, 11–2 on Wed, Sat and Sun, further info from the Warden, tel: Rhandirmwyn 228

LLYN CEFNI, Llangefni, Gwynedd
1950, 70 hectares, 1,800 Ml
An attractive reservoir surrounded by
mature conifers, good for wintering
wildfowl and passage waders.
Birdwatching (hide available, special
facilities)
Trout Fishing (fly only, day tickets
available in Llangefni)
    Cefni Angling Association
Car park
    enq. to Llyn Alaw visitors' centre as
    above

LLYN CELYN, nr Bala, Gwynedd in
the Snowdonia National Park
1964, 336 hectares. 80,800 Ml, max depth
43 m
Trout Fishing
    permits, tel: Bala 520368
Picnic area, car parks and toilets

CWM TAFF RESERVOIR AREA,
Brecon Beacons National Park
Beacons (1897, 21 hectares, 1,600 Ml),
Cantref (1892, 17 hectares, 1,500 Ml),
Llwyn-on (1926, 60 hectares, 5,500 Ml)
reservoirs offer quiet recreational activity
in the national park.
Trout Fishing
    fly only, Beacons and Cantref; multi-
    method put and take, Llwyn-on
    Forestry Commission Visitors' Centre
Picnic area and walks (Llwyn-on), car
parks and toilets

THE ELAN VALLEY, Rhayader,
Powys
5 reservoirs, classic examples of Victorian
civil engineering, set in the dramatic,
wild and beautiful Cambrian mountains.
181 sq km of spectacular country where
red kite, merlin and peregrine falcons can
still be seen. Fine oakwoods in the lower
valleys, with a rich variety of birds,
flowers and insects.
1904 (and 1952, Claerwen), Caban Coch
and Garreg-Ddu: 200 hectares, 36,400
Ml. Claerwen: 263 hectares, 48,300 Ml.
Craig Coch: 88 hectares, 9,100 Ml, Pen-
y-Garreg: 50 hectares, 6,050 Ml.

Birdwatching
Game fishing
Guided **walking** with experienced
guides
    May–Sept, Thurs, Sat and Sun, 2.30,
    also Weds in July and Aug
Walking
Waymarked short walks, cafe and craft
shop, picnic areas, visitor and
information centre, describes the valley's
history and wildlife, car parks and toilets
    all enq. to the visitors' centre, tel:
    Rhayader (0597) 810880

LLANDEGFEDD, Pontypool, Gwent
1964, 176 hectares, 24,100 Ml, max depth
36 m
An intensively used reservoir offering the
best inland sailing in South Wales, also
a winter site of national importance
(SSSI) for wildfowl. A well stocked and
impressive fishery.
Birdwatching (hide available by
permit)
Sailing, windsurfing and **canoeing**
(hire and many other facilities)
    1 Mar–31 Oct, 9am-9pm or sunset
    enq. to Gwent Adventures, tel:
    Pontypool (04955)55745, also
    Llandegfedd Sailing Club &
    Llandegfedd Water Start Club.
    Launching facilities for visitors open to
    all on a day or season permit basis
    (special facilities)
Sub-aqua
Trout fishing (fly only, boats can be
    hired) short period tickets available
    from machines
Walking and way-marked walks
Picnic areas (one central with
refreshments, one secluded), car parks
and toilets
    Further info on all the above, except
    sailing, from the Head Ranger, tel:
    Pontypool (04955) 55122

LLIEDI RESERVOIRS (Swiss
Valley), Llanelli, Dyfed
The reservoirs have been developed in a
low-key manner in order to preserve the
peace of the beautiful woodland setting.

Upper Lliedi (1902, 13 acres, 1,136 Ml) is only accessible by permit, the top end being retained as a nature reserve.
Birdwatching and nature study
    Llanelli Naturalists, tel: Trimsaran 628
Fishing (fly only, special facilities)
Lower Lliedi (1878, 14 hectares, 1,136 Ml) is open to the public; several special facilities for the visually and ambulant disabled; noted for herons, kingfishers and common wildfowl.
Waymarked trail for the visually handicapped.
Car parks at both reservoirs (special facilities) toilets (with special facilities)

LOWER LLIW RESERVOIR, nr Swansea
1978, 8 hectares, 1,136 Ml
Located near the city of Swansea, the reconstructed Lower Lliw reservoir provides car parking facilities which give access to views across the reservoir and the surrounding countryside.

LLYSYFRAN, nr Haverfordwest, Dyfed
1971, 76 hectares, 9,100 Ml
Set in gently undulating agricultural land with the Preseli Mountains and Pembrokeshire National Park in the background, the 125-hectare site is managed as a country park. The only large area of lowland water in the region, it retains a varied population of mammals and woodland and water birds. The name means Court of Crows.
Nature trail (shorter way-marked trail), perimeter path (12 km)
Sailing, windsurfing and **canoeing** (in your own craft)
    1 Apr–30 Sept; 10–4 Wed, 12–4 weekends and bank hols
    No rescue service, users must conform the WW's regulations.
    Permits available from the cafe.
Trout fishing, (fly and ledgered worm only, boats for hire)
    Permits and licences from the cafe
Picnic areas (five), cafe and shop (open 20 Mar–17 Oct), car park and toilets enq. to the Ranger, tel: Maenclochog 273

NATIONAL WHITE WATER CENTRE, Afon Tryweryn, nr Bala, Gwynedd
World **slalom** and **wild water racing course**, eleven days' guaranteed water for competition plus about 180 days when water is available for canoeing (subject to normal clearance procedures)
    enq. to Canoeing Management Officer, tel: Bala (0678) 520826

TAFF FECHAN RESERVOIR AREA, Brecon Beacons National Park
Pontsticill, 1927, 102 hectares, 15,450 Ml. Pentwyn, 39 hectares. Neuadd Upper, 1902, 23 hectares, 1,364 Ml. Lower 1884, 4 hectares, 195 Ml.
Upper Neuadd, Neuadd and Pontsticill reservoirs in beautiful scenery
Sailing (Pontsticill, special facilities)
Trout fishing (Neuadd & Pontsticill)
Picnic areas (at Pentwyn, Upper Neuadd and Llyngeren, Pontsticill)
Car parks

TALYBONT, between Brecon and Abergavenny, via A40(T) and B4558
1939, 130 hectares, 11,670 Ml
A reservoir set in WWA's 1,436-hectare estate in Glyn Collwn, part of the splendid national park scenery, good for wildfowl in migration.
Camp site (tents only)
    booking necessary, enq. to supply superintendent, WWA, tel: Talybont-on-Usk 237
Trout fishing (some special facilities)
    enq. as camping above
Walking
Visitor information centre (at Aber Village), picnic sites (also in Forestry Commission valley nearby), car parks and toilets

USK RESERVOIR, nr Trecastle, between Brecon & Llandovery
1955, 117 hectares, 12,270 Ml
Opportunities for quiet recreation and angling
Trout Fishing
Picnic areas, car parks
    enq. to Ranger, tel: Llandovery 20422

Wessex Water Authority

The Wessex Water Authority is one of the smaller ones. Size is not strictly comparable among water authorities because so much depends on whether you look at area, population, finance or other factors, but Wessex Water probably supplies less water to fewer customers than any other authority. It is not the smallest region, however, nor does it have the smallest population; these contradictory figures are caused by the presence of the Bristol Waterworks Company, one of the largest companies, which supplies a very similar number of people within the 'parent' authority's area. Wessex Water's responsibilities and finance have to cover numerous things that are of no concern to the Bristol company, but one gets the feeling in the region of a father with a

Reservoirs with recreational facilities – Wessex Water Authority.

powerful son who might take over the family business one day. With privatisation nearly upon us, it is not inconceivable that Bristol could as well take over Wessex, as Wessex take over Bristol.

Water supplies in the region are rather neatly balanced between agriculture, industry and domestic use. It is a growth area for industry and the resident population is forecast to increase at a rate approximately three times the national average, so demand is expected to increase for the foreseeable future. The new motorways have contributed to the development of the whole area, bringing London, Birmingham and the north within a few hours' drive. Such twentieth-century delights or horrors, according to your needs, contrast uncomfortably with the mystical overtones of Glastonbury Tor and the many burial mounds and barrows that litter the Wiltshire hills. Glastonbury town, though, has taken on an air of commercial self-confidence and now owes its prosperity to business as much as to tourists. The Romans at Bath would certainly have appreciated the new road builders, whom they would surely have seen as the natural heirs to themselves, emerging

The 'line of works', constructed in 1846 by the Bristol Waterworks Company, to bring spring water from the Mendips into Bristol. (Photograph: Bristol Waterworks Company)

from 2,000 years' sleep. Indeed, they should feel the same about our water-supply system. I am actually pleased enough to use the fast roads myself, and they lead into a very unspoilt and warm domestic landscape that wears its long history lovingly, like the Thomas Hardy novels which it helped to inspire.

The Bath Flood Protection Scheme

If the city hopes to escape them [floods] altogether, we believe that only disappointment will be the consequence, for that engineering skill will ever succeed in the work of total prevention is hardly to be hoped for.

anonymous commentator (*c.* 1880)

Flooding may be desirable on the Levels but is not popular in Bath. Seventy-five per cent of the River Avon's catchment area is upstream of the town and this gives it a history of serious floods; one in 1960 caused £1.14 million worth of damage.

The town's concern for its losses over many years, which included some lives, led to the formation of a Flood Relief Committee in 1824 which sought recommendations, 'either from gentlemen conversant with hydrostatics, or Engineers by profession' for a flood prevention scheme. Thomas Telford, 'a Civil Engineer of the first eminence' was chosen to select the most suitable project, but ended up preparing his own report. This recommended a new bridge and some cuts and channel improvements at a cost of £50,000. The high price and conflicts over land interests prevented acceptance and the committee was wound up. Another, much cheaper, scheme was promoted in 1877; this left the channel alone but replaced the solid weirs with others which could be lowered in floods to release the water faster. This also came to nothing.

Serious flooding in 1882 produced a scheme combining both channel and weir improvements at a cost of over £100,000 and proved no more acceptable. Another ignored proposal, made in 1896, was to cut an 8-km bypass tunnel through the hills, partly paid for by the Bath stone that would be excavated. The Land Drainage Act was passed in 1930 and the River Avon Catchment Board set up, largely to serve agricultural interests, and this was to be the authority to finally accept a new scheme similar to the earlier improved weir and channel idea. The war intervened, however, and prices rose dramatically after it.

A new chief engineer, Frank Greenhalgh, took office in 1953. He assessed the scheme and suggested to the River Board that it should consider improvements capable of handling the maximum flood for which any record existed and checking its potential with a hydraulic scale model. This idea was accepted and Bristol University agreed to prepare such a model. It was felt that Bath's buildings and amenities

Pulteney Weir and Bridge, part of the Bath Flood Protection Scheme, planned by the Bristol Avon River Authority, with advice from the Royal Fine Art Commission. (Photograph: Wessex Water)

should remain as undisturbed as possible and the scheme differed little in intention from the previously accepted one to improve the channel and weirs to carry all the flood water. Where it differed was in the dedicated and thorough analysis and testing which was applied to the problem.

Marks showing the highest flood levels had been placed on Pulteney Weir crest thirteen times since the beginning of the nineteenth century, and because the discharge from some of these floods had been measured, it was fairly straightforward to calculate the highest flow. This turned out to be in 1882 and amounted to 367 cu m per second. It was decided to take this figure, plus an extra 60 cm on embankments, to allow for the highest likely flood.

If you can make a working hydraulic scale model that will accurately reproduce all known situations applied to it, you can assume it will accurately reproduce the effects of planned changes to the river. A model over 50 m long was constructed and this accurately reproduced the river's actions. It was made so that the channels could be altered to test out the new scheme. This took two years' work and satisfactorily proved the suitability of the new plans. It would have been an occasion for celebration and congratulation but for the fact that Bath Corporation were unimpressed and yet another scheme was rejected on the grounds of cost.

At this point fate intervened – floods, reaching a peak on 4 and 5 December 1960, almost equalled the worst ever recorded, and by 13 December the Corporation agreed to the new scheme. The only proviso was that special consideration should be given to the aesthetics of the scheme at sensitive sites like Pulteney Weir. The Royal Fine Arts Commission suggested that an architectural and landscape consultant 'of the highest standing' be appointed to collaborate with the engineers on the construction of Pulteney Weir. This was accepted by the River Board and the Corporation. The work was phased over a long period and finally completed in 1974 at a cost of well over £2 million. The technical details of the engineering work were surprisingly complex and demanding and readers interested in more detailed information are referred to chief engineer, Frank Geenhalgh's book, *Bath Flood Protection Scheme*.

The success of the collaboration with the Royal Fine Arts Commission was demonstrated by the Pulteney Weir section of the scheme receiving a Civic Trust Award in 1972. Part of the citation read,

In one of the most beautiful, and thus vulnerable settings in Europe . . . here the designers have given Bath, already rich in wonders, a new wonder . . . [the weir] is a triumph both visually and accoustically. Its steps, three great crescents cascading across the Avon, are rims of foam in sparkling contrast to the quiet water above them reflecting Pulteney Bridge.

Avonmouth Nature Reserve

Avonmouth must be one of the most bizarre sites for a nature reserve, happily settled in the sewage works lagoons, between Europe's largest smelting works and the county council's rubbish incinerator. The Avonmouth Wildlife Trust runs the 10-hectare site which forms the largest area of freshwater for many kilometres and provides a useful haven for many passing (and some resident) birds amongst the heavy industry of the area.

The water there has other functions. There are two lagoons where Wessex Water have been rearing coarse fish since 1976 – they have been found to thrive on the nutrients from the treated effluent! A special reservoir holds more effluent which is sprayed into the chimneys of the incinerator to 'scrub' the smoke. The continual flow of fresh effluent through this reservoir always keeps its temperature above freezing point, encouraging aquatic life throughout the year and providing food and warmth for visiting birds in winter. Another shallow pond popular with birds was created by accident. When the fish lagoons were constructed, an old rhyne (drainage channel) was blocked which flooded a depression in the meadows that form part of the site. Its shallow margins encourage the colonisation of water-loving plants and it is popular with 'dabbling' ducks and waders.

The fields and waste ground surrounding the ponds have become overgrown and make an ideal home for small mammals which, in turn, attract kestrels, barn owls and foxes. Skylarks, yellow wagtails and other small birds nest in the meadows and it is hoped that more waterbirds will breed when the cover around the pond margins grows up. A total of 120 different species of bird had been identified by 1983 and the list will undoubtedly be longer now. Although the site epitomises the extreme marginalisation that can take place when 'nature' is confined to reserves, its existence at all in such an area encourages optimism.

Bournemouth and District Water Company

Population served: 256,000 (winter) 356,000 (summer)
Length of mains: 1,046 km
Area: 352 sq km
Water from chalk aquifers and the Stour and Avon rivers.

The supply of water to Bournemouth was coincidental to the supply of gas; the original company intended to supply only gas but the civic authorities insisted that one should not be supplied without the other, so the Bournemouth Gas and Water Company was formed in 1863. The company had more success with its gas than with water; the chief difficulty was in finding a reliable supply that would keep up with the rapidly expanding population on the south coast in the last century and in this one. Geological assessments were much less reliable than today and several of the company's schemes were disappointing. In 1928 the company decided to withdraw water directly from the River Stour. Although it needed fairly sophisticated treatment for purification, the scheme successfully produced the necessary supplies and, on the basis of this experience, a similar abstraction from the River Avon was added in 1949, the same year that gas was nationalised, and the company then became the Bournemouth Water Company.

Bristol Waterworks Company

Population served: 1,019,000
Water supplied: 340 Ml/d
Length of mains: 5,995 km
Area: 2,391 sq km
Water from impounding reservoirs in the Mendips, springs, wells and boreholes in sandstone and limestone, and the River Severn.

Bristol is one of England's older ports. No Roman remains have been found here but its strategic position, easily defensible, made it a desirable haven and it was in use by the Saxons from a very early date. In 1353 it was made one of the staple towns for the export of wool and, in recognition of its importance, was granted a charter by Edward III, recognising the town and its suburbs as a separate county. Its position, on the edge of the limestone, made simple water supplies relatively straightforward, although their construction must have needed imagination and resourcefulness.

All the early wells and conduits were constructed by the religious houses for their own and public benefit, as their names reveal. Saint Edyth's Well, Carmelite Pipe, Austin Friars, Franciscan Pipe, Abbey Pipe, Saint Thomas Pipe and Saint Marie's Well, among many similar. After the dissolution of the monasteries some of these supplies were taken over by the corporation and some by the parishes, but their upkeep was neglected and an increase in population began to create problems of pollution.

The first public undertaking was given the assent, by Act of Parliament in 1696, for the Bristol Water Works Company to bring water from Hanham Mills (at the town's edge) via hollow elm pipes into the city. A waterwheel operating force pumps was set up 'for throwing water' into a reservoir that would then allow it to flow downhill into the town. The engineer responsible was the celebrated George Sorocold and the scheme appeared to work, but weak management and inadequate control led to unreliability; its spasmodic supplies seem to have been unpopular with the council – who were at best unhelpful. The company struggled with debts and gave up in 1782.

An enterprising proposal was put forward in 1811 to construct a canal from Bath to Bristol, which, by carrying merchandise and water, would bring a double return. The cost, assessed at about £500,000, proved too great, which was probably fortunate as no provision was made for cleaning the water, which would have been badly polluted by the time it reached Bristol.

Some small-scale supplies were undertaken but the situation must have been unsatisfactory, as a Government commission reported in 1840 that,

... viewed as a sanitary question, there are few if any large towns in England in which the supply of water is so inadequate as at Bristol. The labour and consequent expense attached to the system of obtaining a supply of water from the draw-wells or pumps engenders filthy habits directly acting upon the health, and indirectly upon the morals of the people ...

This presumably encouraged the next attempt to supply water, which was made by certain members of the Merchant Venturers Society, a scheme involving Clifton and 'the more wealthy parts of Bristol' with Brunel engaged as a consultant. This, in its turn, seems to have stimulated a rival scheme that would supply the whole town. Both schemes were put before a parliamentary committee, who chose the latter, and in 1846 the Bristol Waterworks Company was formed.

An ambitious plan was executed, bringing water in from the Mendip Hills to the south of Bristol, where high rainfall over a large area of the limestone produces several strong springs – the strongest was at Watery Coombe at Chewton Mendip, 23 km away. A 76-cm diameter pipe could bring 18 Ml daily over valleys on aqueducts and through hills in tunnels. Known as the 'Line of Works', it was described by a Government health inspector as 'the most magnificent work of its kind in England'. The demand for water increased and in 1865 it was decided to take it from the red sandstone aquifer at Chelvey, 14 km to the west. Three steam engines were installed, with a maximum pumping capacity of 27 Ml a day.

The next large undertaking by the company was the construction of a dam impounding the drainage area of the River Yeo and forming the 178-hectare reservoir now called Blagdon. It was completed in 1901 and opened to the public for fishing in 1904, an historic occasion – the first time a water company allowed the public to have access to its property for recreational pursuits. Another larger impounding reservoir was built in 1957 in the Chew valley, also in the Mendips. Both are now celebrated for their fish, which are reared and stocked from the company's own hatchery.

Further supplies have been found, enabling water resources to keep up with the increasing demands of population and industry. The company is a part shareholder in the Llyn Clywedog regulating reservoir at the head of the River Severn. Water can be released from here to the headwaters, allowing Bristol, among others, to abstract water lower down. Bristol's share is brought across country by the Gloucester to Sharpness Canal. In total about 30 per cent now comes from the Severn, 45 per cent from the Chew and Blagdon reservoirs, with additional storage at Cheddar, and the remaining 25 per cent from springs, wells and boreholes.

West Hampshire Water Company

Population served: 167,000
Water supplied: 85 Ml/d
Length of mains: 1,432 km
Area: 707 sq km
Water mostly from the River Avon but also from boreholes – in chalk at Hale, and in the Bracklesham beds near Lymington.

The company originally served the town of Christchurch and was a late starter, probably resulting from the 1875 Public Health Act requirement that local authorities should see that their areas were provided with a supply of wholesome and sufficient water. A London civil engineer, John Howard, in collaboration with local townsmen, proposed a scheme to abstract water from the River Avon and this was granted an Act of Parliament in 1893 – the first water appears to have flowed in 1895. It does not seem to have been easy to raise money in the early years, and in addition to the usual expansion into other local parishes this company twice sold parts of its supply area to the South Hants Water Company.

Cholderton and District Water Company

Population served: 2,500
Length of mains: 42.3 km
Area: 21 sq km

I cannot do better than quote from the letter kindly sent to me by the director, Henry Edmunds:

... this Company has the unique distinction of being the smallest Statutory Water Company in the country. It was started by my Great Grandfather Henry Charles Stephens who was particularly interested in public amenities. He was M.P. for Finchley for many years before resigning due to what he considered was the Government's bad faith during the Boer War. Incidentally he also owned the Stephens Ink Company. Presumably due to his Parliamentary connections he got the Cholderton and District Water Company Act passed in 1904 ... Briefly the Company was originally formed to supply water for the Estate and for the two villages, that is Cholderton and Shipton Bellinger (which were at that time part of the Estate). Today Shipton Bellinger has considerably expanded and though it is no longer part of the property the company still supplies the water. There are various archives relating to the Company in the hands of the Wiltshire Records Office at Trowbridge.

Reservoirs Open to the Public

AVONMOUTH SEWAGE TREATMENT WORKS
Birdwatching (restricted access)
  tickets from Avon Wildlife Trust

THE BARROWS (3 small separate reservoirs)
Fishing
  Bristol Waterworks Fishing, Woodford Lodge, Chew Stoke, Bristol BS18 8XH, tel: Chew Magna 332339
Sub-aqua (during fishing close season)
Car park and toilet

BLAGDON (SSSI)
178 hectares, 7,700 Ml, max depth 13 m
Birdwatching (restricted access)
  permits required from BWC as above
Game fishing
Bristol Waterworks Company, details as The Barrows above
Car parks and toilets

CAMELEY TROUT LAKES, Temple Cloud, Avon (privately owned)
Fishing with special facilities for the disabled.
  enq. John Harris, tel: Temple Cloud 52790

CANFORD POND, Little Canford, nr Wimbourne, Dorset
Coarse fishing with special facilities for the disabled
  enq. to Avon & Dorset Rivers, tel: Poole (0202) 671144

CHEDDAR (Bristol Waterworks Company)
Canoeing
Coarse fishing
Sailing

CHEW MAGNA (Bristol Waterworks Company)
Model boat sailing

CHEW VALLEY LAKE (SSSI)
486 hectares, 20,500 Ml, max depth 11 m
Birdwatching (restricted access)
  permit required from Woodford Lodge

Game fishing
  Bristol Waterworks Company, details as The Barrows above
Nature reserve
Avon Wildlife Trust
Sailing
Visitors' centre and refreshments, shop picnic areas, car parks and toilets

CLATWORTHY, nr Wiveliscombe, A361 Taunton-Bampton road
52 hectares, 5,364 Ml, max. depth 30 m
Game fishing
  enq. to Fishing Lodge, Wiveliscombe, tel: (0984) 23549
Nature trail (2.5 km)
Perimeter track (8 km)
Picnic site and shelters, car parks and toilets

CONHAM RIVER PARK, nr Bristol
Fishing with special facilities for the disabled
  enq. Kingswood District Council planning office, tel: Bristol (0225) 601121

HAWKRIDGE, nr Spaxton, A39 Bridgwater-Minehead road
13 hectares, max. depth 20 m
Game fishing
  enq. to the Ranger, tel: Bridgwater (0278) 424786
Sailing
  Hawkridge Sailing Club (sec. G. Thompson, Quarry Breach, Over Stowey, Bridgwater)
Car park and toilet

HUTTON PONDS, nr Weston-super-Mare, Somerset
Fishing with special facilities for the disabled
  enq. to the secretary, tel: Nailsea 6107

OTTERHEAD LAKES, nr Churchingford, off B3170 Taunton-Honiton road
2 small lakes on the River Otter (213 m above sea level)

Game fishing
    permits from Fishing Lodge
Nature reserve and **nature trail**
    Somerset Trust for Nature
    Conservation
Picnic area, car park and toilets

SUTTON BINGHAM, off A37 Yeovil-
Dorchester road
57 hectares, 2,270 Ml, max. depth 11 m
Birdwatching
Game Fishing
    enq. to Fishing Lodge, tel: Yetminster
    (0935) 872389
Sailing and **canoeing** (facilities)
    Sutton Bingham Sailing Club (sec.
    Mrs J. Davies, Walnut Tree House,
    Somerton)

TUCKING MILL LAKE, Monkton
Combe, nr Bath
Fishing with special facilities for the
disabled
    enq. to Div. Fishing Officer, tel: Bath
    (0225) 313500
Nature trail and **William Smith trail**,
traverses locations of geological and wildlife interest. (William Smith, the eigh-
teenth-century father of English geology,
lived in a cottage by the lake.)

Wessex Water run 4 nature trails on their
Char my Down Estate, which recognised
conservation bodies may use by prior
arrangement. Monkswood Valley Trail,
Chilcombe Bottom Trail, Sutton
Bingham Trail, Otterhead Trail.

Yorkshire Water Authority

Reservoirs with recreational facilities – Yorkshire Water Authority.

Yorkshire is another region showing the contrasts that are so characteristic of the UK. In Yorkshire can be found some of the most beautiful landscape and some of the worst unemployment in Britain. North Yorkshire's moors are one of the great features of England and include the North York Moors and the Yorkshire Dales National Park. South

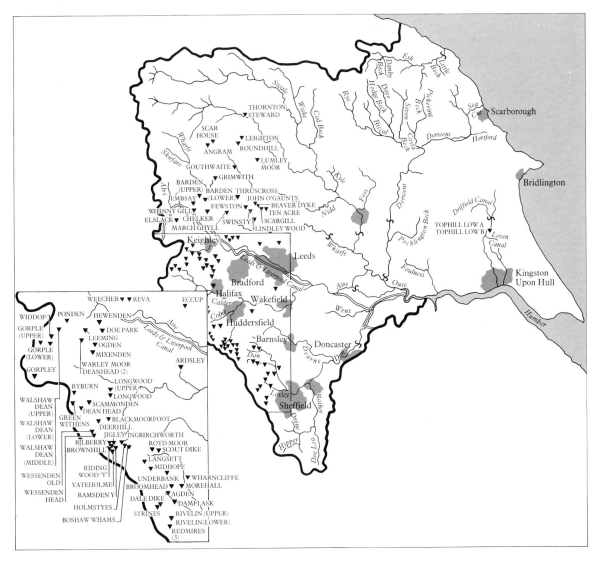

Yorkshire is a heavily populated area whose manufacturing skills have grown directly out of the industrial revolution which developed in its valleys. Textiles have been the great traditional industry, with mining and its associated metal and steel works gaining in importance as mechanisation developed in the last century. Power stations and chemical production have increased in importance in this century, and food processing and brewing are now significant. Most of the heavy industry associated with coal is now in decline and recent developments in smaller-scale manufacturing, like the business parks, are being looked to for a future employment base. As yet the unemployment rate remains one of the highest in the country. It is sad that this should be one of the factors which have contributed to the improvement of water quality in the rivers, although remaining sources of pollution are the worked-out lead and coal mines.

One river that sums up many aspects of Yorkshire is the Aire. It descends from Malham Tarn, through wild limestone rocks in open uninhabited country, to the Bradford/Leeds conurbations where it picks up 80 per cent of the waste of Yorkshire's industry and the sewage of almost 2 million people. It is hardly surprising that it contains more effluent than water in places. Once supporting a thriving salmon fishing industry, by 1840 it was described as being full of the refuse from water closets, cesspools, privies, common drains, dung-hill drainings, infirmaries, wastes from slaughter houses, chemical soap, gas, dye-houses, manufacturers, pig manure, old urine wash, with dead animals and the occasional human body. It is still known to change colour from red to blue to green in a 24-hour period because of the dye pollution in the water. Yorkshire admits that most of its sewers discharging into the Aire are out of date and unable to cope with the large increases in population; £100 million is being spent over 25 years to build new works and improve old ones, and it is predicted that the river will be clean enough for fish to survive along its whole length by the end of the century.

Some Yorkshire Experiments with Sewage Sludges

Yorkshire took over a particularly large number of unsatisfactory local council sewage treatment works in 1974. The new foreman at Featherstone is reported to have had to burn off the brambles and overgrowth before he could find the works! In the same year the authority published a feasibility study and report into methods of treatment and disposal and has since put a number of experimental ideas to the test in practice. These range from small-scale and low capital cost trials of lagoons for improving sludge drying – which can halve the cost of disposal; to multi-million-pound state-of-the-art sludge incinerators.

Sludge is digested to destroy pathogens and improve its smell. The

A typical Victorian dam at Gouthwaite near Pateley Bridge. The 134-hectare reservoir is an important site for birds. Over 200 species have been observed there including ospreys, great northern divers and peregrine falcons. (Photograph: Charles Hall)

common anaerobic method can leave a few surviving bacteria, including some *Salmonella*, and it has been known for these to multiply quite rapidly after treatment, when other competing bacteria have been eradicated. Aerobic digestion can become 'exothermic' (i.e., heat producing) and this can raise the sludge to a high enough temperature (60 and 70°C) effectively to pasteurise it. Two treatment plants are being run side by side at Harrogate, in conjunction with the DOE and the WRc, to compare the aerobic approach with the conventional anaerobic one. Preliminary results suggest that the aerobic method may be best suited to small works, but that the methane produced by anaerobic methods may make works treating populations of over 25,000 a more economical proposition. A combined system is a possibility – where methane from one process might be used to drive air compressors on the other.

It was suggested that the results from these trials may not be publicly available from a new, privatised commercial industry. If this is true, it could confirm fears that experimental work, valuable to public health for instance, might be exploited for private gain.

Colburn Sewage Treatment Works

This works won a pollution abatement technology award in 1987 for its process of pasteurisation combined with anaerobic digestion, which also incorporates a number of other innovations. Some of the methane gas produced by digestion is burnt within the sludge in a submerged combustion unit. This raises the sludge to a temperature of 70°C and maintains it there for 30 minutes, long enough to destroy all bacteria and effectively pasteurise it. The sludge is then cooled to 35°C by a stream of cold effluent and is digested at that temperature for between fifteen and 30 days, the exact number depending on the volume of sewage entering the works.

Other features at the works include a continuous gravity thickener which halves the volume of raw sludge entering the digesters, a method of pumping sludge in and out of the digester which allows great flexibility in the volume treated. There is also an automatic computer control system which will eventually be run from Yorkshire's central control room. This allows the 'remote interrogation of plant operating conditions and status and identification of alarm conditions'.

Versatile plant was necessary because the works treat the sewage from Catterick army camp, whose numbers not only fluctuate greatly but are also secret classified information! The design, which again involved the WRc, has worked successfully, although it was seen as a prototype. Some initial problems have been ironed out and a second version is expected to be more efficient and more economical, in both capital and operating costs.

Incineration

Sewage sludge has been incinerated since 1934 in America and this method has remained popular there, several hundred furnaces being in regular operation. Twelve plants were built in the UK, but only four remain in use. Some of them were closed down even before going into full commission. One of the plants still operating is at Sheffield. Built in 1968, it could dispose of sludge in 1970 at a cost of £28 per dry tonne; this had risen to £73 by 1982 and £107 in 1986. Incinerators are expensive to run. Improvements have brought the cost down to about £85, but this still compares badly with the cost of disposing of treated sludge on land at between £25 and £40 per dry tonne. Unfortunately, land may not be conveniently available and sludge contaminated with metals or toxic waste cannot be disposed of on land anyway, so alternatives are necessary. A computer model, called WYSDOM (West Yorkshire simulation, disposal and optimisation model), was made to examine disposal routes and the results suggested a re-evaluation of incineration.

Recent developments in drying sludge have made the economics of incineration more attractive. If sludge can be dried to at least 30 per cent dry solids it will burn without the use of supplementary fuel (autogenous combustion). If the heat from burning can be recovered to help drying and to generate some power – better still. So a modern incinerator is seen as a plant integrating dewatering, pre-drying, waste heat recovery, flue gas cleaning (very important environmentally), ash handling and ash disposal. Some German units can dry sludge to 50 per cent dry solids before burning, waste heat recovery is efficient and modern flue gas cleaning technology can produce acceptable emmision standards.

Problems remain however. Large quantities of possibly contaminated ash have to be disposed of – you cannot 'get rid of' metals. Cadmium and mercury cannot safely be burnt, and the equipment is expensive, needs skilled control and is inflexible to the extent that it only works at its best on full continuous loads. The economics look sufficiently promising, however, for Yorkshire to renew the plant at Sheffield, and they have built an entirely new one at Bradford, which was due to start work in December 1988. It is hoped to make these plants 'a major sludge disposal route' in the region and costs of about £40 per dry tonne processed are predicted.

Beer effluent in Tadcaster

One of the common criticisms of the water authorities is that they do not use sufficient vigour to pursue those industries that exceed their effluent discharge consents. Consents for the authorities' discharges are given by the Secretary of State and those for industry are given by the water authorities themselves – the generally accepted reason for the authorities' leniency is that they cannot keep their own consents and are therefore not morally justified in prosecuting others. A unique example of co-operation between industry and a water authority is in operation at Tadcaster, however, where three brewers, Bass, Courage and Samuel Smith, have combined with the Yorkshire Water Authority to process the effluent from their brewing operations.

The authorities prefer to treat trade effluents in their own sewage works and to make a direct charge for this to the customer. Recently, several industries have invested in their own custom-designed works, paid for by them but run by the water authorities. In this way, the industry has retained financial control and the authority is responsible for process and environmental controls. Tadcaster produces more beer per head of population than any other town in the world and the organic load of the effluent resulting from one production plant can be equivalent to that of 250,000 people.

A treatment plant has been designed which is capable of processing 15,000 kg per day BOD and produces between 35 and 50,000 tonnes of wet sludge annually. This is disposed of on land at present but studies are underway to dry it sufficiently to form a cake. It has a 33 per cent protein content and, because it is a pathogen-free brewery waste, may be suitable for animal feed.

Sludges are 'digested' or 'stabilised' biologically (by bacteria) to break down solids, destroy disease-giving organisms and reduce the smell – for brewery waste the last is the most important. Most sewage treatment pants in the UK work anaerobically because the process produces methane, often in large enough quantities to be a cost saving byproduct, but it was thought that this particular sludge might not produce enough gas to be useful. The treatment chosen for trials was therefore aerobic, since this was thought to be the more economical option. Trials have been successful and an inoffensive sludge produced. Running costs were found to be a little lower than for anaerobic treatment and capital costs may be as much as £700,000 less.

River Pollution

A beauteous stream ...
The Rother now, as if the very water could be glad,

> Pursues with placid brilliancy its way. John Holland (1836)

The River Rother is by far the most polluted river in Britain and a strong contender for the filthiest river in Europe.

Yorkshire Post (1988)

Reports of river pollution in nineteenth-century England make shocking reading but one is comforted by the cosy thought that things must be different nowadays. They are not. There remain stretches of river that are so badly polluted that it seems almost beyond the capacity of an authority to improve matters. The River Rother in South Yorkshire, running through Chesterfield and Sheffield, is so dead that nobody seems to care what goes into it because it cannot make things any worse. It is precisely the sort of situation that the Control of Pollution Act

(COPA) should have remedied and its condition precisely shows that no legislation is likely to be effective without a wholehearted desire for improvement.

Water authorities have an obligation under COPA to keep public registers of all discharges into rivers, and the DOE have stated that the data should be comprehensible! The registers are there to be read, but in practice it is difficult to build up an overall picture of a region without some specialised knowledge and a lot of dedication. Authorities do publish details of how far their sewage works' discharges keep to their consents (around 80 per cent) but, at most, only give summaries of industrial discharges. With almost 30,000 registered separate industrial effluent discharges in England and Wales, it may well be impractical to give details of the consent conditions and the extent to which they are complied with. Even if this was easily available, the public registers do not include information on industrial effluent discharged to sewers, nor do they include, for instance, results of analysis for substances not listed on the consents – there are large areas of information not available to the public.

Where enough information has been obtained by the public to form a general picture, it has made depressing reading, particularly in the Yorkshire and North West Water Authority's areas. The *Yorkshire Post* has published details of the extent to which consents have been broken in the last year in their area. It records that 142 companies and public bodies were involved, which include the following, listed with the number of effluent samples taken and the number of times the samples failed their consent.

	samples	*failed*
Stocksbridge Enginering	11	11
British Steel	27	25
British Coal	53	28
BP	20	9
Laporte	14	8
Buxted (poultry)	10	10

Some of these breaches may have been minor but many were several hundred times the agreed limit, while others included toxic metals – even cadmium, one of the most dangerous known.

The House of Commons Environment Committee's 1987 report stated that,

industrial effluents discharged to water from fixed pipelines are generally regarded as well controlled under COPA, and do not appear to pose a pressing threat to water quality.

When they were given the details published by the *Yorkshire Post*, the committee's chairman, Sir Hugh Rossi, said

No evidence of this sort of scale of breaches was brought before the committee when we were carrying out our inquiries; we were not told of anything like this at all ... It is quite clear the water authorities are falling down.

Between March 1986 and December 1987, 25.4 per cent of all trade effluent and private sewage works failed their consents in the Yorkshire Water area. Add to this the 20.3 per cent failure of their own sewage works and well over 2,000 water pollution accidents a year and the scale of the problem is clear. There were very few prosecutions: eleven out of 763 breaches of consent in 1987. It is very hard to see why very large, in many cases international, companies should not conform to the law – the control of pollution has not arrived unexpectedly overnight.

Good river conditions are not a desirable social extra, they directly reflect our social conditions – and their opposite can be a serious danger to society. Two policemen and an engineer who jumped into the River Aire to save a drowning man in 1986 subsequently suffered similar symptoms of illness, which appear to have resulted from contact with sewage in the water. One policeman was off work for several weeks, the engineer was very ill for several months, lost a great deal of weight and finally had to give up his job after temporarily losing the use of both arms; he is working again now but is still not fully recovered. The second policeman, Malcolm Beavers, lost all his strength and began to lose his memory and concentration; he can still barely walk and has difficulty in talking. He was awarded a Royal Humane Society award for bravery, but has had to give up his police career. The condition is thought to be Post Viral Fatigue Syndrome, in which the immune system does not reject viral infections in the normal way. Other such cases have been documented where bathers have been in contact with polluted seawater. An environmental health officer has said that the case,

... has important public health implications for the safety of rivers polluted by sewage ... no one should take part in any recreational activities where they could come into contact with the water in severly polluted rivers.

Some panic has taken place within the Government at the prospect of selling off the water industry in this less than desirable state and they have allowed the authorities to spend an extra £300 million on improvements to sewage works. Staff at Yorkshire are 'working 26 hours a day' to spend the money, but it does not seem like good housekeeping to deprive the water authorities of resources for years and then expect them to make up for this neglect immediately. The industries are also taking steps to improve their effluents but their record is poor and in today's money-orientated climate it is cheaper and easier to pollute. The *Yorkshire Post* first campaigned for cleaner rivers in 1972 and were told by the Secretary of State for the Environment that if they returned 'to the subject of river pollution in five years the headline is likely to read "Yorkshire's Living Rivers".' They have returned sixteen years later and found the situation worse; it now seems unrealistic to expect any real improvements to the worst areas before the end of the century.

The Bilberry and Dale Dyke Dam Disasters

The two famous disasters of British dam building both occurred in the Yorkshire area – not through the fault of Yorkshire Water, one should quickly say, as they took place a good 100–150 years before the authority was formed. The reservoirs at Bilberry, south of Huddersfield, and Dale Dyke, west of Sheffield, both stand rebuilt today, though with their dams moved to slightly different places.

Before the widespread use of steam in industry, all power for the larger factories came from water, and mills were grouped together in the valleys close to any suitable streams. Like many water-supply undertakers, they suffered from poor dry-weather flows in the summer and often had an additional problem with excessive flood water in the winter. A number of 'master clothiers' manufactured fancy woollens in the Holme valley, now given over to 'last of the summer wine' consumption. In 1836, they joined together with other manufacturers and formed the Holme Reservoirs Commission to build, 'with Royal Assent', eight reservoirs to regulate the Rivers Holme and Colne. These would store some of the excess water in winter for release in the summer. The scheme's administration seems to have been haphazard, some decisions being left to committees and others to the commissioners, with no firm financial arrangements.

No engineer was consulted on the siting of the dams, some of which were very large by the standards of the day. A surveyor drew up the plans and the well-known engineer George Leather was engaged, on very ambiguous terms, to 'manage' the work at the Bilberry dam. A cheap tender was accepted, against Leather's advice, and work commenced with no experienced supervision, the commissioners apparently unwilling to finance regular visits from Leather. He worked from Leeds, the return journey from where, before the railway, would probably have taken three days. He was busy, much in demand, and pressure of work may have made him willing to accept such an unsatisfactory arrangement. This loose organisation makes it difficult to know who was to blame, but the dam was undoubtedly badly supervised; a spring was found in the earth wall and not properly contained, and problems arose where the masonry outlet culvert ran under the embankment.

The dam was complete by 1843, but leaking badly, and the contractor's contract was terminated following disputes over repairs. A second contractor was engaged between 1843 and 1845, who made further unsuccessful attempts to stop the leaking. A parliamentary Bill was prepared to alter the existing financial arrangements, which were a cause of bitterness among the mill owners, and to allow further money to be raised for remedial work which Leather estimated at £7,800 for Bilberry. The Bill was shelved in 1846 by the commissioners, who said it was 'unexpedient to proceed with such a Bill and no further proceedings were taken therein'.

Leather had nothing further to do with the work and the situation was left to deteriorate. The most dangerous development was a settlement of the dam crest by 3 m which brought it below the top of the overflow. The overflow could have been altered to bring it safely below the crest but the commissioners would not agree to any reduction in storage capacity. They were forced to agree at one time that the water level should be brought down to 11 m to make the reservoir safe, but the work party who turned out to make the necessary alterations were told by some of the commissioners that any attempt to do so would be resisted by force. A disaster was inevitable and it is only surprising that it did not take place until 1852.

After two weeks of heavy rain, the water level on the night of 14 February was rising at about 46 cm an hour. When the water started to run over the top,

... it began to wash away the outer embankment in small quantities. It ran over very slowly at first. Afterwards the embankment came down in larger quantities. After the stream had run over some time, a stream burst out at the bottom of the embankment, I did not stay until it burst, I saw it heave a large quantity of water from the bottom, and then I ran off ...

inquest witness

The results were horrific. The flood wave destroyed 4 mills, 10 dyehouses, 27 cottages, 7 tradesmen's houses, 7 bridges and 18 barns, with 81 lives lost. In addition to this there was serious damage to 17 mills, 5 dyehouses, 44 large shops, 139 cottages, 11 public houses, 3 churches, 6 bridges and 2 iron foundries. With so much damage to property, one of the immediate results was widespread unemployment, which, at that time, meant no money. There was, however, nationwide sympathy and a public appeal brought in £31,345 for the homeless and destitute and, surprisingly, £7,000 for the repair of the reservoir.

An inquest was held that found:

> ... the Bilberry reservoir was defective in its original construction, and that the Commissioners, engineer, and overlooker, were culpable in not seeing to the proper regulation of the works: and we also find that the Commissioners, in permitting the Bilberry reservoir to remain for several years in a dangerous state, with the full knowledge thereof, and not lowering the waste pit, have been guilty of gross and culpable negligence; and we regret that the reservoir, being under the management of a corporation, prevents us bringing in a verdict of manslaughter, as we are convinced that the gross and culpable negligence of the Commissioners would have subjected them to such a verdict had they been in the position of a private individual or firm. We also hope that the legislature will take into its most serious consideration the propriety of making provision for the protection of the lives and properties of Her Majesty's subjects exposed to danger from reservoirs placed by corporations in situations similar to those under the charge of the Holme Reservoir Commissioners.

The second collapse was a water-supply reservoir for the Sheffield Waterworks Company. Work began in 1859 and was completed by 1863 without any of the financial or supervisory problems associated with Bilberry. Filling commenced that year but did not approach the crest of the overflow until March 1864. On the afternoon of 11 March, the dam was practically full when a crack was noticed on the side of the embankment. At 11.30 that night the dam gave way and nearly 250 people lost their lives.

The reasons for the collapse were the subject of much professional debate at the time; they are now thought to relate to the construction of the clay wall that forms the heart of the embankment and the quality of the materials used to build the slopes. The arguments are very technical and the reader is referred to G. M. Binnie's thorough and fascinating study of Bilberry and Dale Dyke in *Early Victorian Water Engineers*.

A very brief inquest was held, which appeared anxious not to blame the water company or ask any embarrassing questions. No enquiry was held nor was there any pressure for one from local MPs. Binnie points out that all those killed were labourers, at that time without the vote, while any constituents were more likely to be shareholders of the water company.

It was not until 1930 that the Reservoirs (Safety Provisions) Act ordered that all reservoirs over 23 Ml capacity must pass stringent checks for safety at least every ten years, and gave licensed inspectors the power to enforce their recommendations. Since 1975 all reservoirs have to have an additional annual check by a qualified engineer.

York Waterworks Company

Population served: 173,000
Water supplied: 50–60 Ml/d
Length of mains: 910 km
Area: 340 sq km
Water taken entirely from the Ouse.

York's water supply has a long history, distinguished by often having been at the forefront of technical development. Although the York Waterworks Company itself only dates from 1846, its Lendal Tower has been supplying water for at least 300 years and possibly longer since the original lease of the tower describes it as 'that auntient building or tower called the Water House Tower'. This lease was given to Henry Whistler, a London merchant, for 500 years under a charter from King Charles II, to 'erect and make a waterhouse and waterwork for the service and accommodation of the inhabitants'. A pump, operated by a windmill and later by horses, lifted water to the top of the tower from where it was distributed on alternate days to different parts of the town.

The tower was purchased in 1779, for £7,000, by a group that included the famous engineer John Smeaton. He designed and built a steam engine at the tower capable of lifting 77,000 litres an hour, a dramatic achievement at the time. Wooden pipes distributed the water through the town. In practice, the supply, drawn from so near the town centre, was polluted and the distribution inefficient, resulting in 'plagues and many other evils'.

The present company was later formed and employed Thomas Hawksley and James Simpson as engineers. Hawksley chose a new intake further upstream and Simpson installed slow sand filters, their earliest use in England outside London. Further improvements from that time onwards, to the pumping plant and filtering system, often made the company a leader in technology.

York's exclusive use of river water has always carried a high risk of pollution and made efficient filtering a priority. Its 1902 rapid gravity filters were the first of their kind in the world and the company pioneered work on activated carbon filters in 1932. Chemical filtering aids and chlorination were introduced at about the same time. The Siward's How water tower is the largest in Britain and holds 4.5 Ml of water.

Reservoirs Open to the Public

AGDEN, nr Bradfield
25 hectares
Birdwatching

ARDSLEY, nr Morley
24 hectares
Birdwatching (permit required)
    enq. to Central Div., tel: (0532) 781313

BARDEN Lower and **Upper**, nr Skipton
23 and 22 hectares
Birdwatching

BEAVERDYKE, nr Harrogate
Game fishing
    Yorkshire A.C., c/o E. Quayle, 47 West Busk Lane, Otley
Birdwatching

BILBERRY, nr Holmfirth
3.6 hectares
Birdwatching

BLACKMOOR FOOT, nr Meltham
An important bird site
34 hectares
Birdwatching
    access for Huddersfield Birdwatchers Club only, otherwise view from the road

BOSHAW WHAMS, Longley, nr Holmfirth
6 hectares
Game fishing
    Huddersfield A.A., c/o C. Clough, 38 Holly Bank Avenue, Upper Cumberwell, Huddersfield
Sailing
    Huddersfield Sailing Club, The Clubhouse, Boshaw Whams Reservoir, Hade Edge, Holmfirth HD7 1RS

BROOMHEAD, nr Stocksbridge
50 hectares
Birdwatching

BROWNHILL, nr Holmfirth
10 hectares

Game fishing
    Yateholme A.C., c/o J. Stead, 1028 Leeds Road, Woodkirk, Dewsbury

CHELKER, nr Addingham
On bird migration route, particularly good if low water levels coincide with spring and autumn passage.
23 hectares
Birdwatching
    from adjacent highway
Game fishing
    Bradford Waltonians A.C., c/o H. Swarbrick, 43 Hawksworth Drive, Menston, Ilkley

DALE DIKE, nr Bradfield
25 hectares
Birdwatching

DAMFLASK, Low Bradfield, Sheffield
46 hectares
Birdwatching
Mixed fishing
    tickets available on site
Sailing, windsurfing and rowing
    Viking Sailing Club, J.W. Chapman, Clarendon, 241 Millhouses Lane, Sheffield S11 9HV
Picnic area

DEANHEAD, nr Rippoden
7 hectares
Birdwatching

DEAN HEAD Lower and Upper, nr Hebden Bridge
4 hectares each
Birdwatching

DEERHILL, nr Marsden
15 hectares
Birdwatching

DIGLEY, nr Holmfirth
17 hectares
Birdwatching
Picnic area

DOE PARK, nr Denholme, Bradford
8 hectares
Mixed fishing

Sailing
   Denholme Sailing Club, J. Bellaby, 22 Glenlee Lane, Keighley, West Yorkshire

ECCUP, nr Leeds
A significant site for winter wildfowl, particularly goosander, regarded as 'a site of outstanding regional importance'
80 hectares
Birdwatching (restricted access to part of the site)
   Leeds Birdwatchers Club

EMBSAY, nr Skipton
11 hectares
Game fishing
   Skipton A.A., c/o J. Preston, 18 Beech Hill Road, Carleton, Skipton
Sailing and **windsurfing**
   Craven Sailing Club, R.D. Hind, 6 Bannister Walk, Cowling, Keighley

GORPLE Lower and Upper, nr Hebden Bridge
21 and 22 hectares
Birdwatching

GORPLEY, nr Todmorden
6 hectares
Birdwatching

GOUTHWAITH, nr Pateley Bridge
YWA's most important ornithological site, over 200 species recorded including ospreys, **nature reserve**.
134 hectares
Birdwatching (no public access to reservoir)
   view from the public road following the entire western side, or the bridleway on the east.
Game fishing (syndicate only)

GREEN WITHENS, Rishworth, nr Ripponden
21 hectares
Sailing
   Green Withens Sailing Club, G. Rhodes, 70 Prune Park Lane, Allerton, Bradford BD15 9JA

GRIMWITH, large new reservoir
150 hectares

Dinghy sailing and **windsurfing**
Walking
Picnic area, car park

HEWENDEN, nr Denholme
6 hectares
Game fishing
   Central Division WMCA

HOLMSTYES, nr Holmfirth
4 hectares
Game fishing
   Huddersfield A.A., see Boshaw Whams above

INGBIRCHWORTH, nr Denbigh Dale
23 hectares
Birdwatching

JOHN O'GAUNTS, nr Harrogate
5 hectares
Birdwatching

LANGSETT, nr Penistone
52 hectares
Birdwatching
Picnic area, visitors' centre (1989)

LEEMING, nr Oxenhope
8 hectares
Game fishing
   Bradford City A.A., c/o M. Briggs, 4 Brown Hill Close, Birkenshaw, Bradford

LEIGHTON, nr Masham
an important winter wildfowl site
42 hectares
Birdwatching
   from the public road skirting the western margin only
Game fishing
   Swinton Estates, tel. Ripon 89224

LONGWOOD, nr Huddersfield
4 hectares
Coarse fishing
   Huddersfield A.A., see Boshaw Whams above

LUMLEY MOOR, nr Ripon
12 hectares
Birdwatching

MIDHOPE, nr Stocksbridge
21 hectares
Birdwatching

MOREHALL, Ewden, Sheffield
26 hectares
Birdwatching
Game fishing (fly only)
    tickets available on site
Sailing and **windsurfing**
    South Yorkshire Sailing Club, B. Gill,
    The Brinks, Woodlands Road, Hope
    S30 2RF
Car park

MIXENDEN, nr Halifax
9 hectares
Birdwatching

OGDEN, nr Denholme
1857, 1,000 Ml, 15 hectares water in 70
hectares mixed semi-mature woods and
open moorland
Birdwatching
Walking and picnics
Car park

PONDEN, Stanbury, nr Haworth
12 hectares
Sailing and **windsurfing**
    Ponden Boat Users Assoc., J.
    Kennedy, 116 Ryedale Way, Allerton,
    Bradford BD15 9AU

RAMSDEN, nr Holmfirth
5 hectares
Game fishing
    Yateholme A.C., see Brownhill above

**REDMIRES Lower, Middle and
Upper**, nr Hallam
12, 19 and 23 hectares
Birdwatching

REVA, Hawksworth, Menston, nr
Guiseley
7 hectares
Sailing (scouts only)
    Wharfdale District Scouts Council

RIDING WOOD, nr Holmfirth
4 hectares
Game fishing
    Yateholme A.C., see Brownhill above

RIVERLIN, Lower and Upper, nr
Hallam
12 and 4 hectares
Birdwatching

ROUNDHILL, nr Masham
Elevated and exposed winter wildfowl
site
23 hectares
Birdwatching
    from public paths only, permit
    required elsewhere, enq. North & East
    Div., tel: (0904) 642131

ROYD MOOR, nr Penistone
15 hectares
Birdwatching

RYBURN, nr Ripponden
11 hectares
Game fishing
    Ripponden Flyfishers, c/o H. Hamer,
    The Hollies, Greetland, Halifax

SCAMMONDEN, nr Ripponden,
Huddersfield
42 hectares
Sailing and windsurfing
    Scammonden Water Sailing Club,
    G.A. Dixon, 13 Roseberry Street,
    Pudsey, Leeds LS28 7JR
Picnic area, car park

SCARGILL, nr Harrowgate
12 hectares
Birdwatching

SCAR HOUSE and Angram,
Lofthouse, nr Pateley Bridge
Remotely sited in 2,750 hectares of
upland river valley with moorland
habitat for birds of prey and others. Long
walks in magnificent scenery. Several
picnic areas, shelters and toilet.
Scar House, 1936, 10,000 Ml, 70
hectares
Game fishing
    Nidderdale A.C., tel: Harrogate
    711638
Angram, 1913, 4,700 Ml, 34 hectares
Birdwatching
    from footpaths or by permit from
    Western Div., tel. (0274) 691111

SCOUT DIKE, nr Penistone
16 hectares
Canoeing (schools only)
Game fishing
   permits available on site
Sub-aqua (strictly club use only)
Car park

STRINES, nr Bradfield
22 hectares
Birdwatching

WASHBURN VALLEY RESERVOIRS

4 reservoirs with extensive catchment areas which support a number of winter wildfowl and woodland birds in the mixed plantations of the lower valleys. Long walks, picnic areas and car parks.
   enq. for all reservoirs to YWA Recreation officer, tel: (0904) 642131

FEWSTON, Nr Blubberhouses
1879, 63 hectares
Birdwatching
Game fishing (fly only)
   permits from vending machines on site

LINDLEY WOOD, nr Otley
1875, 47 hectares
Birdwatching

SWINSTY, nr Blubberhouses
1876, 63 hectares
Birdwatching
Game Fishing (fly only)
   permits as Fewston

THUSCROSS, nr Blubberhouses
58 hectares
Birdwatching
Sailing and **windsurfing**
   Leeds Sailing Club, P. Turner, High Rising, Queens Drive, Ilkley

TEN ACRE, nr Harrogate
4 hectares
Birdwatching
Game fishing (syndicate only)

THORNTON STEWARD, Bedale
14 hectares
Game fishing (fly only)
   permits from Finghall sub-PO, tel: Bedale 50245

Sailing and **windsurfing**
   Thornton Steward Sailing Club, J. Jackson, 6 The Avenue, Richmond, North Yorks.

TOPHILL LOW A and LOW B, nr Beverley
Good for wildfowl
24 and 11 hectares
Birdwatching (very restricted access)
   enq. to North & East Div., tel: (0904) 642131

UNDERBANK, nr Stocksbridge, Sheffield
42 hectares
Birdwatching
Mixed fishing
   permits available on site
Sailing and **windsurfing**
   Pennine Sailing Club, J.C. Gentry, 52 Haywood Lane, Deepcar, Sheffield S30 5QF
Car park

WALSHAW DEAN Lower, Middle and Upper, nr Hebden Bridge
10, 15, and 11 hectares
Birdwatching

WARLEY MOOR, Oxenhope, Haworth
28 hectares
Birdwatching
Sailing
   Halifax Sailing Club, J. Dixon, 18 Crawshaw Park, Pudsey, Leeds

WEECHER, High Eldwick, nr Baildon
3 hectares
Windsurfing
   Weecher Windsurfing Club, I. Platts, 18a Hodgson Fold, Myer Lane, Bradford BD2 4EB

WESSENDEN HEAD and WESSENDEN OLD, nr Meltham
6 and 7 hectares
Birdwatching

WHARNCLIFFE, nr Stocksbridge
3 hectares
Birdwatching

WHINNY GILL, nr Skipton
3 hectares
Mixed fishing
   Skipton A.A., as Embsay above

WIDDOP, nr Hebden Bridge
38 hectares
Birdwatching

YATEHOLME, nr Holmfirth
7 hectares
Game fishing
   Yateholme A.C., as Brownhill above.

Museums and Places of Interest

Most of the more important historical sites have now been opened as museums, but some of the others may only be open to special interest groups by appointment.

Anglia

Berney Arms Drainage Windmill
Berney Arms, Reedham, Nr Great
Yarmouth, Norfolk
Land drainage windmill, 21 m high
Open Apr–Sept, 9.30–6.30 Mon–Sat,
Sun morning.
Access via Berney Arms station or boat
from Gt Yarmouth.
Enq. English Heritage

Cambridge Museum of Technology
Riverside, Cambridge CB5 8HN,
formally Cheddars Lane Pumping
Station.
Victorian sewage pumping station
containing various engines dating from
1895, plus other local industrial exhibits.
Open 1st Sun in every month, 2–6.
Working steam weekends: Apr 19–20;
May 24–25; Jul 25–26; Aug 30–31; Oct
17–18, 11–5.
Enq: Chris Webb, Engineers House,
Riverside, Cambridge CB5 8HN, tel:
(0223) 68650

Dogdyke Pumping Station
Bridge Farm, Tattershall, nr Coningsby,
Lincs
1856 beam engine for land drainage plus
other more recent machines.
open and in steam: Easter Sun, then
1st Sun in month May–Oct, 2–5.
Enq. Hon. Sec., Dogdyke Pumping
Station Preservation Trust, c/o J.
Parkinson, 124 London Road, Long
Sutton, Spalding, Lincs PE12 9EE

Forncett Industrial Steam Museum
Forncett St Mary (16 km south of
Norwich)
An unusual collection of large stationary
engines including several from
waterworks.

Open: Sundays from May to end Sept.
Open and in steam: 1st Sun in month
May-Oct, plus 3rd Sun in July, Aug
and Sept, plus spring and August bank
holiday Sun and Mon, 2–6.
Enq. Forncett Ind. Steam Mus., Low
Road, Forncett St Mary, Norwich
NR16 1JJ, tel. (0508) 418277

Horsey Drainage Mill
Horsey Mere, Nr Stalham, Norfolk
1912 brick drainage windmill replacing
earlier structure.
Open Easter to end Sept, 11–5, check
details.
Enq. National Trust

Langford Pumping Station
Langford, Essex
1930 vertical triple expansion engine for
water supply.
EWC by appointment

Normanton Church Water Museum
Rutland Water
Illustrates the history of the water
industry.
Open 1 Apr to end Sept, 11–5.
Winter season Sun only

Pinchbeck Marsh Pumping Station
Marsh Road, off Wardentree Lane,
Pinchbeck, Spalding, Lincs
1833 A-frame simple rotative beam
engine for drainage.
Enq. to Welland & Deepings Internal
Drainage Board, tel: Spalding 5861

Stretham Drainage Engine
Stretham, nr Ely, Cambs
1831 beam engine driving 11-m scoop
wheel.
Open every day 9.00–6.00
Enq. O. Jakes, superintendent

Willingham West Fen Drainage Pump
Earith Road, Willingham, Cambs
1936 34hp diesel engine and small drainage museum.

By appointment: K.S.G. Hinde, Denny House, High Street, Waterbeach, Cambs., tel: Cambridge 860895

North West

Barton Pumping Station
off Moss Lane, Barton, Downholland, Lancashire
1923/4 single cylinder diesel engines for land drainage.

Enq. to Merseyside area engineer, Rivers Div., NWWA

Northumberland

Ryhope Pumping Station, Ryhope
Sunderland, Tyne & Wear
1868 compound beam engines and water supply museum.
> Open Sat-Sun, 2–5, Easter to end of year.
> In steam bank holiday weekends.
> Enq. M. J. Robinson, custodian

Dalton Pumping Station
Cold Hesledon, Seaham Harbour

1879 Cornish beam engine (only one run on super heated steam).
> By appointment S&SSWC

Broken Scar Waterworks
Darlington
1904 Compound rotative beam engine and 1913 gas engine.
> by appointment NWA

Severn Trent

Basford Beam Engine
Nottingham Industrial Museum, Wollaton Park, Nottingham
Water-supply beam engine by R. Hawthorn 1858.
> Open Apr–Sept, Mon to Sat, 10–6, Sun, 2–6. Oct–Mar, Thurs and Sat, 10–6.30, Sun 1.30–6.30.
> Steam days last Sun of each month and bank hols

Brindley Bank Pumping Station
Wolseley Road, Rugeley, Staffs (near A51)
Water supply museum with Hathorn Davey 1907 steam engines.
> Open by appointment: South Staffs Waterworks Co, Green Lane, Walsall WS2 7PD, tel: (0922) 38282

Clay Mills Pumping Station
Meadow Lane, Clay Mills, nr Burton-on-Trent, Staffs
1885 Compound rotative beam engines for sewage pumping, among others.
> STWA by appointment

Coleham Pumping Station
Coleham Head, Shrewsbury
1898/1900 compound rotative beam engines for sewage pumping.
> Open mid-May–mid-Sept, Mon to Sat, 2–5.
> Curator Miss V.M. Bellamy, tel: (0743) 61196

Hopwas Pumping Station
Tamworth, Staffs
1879 simple rotative beam engines for water supply.
> SSWC by appointment

Leicester Museum of Technology
Abbey Pumping Station, Corporation Road, off Abbey Lane, Leicester LE4 5PX
Former sewage pumping station with 4 compound beam engines with local industry and transport displays.
> Open Mon to Sat, 10.00–5.30, Sun, 2.00–5.30. Regular steam days.
> Tel: (0533) 661330

Maplebrook Pumping Station
Chorley Wood, Burntwood, Walsall,
Staffs
1915 inverted triple compound expansion
surface condensing rotative steam engine
for water supply.
   SSWC by appointment

Mill Meece Pumping Station
Eccleshall, 10 km south of Stoke-on-
Trent off the A519
1913 tandem compound rotative steam
engine and water-supply museum.
Winner 1987 Steam Heritage Award.
Steamed on occasional weekends.
   Details from D. E. Baddeley, tel: (0785)
   822523

Papplewick Pumping Station
Longdale Lane, Ravenshead,
Nottingham, NG15 9AJ
Exceptionally fine and ornate pumping
station (1884).
   Open Easter to end Oct, Sun only, 2–
5.
   In steam bank holidays and occasional
weekends.
   Tel: (0602) 632938

Sandfields Pumping Station
Chesterfield Road, Lichfield, Staffs
1873 Cornish single acting condensing
beam engine for water supply.
SSWC by appointment

Southern

Amberley Chalk Pits Museum
Amberley, nr Arundel, West Sussex
BN18 9LT
35-hectare regional industrial heritage
centre, several water and sewage pumps
and engines, sewage works railway locos
etc.
   Open Wed-Sun (+ bank hol Mon),
   10–6. 1 Apr-1 Nov.
   Also daily during school summer
   holidays.
   Enq. Ian Dean, director, tel: (0798)
   831370

The British Engineerium
off Nevill Road, Hove, East Sussex BN3
7QA
A working steam museum of Britain's
engineering heritage in the fully restored
Goldstone water pumping station.
Hundreds of engines and other
mechanical antiquities.
   Open every day 10–5 except week prior
   to Christmas.
   Engines in steam every Sun and bank
   holiday.
   Frequent special exhibitions and
   events.
   Tel: (0273) 559583

Burton Mill
as Coultershaw Pump
Blake compound ram, working and left
running Apr–Oct. Any time.

Carisbrooke Castle Donkey Wheel
Carisbrooke, Isle of Wight
Water-supply donkey wheel in
wellhouse.
   Enq. English Heritage

Cherry Garden Waterworks
Cherry Garden Lane, Folkestone, Kent
1865 single cylinder beam engine for
water supply, and large collection of
steam plant.
   FADWC by appointment

Connaught Pumping Station
Connaught Road, Dover, Kent
1939 compound triple expansion steam
engine for water supply.
   FADWC by appointment

Coultershaw Water Pump
3 km south of Petworth, West Sussex
Triple beam pump driven by water
installed in 1784.
   Open 1st and 3rd Sun Apr–Sept inc.,
   11–4.
   Sussex Industrial Archaeological Soc.,
   tel: (0903) 505626

Eastney Pumping Station
Henderson Rd, Eastney, Portsmouth
PO4 9JF
Restored 1887 Boulton & Watt beam
engines for sewerage.
In steam at weekends.

Adjacent building houses 1904 Crossley gas engines.

> Open daily Apr–Sept, 1.30–5.30, Oct–Mar 1st Sun in month only, 1.30–5.30.
> Tel: (0705) 82761

Garnier Road Pumping Station

Winchester, Hants
1930 ram pumps for sewage and other technological artifacts in listed 1878 building.

> Enq. to SW Hampshire Div.

Henwood Pumping Station

Ashford, Kent
1870 rare Woolf compound rotative beam engine for water supply.

> MKWC by appointment

S.S. Shieldhall

Ocean Village, Southampton

Historic sludge transporting ship, built 1955 with two Lobnitz triple expansion engines and numerous auxiliary steam engines. A unique exhibit.

> Shieldhall Preservation Trust

Stanmer Donkey Wheel

Stanmer, Sussex (nr Brighton)
4 m wheel for community water supply. Also a horse engine. Both can be seen anytime outside the village rural museum.

> Museum open: Easter–Oct, Sunday only, 2–5

Twyford Pumping Station

1898 triple expansion steam engine, also 5 unique lime kilns for water softening.

> Twyford Waterworks Trust

Thames

Abbey Mills Pumping Station

Access details available from TWA

Addington Pumping Station

Addington, Surrey
1887 compound beam engine

Crossness Sewage Treatment Works

Crossness
Four 11865 compound rotative beam engines

Eton Pumping Station

Tangier Lane, Eton, Windsor, Berks
1873 two water-driven turbine pumps for water supply, plus others.

> TWA by appointment

Fobney Water Treatment Works

Manor Farm, Reading, Berks
1922/23 two vertical water-driven turbines for water supply.

> TWA by appointment

Greys Court Donkey Wheel

Greys Court, Rotherfield Greys, Henley-on-Thames, Oxon
579 cm donkey wheel in Tudor well house, 61 m well.

> Open Apr–end Sept, Mon–Sat, 2–5.30.
> Enq. National Trust

Hampton Pumping Station

Sunbury Way, Hanworth, Middx
1938/47 eight impulse steam engines for water supply.

> TWA by appointment

Kew Bridge Steam Museum

Green Dragon Lane, Kew Bridge Road, Brentford, Middx
Beam and other water-supply engines dating from 1820.

> Open daily inc. bank holidays, 11–5. In steam at weekends.
> Enq. tel: (01) 568 4757

Kempton Park Pumping Station

Feltham Hill Road, Sunbury Way, Feltham, Middx
1929 inverted compound triple expansion engines, largest waterworks engines in Europe. Two impulse reaction steam turbines (1930).

> TWA by appointment

King George's Pumping Station

Enfield Lock, nr Waltham Abbey, Middx
1913 gas pumps for water supply.

> TWA by appointment

Littleton Pumping Station

Ashford Road, Laleham, nr Staines, Middx

1925 two horizontal uniflow steam engines for water supply.
   TWA by appointment

Markfield Road Pumping Station
Tottenham, London N15
1884/85 two cylinder compound rotative beam engine for sewage.
   Enq. River Lea Ind. Arch. Soc., c/o Lea Valley Reg. Park,
   Tel: Lea Valley 717711

Thames Barrier Visitors' Centre
Unity Way, Woolwich, London SE18 5NJ
Display, information, history etc., boat trip available, shop and refreshments.
   Open daily, 10.30–5.00, 10.30–5.30 weekends.
   Enq. (01) 854 1373

Turnford Pumping Station
Canada Lane, Great Cambridge Road, Turnford, Wormley, Herts
Beam engine.
   TWA by appointment

Waddon Pumping Station
Waddon Way, off Purley Way, Croydon, Surrey 1911/15 rare tandem cross compound horizontal engines for water.
   TWA by appointment

Walton Pumping Station
Hurst Road, Walton-on-the-Hill, Surrey 1911 Triple exp. inverted vertical marine engine for water supply.
   TWA by appointment

West Ham Pumping Station
London E15
1895 two compound rotative beam engines for water supply

Wales

Hereford Waterworks Museum
Lower Pumping Station, Broomy Hill, Hereford
1895 compound triple expansion engine and others. Water supply museum in 1856 pumping station.
   Enq. to the Curator, tel: Hereford (0432) 274104

Milton Carew Pumping Station
1932 Gas/oil and triple ram pump.
   Enq. to WWA

Pembrey Pumping Station
Pembrey, Dyfed
1931 Plurovane turbine pump and twin horizontal diesel engine.
   Enq. to the Divisional Manager, Gower Div., WWA

Welsh Industrial & Maritime Museum
Bute Street, Cardiff
Large collection of engines from 1851 single cylinder beam onwards.
   Open all year Mon–Sat, 10–5, Sun, 2.30–5.00

Wessex

Allermoor Pumping Station
Burrowbridge, Bridgwater, Somerset.
1869 vertical twin-cylinder steam engine and pumps for land drainage, plus several other early engines.
   By appointment L. W. Musgrave, Allermoor Pumping Station, tel: Burrowbridge 324

Bristol Avon Divisional HQ
Quay House, Bath
1910 Campbell diesel engine (on display in foyer).

View by appointment with Bath divisional general manager, tel: (0225) 313500

Blagdon Pumping Station
Blagdon, nr Bristol, Avon
1902 compound rotative beam engines for water supply.
   View by appointment with Bristol Waterworks Company, tel: (0272) 665881

Chelvey Pumping Station
Chelvey, nr Nailsea, Avon

1923 compound triple expansion engine for water supply.

Viewing as Blagdon above

Currymoor Pumping Station

Athelney, Bridgwater, Somerset
1864 vertical twin-cylinder steam engine and pump for land drainage.

Viewing as Allermoor Pumping Station above

Dorchester Water Tower

Dorchester, Dorset
1870, 0.36 Ml water tower (still in use).

View by appointment with Avon & Dorset divisional general manager, tel: (0202) 671144

Friar Waddon Pumping Station

Friar Waddon, Portesham, nr Weymouth.
1936 Ruston Paxman diesel engine for water supply.

Viewing as Dorchester Water Tower above.

Milborne St Andrew Pumping Station

Blandford Forum, Dorset
1928 three stage ram pump for water supply.

Viewing as Dorchester Water Tower above

Milton Road Depot

Milton Road, Weston-super-Mare, Avon
1923 air blast diesel engines for water supply.

Viewing as Blagdon above

Rodney Stoke Pumping Station

Rodney Stoke, Cheddar, Somerset
1915 Campbell single-cylinder diesel and pump for land drainage.
View by appointment with Somerset rivers division general manager, tel: (0278) 457333

Sutton Poyntz

Weymouth, Dorset (museum in course of alteration)
1857 water-supply turbine and several other engines and exhibits connected with water supply.

Viewing as Dorchester Water Tower above

Salisbury Devizes Road Pumping Station

Salisbury, Wilts
1934 targe horizontal single-cylinder diesel engine and pumps for water supply.

Viewing as Dorchester Water Tower above

Victoria Pumping Station

Oakfield Road, Clifton, Bristol
1913 Inverted compound triple expansion engine for water supply.

Viewing as Blagdon above

Westford Pumping Station

Rockwell Green, Wellington, Somerset
1936 horizontal Ruston single cylinder diesel engines for water supply and two 3-ram pumps.

View by appointment with Bath divisional general manager, tel: (0225) 313500

Westonzoyland Pumping Station

Westonzoyland, Bridgwater
1861 vertical two-cylinder steam engine and pumps for land drainage, plus several other engines and exhibits.

View by appointment with Mrs M. Miles, Hon. sec., Westonzoyland Engine Trust, Rose Cottage, Lower Durston, Taunton, tel: (0823) 412713

Yorkshire

Brayton (south) Pumping Station

Thorpe Willoughby, nr Selby, North Yorkshire
1906 Compound triple exp. steam engine and others.

Enq. to The Director, S.E. Div., YWA

Cottingham Pumping Station

Millhouse Woods Lane, Cottingham, N. Humberside HU16 4HD
1934 compound triple exp. steam engine also an 'eroder' boat used to scour the channel at Patrington Haven.

Enq. to The Director, E. Div., YWA

Roall Waterworks
Whitley Bridge, nr Goole, N. Yorkshire
1891 compound rotative beam engine.
   Enq. as at Brayton above

Springhead Pumping Station
Springhead Avenue, Willerby Road,
Kingston-upon-Hull HU5 5HZ
1876 Cornish beam engine in water
supply museum.
   View by appointment with the North
   & East Division Office, tel. (0904)
   642131

List of Abbreviations used in the Text

BOD	Biochemical oxygen demand
BPEO	Best practical environmental option
CBI	Confederation of British Industry
CC	Countryside Commission
COD	Chemical oxygen demand
COPA	Control of Pollution Act
CPRE	Council for the Protection of Rural England
DOE	Department of the Environment
EEC	European Economic Community
EQO	Environmental quality objective
EWC	Essex Water Company
FADWC	Folkestone and District Water Company
IDB	Internal Drainage Board
MAFF	Ministry of Agriculture, Fisheries and Food
MKWC	Mid Kent Water Company
MSC	Manpower Services Commission
NERC	Natural Environmental Research Council
NCC	Nature Conservancy Council
NFU	National Farmers Union
NRA	National Rivers Authority
R&CO	Recreation and Conservation Officer
RQO	River quality objective
RSPB	Royal Society for the Protection of Birds
SSWC	South Staffordshire Water Company
WAA	Water Authorities Association
WRc	Water Research Centre

Useful Addresses

British Waterways Board, Melbury House, Melbury Terrace, London, NW1 6JX tel. 01– 262 6711

Central Electricity Generating Board, Sudbury House, 15 Newgate Street, London, EC1A 7AU tel. 01– 634 5111

Council for the Protection of Rural England, 4 Hobart Place, London, SW1W 0HY tel. 01– 235 0511

Countryside Commission, John Dower House, Crescent Place, Cheltenham, GL50 3RA tel. 0242– 521381

Forestry Commission, 231 Corstorphine Road, Edinburgh, EH12 7AT tel. 031– 334 0303

Friends of the Earth, 26–28 Underwood Street, London, N1 7JQ tel. 01– 490 1555

Greenpeace, 30–31 Islington Green, London, N1 8XE tel. 01–354 5100 & 01– 359 7396

Inland Waterways Association, 114 Regents Park Road, London, NW1 8UQ tel. 01– 586 2556 & 2510

Marine Conservation Society, 4 Gloucester Road, Ross-on-Wye, HR9 5BU

The Nature Conservancy Council, Northminster House, Northminster, Peterborough, PE1 1UA tel. 0733– 40345

Royal Society for the Protection of Birds, The Lodge, Sandy, Bedfordshire, SG19 2DL tel. 0767– 80551

The Sports Council, 16 Upper Woburn Place, London, WC1H 0QP tel. 01– 388 1277

Water Authorities Association, 1 Queen Anne's Gate, London, SW1H 9BT tel. 01– 222 8111

Water Companies' Association, 14 Great College Street, London, SW1P 3RX tel. 01– 222 0644

Water Research Centre, PO Box 16, Marlow, Bucks, SL7 2HD tel. 0491– 571531

Water Authorities

Anglian Water, Ambury Road, Huntingdon, PE18 6NZ tel. 0480– 56181

North West Water, Dawson House, Great Sankey, Warrington, WA5 3LW tel. 092– 572 4321

Northumberland Water, PO Box 4, Regent Centre, Gosforth, Newcastle upon Tyne, NE3 3PX tel. 091– 2843151

Severn Trent Water, Abelson House, 2297 Coventry Road, Sheldon, Birmingham, B26 3PU tel. 021– 743 4222

South West Water, Peninsular House, Rydon Lane, Exeter, EX2 7HR tel. 0392– 219666

Southern Water, Guildbourne House, Worthing, West Sussex, BN11 1LD tel. 0903– 205252

Thames Water, Nugent House, Vastern Road, Reading, RG1 8DB tel. 0734– 593333

Welsh Water, Plas-y–ffynnon, Cambrian Way, Brecon, Powys, LD3 7HP tel. 0874– 3181

Wessex Water, Wessex House, Passage Street, Bristol, Avon, BS2 0JQ tel. 0272– 290611

Yorkshire Water, West Riding House, 67 Albion Street, Leeds, LS1 5AA tel. 0532– 448201

Water Companies

Bournemouth and District Water Company, George Jessel House, Francis Avenue, Bournemouth, BH11 8NB tel. 0202– 572261

Bristol Waterworks Company, PO Box 218, Bridgewater Road, Bristol, BS99 7AU tel. 0272– 665881

Cambridge Water Company, Rustat Road, Cambridge, CB1 3QS tel. 0223– 214052

Chester Waterworks Company, Aqua House, 45 Boughton, Chester, CH3 5AU tel. 0244– 320501

Cholderton and District Water Company, Estate Office, Cholderton, Salisbury, Wilts tel. Cholderton 0980– 64203

The Colne Valley Water Company, Blackwell House, Aldenham Road, Watford, Herts, WD2 2EY tel. 0923– 223333

East Anglian Water Company, 163 High Street, Lowestoft, Suffolk, NR32 1HT tel. 0502– 517039

East Surrey Water Company, London Road, Redhill, RH1 1LJ tel. 0737– 765933

East Worcestershire Waterworks Company, 46 New Road, Bromsgrove, Works, B60 2JT tel. 0527– 75151

The Eastbourne Waterworks Company, 14 Upperton Road, Eastbourne, Sussex, BN21 1EP tel. 0323– 411411

Essex Water Company, Hall Street, Chelmsford, Essex tel. 0245– 266622

Folkestone and District Water Company, Cherry Garden Lane, Folkestone, Kent, CT19 4QB tel. 0303– 76712

Hartlepools Water Company, 3 Lancaster Road, Hartlepool, TS24 8LW tel. 0429– 274405

Lee Valley Water Company, PO Box 48, Bishops Rise, Hatfield, Herts, AL10 9HL tel. 0702– 268111

Mid Kent Water Company, PO Box 45, High Street, Snodland, Kent, ME6 5AH tel. 0634– 240313

Mid Southern Water Company, Frimley Green, Camberley, Surrey, GU16 6HZ tel. 0252– 835031

Mid Sussex Water Company, PO Box 129, 1 Church Road, Haywards Heath, Sussex, RH16 3DX tel. 0444– 457711

Newcastle and Gateshead Water Company, PO Box 10, Allendale Road, Newcastle upon Tyne, NE6 2SW tel. 091– 2654144

North Surrey Water Company, Millis House, The Causeway, Staines, Middlesex, TW18 3BX tel. 0784– 55464

Portsmouth Water Company, PO Box 8, West Street, Havant, Hants, PO9 1LG tel. 0705– 486333

Rickmansworth Water Company, London Road, Rickmansworth, Herts, WD3 1LB tel. 0923– 776633

South Staffordshire Water Company, Green Lane, Walsall, West Midlands, WS2 7PD tel. 0922– 38282

Sunderland and South Shields Water Company, 29 John Street, Sunderland, SR1 1JT tel. 091– 5101050

Sutton District Water Company, 59 Gander Green Lane, Cheam, Sutton, Surrey, SM1 2EW tel. 01– 643 8050

Tendring Hundred Waterworks Company, Manningtree, Essex, CO11 2AZ tel. 0206– 392155

West Hampshire Water Company, Knapp Mill, Mill Road, Christchurch, Dorset, BH23 2LU tel. 0202– 483361

West Kent Water Company, Cramptons Road, Sevenoaks, Kent, TN14 5DG 0732– 452307

Wrexham and East Denbighshire Water Company, 21 Egerton Street, Wrexham, L11 1ND tel. 0978– 291777

York Waterworks Company, Lendal Tower, York, YO1 2DL tel. 0904– 622171

Further Reading

*Binnie, G. M., *Early Dam Builders in Britain*, Telford, 1987.

*Binnie, G. M., *Early Victorian Water Engineers*, Telford, 1981.

Birch, T., *Poison in the System* (A critical review of the role of industry, water authorities, the public and the Control of Pollution Act 1974 in Water Pollution), Greenpeace, 1988.

*Bowers, J., O'Donnell, K. & Whatmore, S., *Liquid Assets* (The likely effects of privatisation of the water authorities on wildlife habitats and landscape), CPRE & RSPB, 1988.

*Briggs, A., *Victorian Cities*, Pelican, 1968.

Dangerfield, B. J., *Recreation: Water and Land*, Institute of Water Engineers and Scientists, 1981.

*Davison, C., *A Woman's Work is Never Done* (A history of housework in the British Isles 1650–1950), Chatto and Windus, 1982.

*Delderfield, E. R., *The Lynmouth Flood Disaster*, ERD, Exmouth, 1953.

*Godwin, Sir H., *Fenland: its ancient past and uncertain future*, Cambridge University Press, 1978.

Greenhalgh, F., *Bath Flood Protection Scheme*, WWA, 1974. *Hartley, D., *Water in England*, Macdonald & Jane, 1978 edition.

*Hawkings, D. J., *Water from the Moor* (An illustrated history of the Plymouth, Stonehouse and Devonport Leats), Devon Books, 1987.

Hill, H., *Freedom to Roam*, Moorland Publishing, 1980.

Holden, W. S., *Water Treament and Examination*, Churchill, 1970.

House of Commons Environment Committee, *Pollution of Rivers and Estuaries*, HMSO, 1988.

*Hoyle, N., *Reservoirs from Rivington to Rossendale*, NWWA, 1987.

*Kirby, C., *Water in Great Britain*, Penguin, revised edition 1984.

Lees, A. & McVeigh, K., *An Investigation of Pesticide Pollution in Drinking Water in England and Wales*, Friends of the Earth, 1988.

*Minchington, W., *Life to the City* (An illustrated history of Exeter's water supply from the Romans to the present day), Devon Books, 1987.

Newson, M. D., *Flooding and Flood Hazard in the United Kingdom*, OUP, 1975.

*Pearce, F., *Watershed* (The water crisis in Britain), Junction Books, 1982.

*Quayle, T., *Reservoirs in the Hills* (The story of the construction of the reservoirs in the Longendale Valley, which feed Manchester with water), NWWA.

*Rackham, O., *The History of the Countryside*, Dent, 1986.

*Robins, F. W., *The Story of Water Supply*, OUP, 1946.

*Royal Commission on Environmental Pollution, *Tenth Report* (Tackling pollution – experience and prospects), HMSO, 1984,

*Storer, B., *The Natural History of the Somerset Levels*, Dovecote Press, 1987.

*Non-technical books suitable for the general reader.

INDEX